Selling Songs and Smiles

Selling Songs and Smiles

The Sex Trade in Heian and Kamakura Japan

Janet R. Goodwin

University of
Hawai'i Press
Honolulu

Printed in the United States of America
12 11 10 09 08 07 6 5 4 3 2 1

Library of Congress Cataloging-in-Publication Data
Goodwin, Janet R.
Selling songs and smiles : the sex trade in Heian and Kamakura Japan / Janet R. Goodwin.
p. cm.
Includes bibliographical references and index.
ISBN-13: 978-0-8248-3068-7 (hardcover : alk. paper)
ISBN-10: 0-8248-3068-7 (hardcover : alk. paper)
ISBN-13: 978-0-8248-3097-7 (pbk. : alk. paper)
ISBN-10: 0-8248-3097-0 (pbk. : alk. paper)
1. Prostitution—Japan—History—To 1500.
I. Title.
HQ247.A5 G58 2006
306.74'209520902—dc22 2006024199

Frontis: *Asobi* Approaching Hōnen's Boat. From *Hōnen shōnin eden.* Courtesy Chion-in, Kyoto. Photograph supplied by the Kyoto National Museum.

University of Hawai'i Press books are printed on acid-free paper and meet the guidelines for permanence and durability of the Council on Library Resources.

Designed by April Leidig-Higgins

Printed by The Maple-Vail Book Manufacturing Group

Contents

Acknowledgments

THE RESEARCH and writing of this book owe much to the encouragement and criticisms of many friends and mentors. I am particularly indebted to the late Professor Matsumae Takeshi, who encouraged my research in its initial stages and gave it a jumpstart by suggesting many valuable primary and secondary sources. I regret that Professor Matsumae did not live to see the completion of this book. I am also grateful to Professor Delmer M. Brown, my research adviser at the University of California, Berkeley, for stimulating my interest in premodern Japan in the first place and for introducing me to the variety of possible research topics in that very fruitful area. I would also like to thank the Fulbright Foundation for generous support during the early stages of this research.

I am grateful to Elizabeth Leicester for reading and critiquing the entire manuscript. Others who provided helpful comments on the manuscript or on the *Monumenta Nipponica* article on which it expands are Andrew Goble, Bettina Gramlich-Oka, Kate Nakai, Yuki Terazawa, and Hitomi Tonomura, as well as Joan R. Piggott and Jason Webb and their students in a graduate seminar in Japanese history at the University of Southern California: Andrew Dyche, Rieko Kamei, Sachiko Kawai, John Leisure, and Mitsuo Maeda. I would also like to thank the two anonymous readers for the University of Hawai'i Press for their constructive criticism and editor Patricia Crosby for her encouragement and patience. The staffs of the libraries at the University of Aizu, the University of Tokyo, and the University of California, Los Angeles, graciously helped me locate materials; in that regard I would like especially to thank Toshie Marra of UCLA. I am grateful to *Monumenta Nipponica* for granting me permission to publish portions of my article, "Shadows of Transgression: Heian and Kamakura Constructions of Prostitution"; to Chion-in in Kyoto for permission to use an illustration from the picture scroll *Hōnen shōnin eden* for the dust jacket and frontispiece; to the Kyoto National Museum for providing me with a photograph of the illustration; and to Stanford University Press for permission to adapt the map of the capital region.

I owe a great deal to my parents, the late W. E. and Ruth I. Durstine, and to my brother, the late Richard M. Durstine, for making educational achievement a priority in our family and intellectual discourse a common occurrence in our household. I am deeply indebted to my husband, Jim Goodwin, for his unflagging encouragement, for his computer expertise, and for the many hours he spent working on the maps. Had it not been for his willingness to learn a new language and experience a new culture in the first place, my "long strange trip" through the landscape of medieval Japan might have never begun.

Los Angeles, California

Periods of Japanese History

Nara period (710 – 794)

Heian period (794 – 1185)

Kamakura period (1185 – 1333)

Kenmu Restoration (1334 – 1336)

Muromachi period (1336 – 1573)

Momoyama period (1573 – 1603)

Edo (Tokugawa) period (1603 – 1867)

Note on Primary Sources

IN CITING PRIMARY SOURCES in the notes, I have decided to privilege convenience to the reader over stylistic consistency. Many primary sources are available in several different editions, and a given library may not necessarily have the ones that I actually used. Therefore rather than citing specific editions and page numbers, I have referred to these sources in some way that will enable the reader to find the reference in any edition: by date for diaries and chronicles; by episode number for tale collections. Only when it would require a long linear search for a given reference have I chosen a particular edition and cited its page number. The editions I used are listed in the bibliography. Although English translations are given for most titles, a few are virtually impossible to translate into comprehensible English.

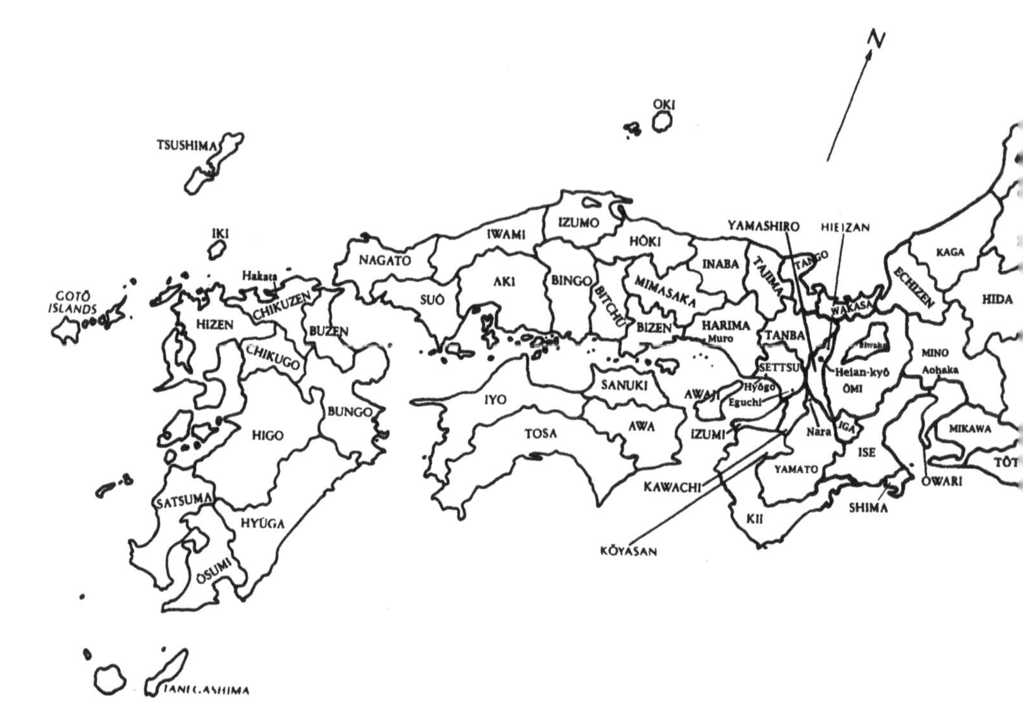

Provinces of Heian and Kamakura Japan. Adapted from the map in George Elison and Bardwell L. Smith, *Warlords, Artists, and Commoners: Japan in the Sixteenth Century* (University Press of Hawai'i, 1981)

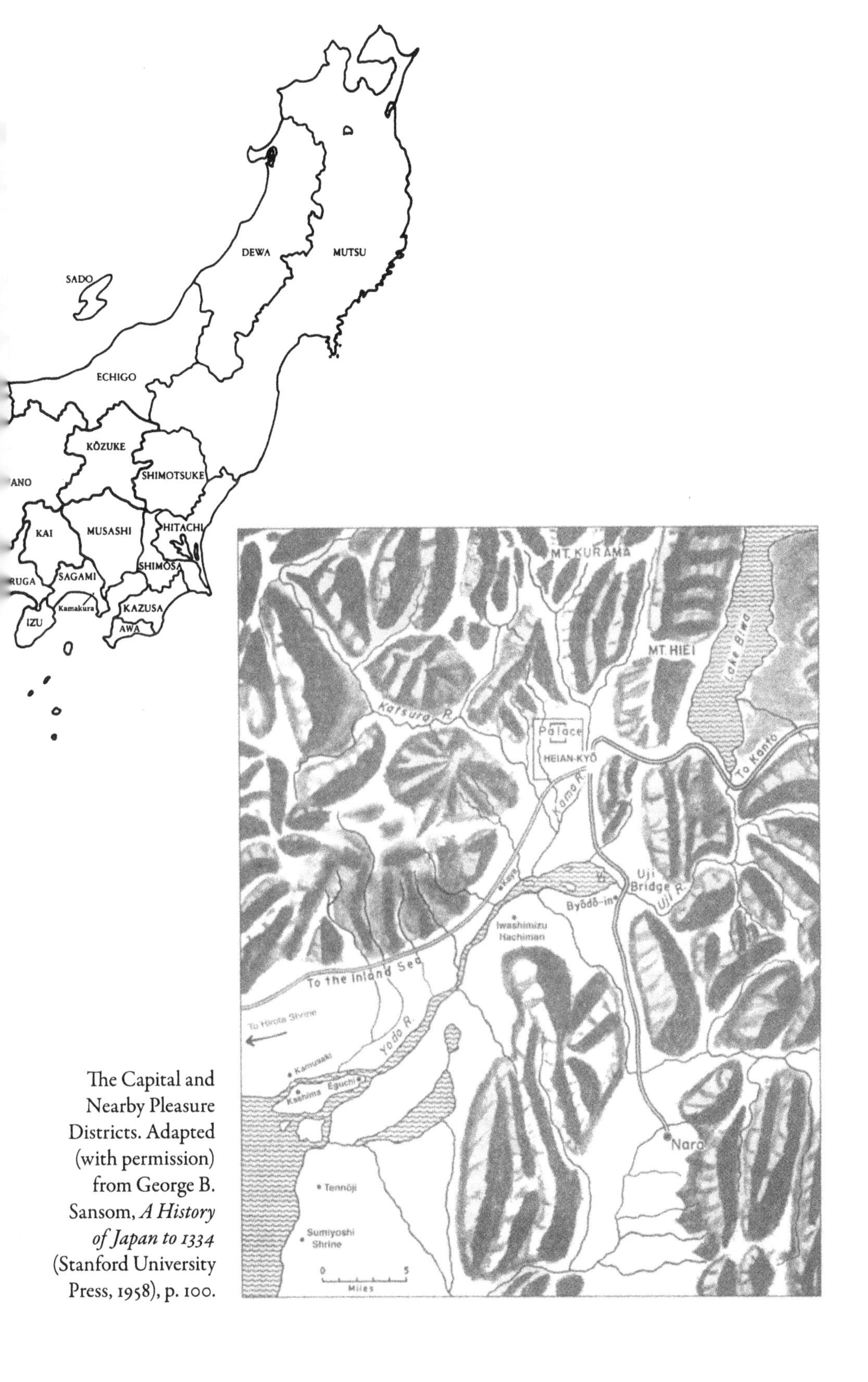

The Capital and Nearby Pleasure Districts. Adapted (with permission) from George B. Sansom, *A History of Japan to 1334* (Stanford University Press, 1958), p. 100.

Introduction

AMONG THE OCCUPATIONAL groups that peopled the landscape of mid- and late-Heian Japan were cohorts of women whose professional services included sexual play and intercourse in exchange for compensation from male patrons. Many of these women were entertainers who specialized in popular song and, later, in dance. They went by several occupational designations, depending on such variables as entertainment style, modes of living, geographic location, and methods used to attract patronage. The most conspicuous among them were *asobi* (also known as *yūkun*), often found entertaining travelers at sea and river ports. Other important groups were women of puppeteers' troupes called *kugutsu,* and dancers known as *shirabyōshi,* who appeared at the end of the Heian period. We know about these women because many of them entertained and became the sexual partners of prominent men whose experiences were recorded in the men's diaries or in accounts written by others.

This book aims to tease out the particular, historically conditioned meanings of professionalized sexual interaction in a society whose sexual taboos, marriage patterns, modes of economic exchange, and gender relations differed sharply from those in premodern Christian Europe and modern Japan. In so doing, the book examines the changing process of defining and dealing with sexual transgression and female sexuality in Japan over a period of some four hundred years from the mid-tenth to the mid-fourteenth centuries—the mid-Heian through the Kamakura periods. During this period, sexual norms were shaped by significant political and socioeconomic transformations in configurations of power, in religious currents, and in marriage and inheritance patterns.

Sexual entertainers played an important part in the history of early Japanese literature, both as lyricists and as subjects of essays, poems, and tales. How they appeared in literary works of their own or others' making is a significant question, and a number of scholars have studied sexual entertainers from this vantage point.[1] However, sexual entertainers were also social actors involved in specific and recognized occupations. As such, they interacted with authorities, developed characteristic methods of doing business, found a place inside (or outside) the social structure, and invited both praise and censure. In this book I examine the dynamics of change in sexual entertainment occupations in conjunction with socioeconomic transformation and attendant changes in sexual norms.

Entertainers or Prostitutes?

I focus primarily on the women's identities as providers of sexual services, although their function as entertainers cannot be disentangled from these identities. Modern scholars sometimes refer to the women as prostitutes or courtesans, but the Japanese language of the mid-Heian period had no common designation for female sexual professionals. Concepts of prostitution were as yet inchoate, and notions of lewdness or illicit sexual activity were inconsistently mapped onto the persons and occupations of sexual entertainers. By the late Kamakura period, sexual entertainers were often considered transgressive individuals involved in a questionable (though not illegal) trade. However, the development of a transgressive identity for them was halting and frequently contested, and it was not based primarily on notions that certain sexual activities or relationships were immoral in and of themselves. Concepts of transgressive female sexuality were shaped by a number of factors: the perceived needs to limit itinerancy and to preserve class boundaries; the intensified competition for resources, especially land; and notions of the female body as polluted and sexual desire as a dangerous snare for men seeking religious fulfillment.

A working definition of a prostitute is one who engages in sex with multiple partners for compensation that provides at least a partial living. Although this definition begs the question of enslavement, it can be applied to various societies and periods. In ancient Roman legal discourse, for example, a prostitute was one "engaging in sexual activity with a large number of customers for money or other material remuneration."[2] The definition can also be applied to the modern Japanese term *baishun* as defined in the 1956 law prohibiting the indiscriminate exchange of sexual services for payment.[3] The ultimate validity of the term "prostitute," however, is a matter of dispute. Shannon Bell approaches the question from a theoretical perspective, arguing that "the flesh-and-blood female body engaged in some form of sexual interaction in exchange for some kind of payment has no inherent meaning and is signified differently in different discourses."[4] Observers in recent times as well as in the past have wrestled with the problems of distinguishing prostitutes from the casually promiscuous, from "courtesans" who might not have offered sex indiscriminately or for direct payment, or from poor women who survived on occasion by turning a trick.[5] Such difficulties are compounded when one studies an economy not yet fully commercialized or a society that may not judge the sale of sex as deviant. Even in the commercialized society of late medieval England, which placed the sale of sex outside of Christian law, the Latin term *meretrix,* usually translated "prostitute," could simply mean a promiscuous woman; and in medieval Europe, according to Ruth Mazo Karras, "it was not the exchange of money, nor even multiple partners, but the public and indiscriminate availability of a woman's body that was the defining feature of prostitution."[6]

If "prostitute" is a slippery term in commercialized societies or those that subject the sex trade to legal and ecclesiastical controls, it is all the more so for Heian and Kamakura Japan. There was almost no legislation regarding the sex trade, and the incomplete commercialization of the economy makes it hard to differentiate prostitutes who were paid from sexual partners who were given gifts. In fact, much literature about sexual interaction with women such as *asobi* maintained at least the appearance that their rewards were considered gifts, not payment. However, even though some scholars argue that sex was not commercialized until the fourteenth century,[7] several eleventh-century accounts refer to the exchange of sexual services for payment as a "sale."[8] By mid-Heian times, in other words, women's sexual bodies could be treated as commodities and women's sexual service as labor for hire. In this sense *asobi* and others can be regarded as prostitutes. However, the term also implies that there are orthodox and unorthodox sexual liaisons distinguished by criteria such as governmental or ecclesiastical sanction, permanence, limits on additional relationships, and quid pro quo payments. Sexual relationships in Heian and Kamakura Japan were not so neatly divided; in particular, as I will discuss in detail shortly, marriage was poorly defined, especially in Heian times, and thus could not serve as a model of orthodoxy against which to contrast other liaisons and label them as transgressive.

Japanese scholars have examined some of the complexities and contradictions in the lives of sexual entertainers and in the ways that society regarded them. Scholars fall roughly into two camps: those who see the women as marginalized and exploited, even when they maintained relationships with men of power, and those who argue that they were integrated into society and included women of wealth, power, and recognized position.[9] Both camps generally concur that the women's status fell sometime between the mid-Kamakura and early Muromachi ages, but they disagree on timing and particulars. Perhaps in part because the women themselves varied in refinement and social class, attitudes toward them were always ambiguous, ranging from delight to dismay at any given time. However, the image of their trade as illicit and the women themselves as transgressors began to affect social policy beginning in the Kamakura period. At first the women's severest critics did little but wring their hands. But by the thirteenth century negative judgments began to generate action, including restrictions on certain sex-related occupations and limits on the inheritance rights of sexual entertainers. The women were not made outlaws or outcastes, however, nor was the sex trade strictly regulated until the sixteenth century, when it was nominally confined to licensed quarters. In general, attitudes toward the trade remained tolerant compared to common views of it as degraded in most European Christian societies.

Sources

I base my work on a variety of evidence. For the early portion of the period, especially, the most important sources are commentaries and diaries written by court aristocrats; didactic stories *(setsuwa)* compiled by literate men, some of them monks; poems, tales, and miscellany, some composed by women; and songs that purport, perhaps falsely, to reveal the voices of women in the sex trade themselves. In the Kamakura period, entertainers and the sex trade appear as objects of legislation and decisions in court cases, adding another dimension to the personal observations that dominate Heian sources. Often the evidence reveals conflicting interests of the major components in the power structure of Heian and Kamakura Japan: courtiers, monks, and, from the mid-twelfth century, warrior elites. Each had its own reasons for defining (or not defining) specific sexual acts as transgressive; moreover, the treatment of sexual professionals was sometimes the product of the multiple and often quite personal intentions of individuals within elite strata.[10] As different as these localized concerns may have been, however, they were subsumed by broad socioeconomic pressures that produced a discernible trend toward marginalization. By using a wide variety of sources, without privileging one type over another, I aim to illuminate this process of historical change.

Most sources indicate far more about the way sexual entertainment and entertainers were perceived than about the way they actually lived. Although many sexual entertainers were literate, they rarely wrote about their own lives. Contemporary sources reveal the ways in which elite men patronized, praised, criticized, restricted, and both legitimized and delegitimized professional sexual entertainment. There is, of course, a great deal more to the story of female sexual professionals than the way in which they were viewed and treated by men of authority; most of this story is available only by inference and dependent on sources that have already been selected and edited by elites. Occasional glimpses of agency—of entrepreneurship, resistance, or even regret—serve as reminders that the women were actual historical subjects, not mere literary tropes or illustrations of moral or social positions. The necessary reliance on elite male discourse reflected in most sources should not negate the reality of the women's lives, even when that reality is difficult to ascertain.

Historical Background: A Brief Sketch

Sexual entertainment as a defined profession first appeared in the middle of the Heian age, a time when a state system based on laws *(ritsuryō)* appropriated from Chinese models was giving way to the *ōchō kokka* or court-centered polity, in which power was still in the hands of the throne and the court but was exercised through institutions that had not been established in the *ritsuryō* codes, such as private landholding systems and a regency for both child and adult sovereigns.[11] Both *ritsuryō* and *ōchō* societies were dominated by a tiny aristocracy that monopolized wealth, land, and high culture, though not basic literacy. From the end of the ninth century, the court itself was dominated by a branch of the Fujiwara family, which married its daughters to crown princes and rulers and controlled access to the throne through regental offices. Fujiwara regents also held superior title to significant tracts of agricultural land, firming their grip on economic as well as political life. Lesser figures of the aristocracy served at court but perhaps more importantly in the provinces as well; as provincial governors and district heads, they both accumulated private wealth and extended tentacles of power into local society.

The agrarian economy of mid- and late-Heian Japan was dominated by privately controlled estates *(shōen)* and public lands *(kokugaryō)* controlled by provincial officials in much the same way as *shōen.* No one owned exclusive title to *shōen* lands; rather, holders including local managers and aristocratic absentee overlords possessed designated rights to a portion of produce from particular fields. Important shrines and monasteries often had overlords' rights. At the very highest level of the landholding hierarchy were powerful nobles at court who wangled exemptions from central government taxes for their fields. However, dues paid to overlords and guarantors were the equivalent of taxes and individual estates became de facto units of government, with localized police and juridical systems.

While the economy of Heian Japan was primarily agrarian, many people made a living in occupations other than farming. Goods shipped to the capital from distant estates required a transportation network peopled by sailors, teamsters, and porters. Ironcasters made and sold metal implements such as farm tools and weapons. Silk thread was produced for sale in regions where mulberry trees flourished. Cohorts of hunters specialized in supplying fowl for the court's tables. The mid-tenth-century dictionary *Wamyō ruijushō,* which contains the oldest known reference to *asobi,* lists other nonagricultural occupations such as potters, fishers, and peddlers.

In the period under study, Japan was emerging slowly from a gift/barter economy to a profit economy based on cash payments and the commodification of services—a transformation that began sometime in the late Heian period in advanced locations and was not complete by the end of Kamakura. Coins had been minted in the realm in the Nara and early Heian periods, although it seems doubtful that the use of cash penetrated very deeply into ordinary society. There is little evidence of cash in the subsequent years of the Heian period, until the mid-twelfth century when land began to be sold for cash, probably in the form of coins imported from China. Most taxes and estate dues were calculated in rice but sometimes in textiles or other manufactured goods. Yet commercial transactions flourished even in mid-Heian times, despite the absence of a standard medium of exchange. Excess goods from estates were often traded at markets in the capital of Heian-kyō. At the highest social level, individuals were rewarded by land rights that enabled them to exploit agricultural and handicraft production; workers, including sexual entertainers, were paid in rice, wine, or clothing. In the Kamakura period, entertainers and artisans were also sometimes paid in cash or given rights to small portions of land.

A civilian aristocracy controlled the court and landed wealth in Heian times, but warriors played an important role in extending state power to remote regions, keeping the peace in provinces and capital, and supporting factions at court. When disputes at court erupted into civil conflicts at the end of the twelfth century, powerful warriors took the opportunity to insert themselves into politics at the level of the realm. After the last of these conflicts ended in 1185, warriors led by Minamoto Yoritomo joined the court in establishing dual control over the archipelago, launching what later historians would call the Kamakura period. Under Yoritomo and his early successors, the administrative organization that we now call the bakufu respected and upheld court prerogatives and land rights but did not hesitate to extend those of warriors.[12] By the middle of the thirteenth century, however, court politics came under bakufu sway. Formally speaking the bakufu governed other warriors and their dependents, doing so in part through a code of laws that regulated their conduct, including aspects of sexual behavior and family organization.

Important religious establishments, which held significant land rights and whose clergy often had family ties to powerful figures at court, joined court and warrior government as a third significant component in the Heian and Kamakura power structure. The political and economic roles of religious institutions influenced their definitions of sexual orthodoxy and transgression, but religious ideology played a significant part as well. Particularly important was the absence of any concept of "sin" as a cosmic moral offense. Buddhism considered all human desires to be illusions that obstructed the path to Buddhahood; Buddhist concerns with female sexuality largely rested on fears that men—especially nominally celibate monks—would be overcome by sexual desire. Strategies proposed for overcoming the power of desire contributed to the definition of sexual transgression in society as a whole. On the other hand, the largely indigenous belief system that predated Buddhism celebrated sexuality as a life-giving force. Many sources suggest that sexual affirmation in Japanese folk religion generated a tolerant attitude toward female sexual activity. Yet the belief that women were ritually polluted was promoted in part by the indigenous system.

One difficulty in defining any given sexual activity as transgressive is the fuzzy boundary between sexual orthodoxy and heterodoxy in Heian and Kamakura Japan. Elite society tolerated a wide range of sexual relationships and behavior. Male-male relations, male promiscuity, and female premarital relationships were well within the bounds of acceptable behavior.[13] Arranged marriages were common, but so too were liaisons based on personal romantic attraction; at the same time, sexual liaisons with someone of higher status were a standard method of advancing one's position and that of one's family. Japanese society in the Heian and Kamakura periods recognized a variety of relationships based on a variety of motives, requiring neither love nor procreation for a socially validated union.

In comparison with other times in Japan and with many other cultures, women held a relatively high position in Heian elite society. Although disadvantaged by the inability to hold important public offices, elite women were neither politically nor economically helpless. They could inherit and hold real estate, movable goods, and rights to land. At court, women exercised informal power through sons, brothers, and fathers; literate female courtiers became formidable cultural and social arbiters. On the other hand, the polygynous marriage system made women a commodity utilized by their male relatives to obtain political influence. The dual role of elite women as agents and tools of power conditioned the way that they and others used their sexuality and the way in which it was regarded by society.

The definition of "marriage" was fluid—as Hitomi Tonomura has remarked about the twelfth century, marriage "was a social process without a name."[14] As readers of *The Tale of Genji* know very well, elite families were based on polygynous liaisons in which a man could have several publicly recognized partners.[15] In addition to long-term relationships, a man might have short-term affairs with women of much lower social status than he. Since women often held property, a man was not necessarily obliged to support his wives financially—in fact he was sometimes supported by a wife's parents; but he did incur both financial and social obligations to his children of a recognized union. For that reason, it seems unlikely that elite marriage patterns were entirely reproduced among ordinary peasants and city dwellers.

Married couples did not necessarily live together, especially when they were young. In Heian times and to some extent in Kamakura, women often remained in their parents' home or a home they had inherited from their parents; their husbands paid them visits, and the children were raised by the mother and her family. The bilateral kinship system, in which the political backing and social status of both the mother's and the father's families were important and property could be passed down from fathers or mothers to both sons and daughters, gave elite women an additional measure of support, even when they did form a household with their husbands. The system had both drawbacks and advantages for women. On the one hand, wives could be easily neglected or abandoned. On the other hand, the uxorilocal marriage pattern gave a woman considerable influence over her children and a degree of freedom from her husband's control. In particular, the pattern made it difficult to enforce monogamy for wives, even though it was formally expected of them. In addition, marriages were not necessarily permanent: although strictly speaking only a husband could initiate a divorce, a wife or her family could pressure the husband for a separation; and there was no unconditional ban on remarriage for divorced women or widows. Polygyny, the wife-visiting system, the ease of divorce and remarriage, and the absence of any required marriage ceremony or authority to legitimize a marriage—all make it difficult to define sexual orthodoxy and transgression clearly in the Heian period.

In the thirteenth and fourteenth centuries, definitions of sexual transgression were shaped in part by emerging patterns of inheritance and marriage. As demands for land rights increased, the bakufu came to favor male unigeniture over partible inheritance patterns and began to restrict the rights of women to inherit and bequeath property. In addition, virilocal marriage patterns were promoted within warrior society but were not firmly established even at the end of the Kamakura period.[16] Even though incompletely realized, these trends contributed to a definition of orthodox sexual relationships that in many aspects resembled the Chinese patriarchal model. Ironically, such a model had been mandated by eighth-century law codes without becoming the norm in practice.[17] A Chinese-style model of marriage gained in strength as other patterns of society and government drifted away from continental standards.

THESE HISTORICAL PATTERNS provide the context for the development of sexual entertainment occupations explored in this book. Chapter 1 provides a general overview of these occupations. Using writings of courtiers who observed—or imagined—sexual entertainers, I discuss the operation of the sex trade and its role in contemporary society. Chapter 2 turns to a broader topic: the construction of concepts of sexual transgression. I examine popular tale literature and law codes—sources that are often thought to contradict one another—for the bases used to identify certain actions and relationships as transgressive. In Chapter 3, I explore the relationship of the sex trade to religious issues such as the sacred nature of sex, ritual pollution, and redemption and salvation. In this chapter I challenge commonly accepted theories of an organic connection between sexual entertainers and female shamans. Chapter 4 examines questions concerning stigma and the construction of a transgressive identity as "prostitute" for sexual entertainers: when and why did this occur, and how was the process related to socioeconomic developments on a larger scale?

In general, I agree with the many Japanese scholars who have posited a historical decline in the social status of the sexual entertainment trade. It is all too easy, however, to characterize this decline as a smooth linear process; at any historical moment during the period in question, sexual entertainment occupied an ambiguous position, both socially and in terms of public mores. Sexual entertainment emerged as a recognized trade during the Heian period, but entertainers themselves were sometimes regarded with suspicion or even contempt. Although they mixed freely with elites, sexual entertainers were not of elite status. Moreover, issues linking some of the women to varieties of societal disorder were raised in middle and late Heian times, even as literate courtiers were extolling the musical performances and sexual pleasures of *asobi* and *kugutsu*. Conversely, although from the mid-thirteenth century sexual entertainers were subjected to discrimination and attitudes expressed toward them were generally less favorable than before, this was also the period in which we find considerable evidence that they possessed land rights and were of sufficiently high status to file lawsuits before court or bakufu judges. While the women were obviously considered functioning members of society and thus objects of legislative and juridical oversight, policies generated by this oversight were negative on the whole. Patterns of decline and incorporation need to be analyzed together, not as contradictions but as modes of interaction with changing social conditions. As I venture to do so, I hope to provide some understanding of the way sexual norms developed in a society very different from those in which we live.

Delightful Sirens and Delighted Patrons

Their voices halt the clouds floating through the valleys, and their tones drift with the wind blowing over the water. Passersby cannot help but forget their families.—Ōe Masafusa, *Yūjoki* (An account of *asobi*)

WITH HYPERBOLIC FLOURISH, a twelfth-century courtier-poet thus describes cohorts of *asobi,* professional sexual entertainers who plied their trade along the river route from the capital to points south and west. In this essay and a companion piece about *kugutsu,* Ōe Masafusa (1041–1111) scrutinizes female performing artists who appeared on the scene in the middle and late Heian period, describing them in florid detail. Masafusa's work occupies a central place in the observations of elite male courtier-literati, some of whom patronized *asobi* and other sexual entertainers, a few of whom criticized or even deplored them. In essays, diaries, poems, and tales, such men explored the delights and perils of professional sexual entertainment. Court women, often among the audience for the musical performances of *asobi,* also offered an occasional view; and lyrics to songs that *asobi* and *kugutsu* used to entertain men provide an additional perspective on the sex trade and its practitioners. This chapter examines these varied sources for both male experiences with sexual professionals and details about the women's lives; Chapter 4 will revisit some of the same sources to examine public policies toward the sex trade and issues of stigma and marginalization.

Speculating on Origins

According to one version of the fourteenth-century *Hōnen shōnin eden* (Illustrated biography of St. Hōnen), the first *asobi* were eight princesses dispatched to "the seven circuits" or regions of Japan by the sovereign Kōkō Tennō (r. 884–887).[1] In positing a royal origin for the *asobi,* the text suggests their relatively high social status as entertainers of aristocratic patrons. Yet it goes on to depict them as prostitutes who used cosmetics and sexual wiles to deceive men, and it concludes that they had fallen into sin.

The authors of *Hōnen shōnin eden* had their own reasons for portraying *asobi* as women who had tumbled from high positions into a moral abyss, a topic I will explore in a later chapter. While no one takes the princess theory seriously today, modern Japanese scholars have vigorously debated other possible origins of both the female performing traditions and the sex trade. Although these are not quite the same issue, the debates have overlapped, and two major theories have emerged: one contends that performers such as the *asobi* traced their lineage from female shamans who turned to secular entertainment and prostitution; the other holds that traditions combining performance and prostitution originated on the Asian continent and were brought to Japan by continental immigrants.

Citing similarities between Chinese entertainer-prostitutes and *asobi,* Takigawa Masajirō argued in the mid-1960s that the *asobi* tradition originated among female entertainers of slave status in China and was transmitted to Japan through Korea, perhaps by immigrants. A similar argument was applied to the *kugutsu.*[2] Fukutō Sanae has criticized Takigawa's theory as both ethnocentric and biased against women, and Amino Yoshihiko has dismissed it as a "short circuit" resulting from prejudice against Korea.[3] However, it seems reasonable to suppose that elements of any performing tradition might have been introduced from other East Asian societies; in particular, Matsumae Takeshi has pointed out similarities between continental puppetry traditions and those practiced by *kugutsu.*[4] But Takigawa's argument that the first *asobi* were of foreign origin has no conclusive evidence to support it. Most modern scholarship locates the origins of female sexual entertainment within Japan. Early-twentieth-century scholars such as Yanagita Kunio and Nakayama Tarō traced the origin of *asobi* to female shamans, an argument that I examine in detail in Chapter 3.[5] Their theories suggest an intriguing connection between religious and sexual practices, but actual evidence is scanty and based on speculation. In fact it seems fruitless to search for one ultimate historical origin for performing traditions and sexual practices that no doubt had multiple roots.

As a trade, however, the sexual entertainment practiced by *asobi* had antecedents in the professional banquet entertainment offered by *ukareme,* women who appear in the eighth-century poetry collection *Man'yōshū.* The *asobi* trade probably developed as *ukareme* organized into groups, expanded their practice beyond official banquets, settled at specific locations, adopted signature methods and performing practices, and added sexual services as a routine component of their entertainment package.[6] *Ukareme* and *asobi* are equated, in fact, in the earliest known reference to the *asobi* profession, an item in *Wamyō ruijushō* (*Wamyōshō;* Topical collection of Japanese terms). Compiled in the mid-930s by Minamoto Shitagō (911–983), a poet and scholar with a modest career at court, *Wamyōshō* is both a dictionary that gives the pronunciation and etymology of terms written in Chinese characters and an encyclopedia of social phenomena in mid-Heian Japan. *Asobi* are listed under the category "beggars and thieves," along with convicts, robber gangs, pirates, and male and female shamans. The text, which reads as follows, is unique among Heian-period depictions of *asobi* in that it explicitly categorizes them as social undesirables:

> *Asobi* 遊女 (*yahochi* 夜発)
>
> [The eighth-century dictionary] *Yōshi kangoshō* lists [the following characters] 遊行女児 (pronounced *ukareme* or *asobi*). According to one source, those who wander about in the daytime are called *asobi,* while those who wait until nighttime and then offer illicit sex *(inbon)* are called *yahochi.*[7]

Wamyōshō lists three terms for the women in this category: *ukareme, asobi,* and *yahochi.* The pronunciations for all three terms are given in an interlinear note, suggesting that they may not have appeared in the original source, a dictionary dated around 717–723 that is no longer completely extant. The term *asobi* is rendered by two of the characters in *ukareme,* indicating the connection between the two types of performers. The *Wamyōshō* citation is the first known reference to either *asobi* or *yahochi,* but *ukareme* have been found in earlier sources: they were traveling performers who entertained guests at banquets, often at provincial headquarters. Literate and accomplished, *ukareme* are credited with some fifty poems in the *Man'yōshū,* such as this one:

> The road to Yamato
> is hidden in the clouds but
> do not think it rude of me
> to wave my sleeve in farewell.

> When the Dazaifu governor-general Lord Ōtomo [Tabito] received a concurrent appointment as major counselor *[dainagon]*, he set out along the highway to the capital. That day he halted his horse at Mizuki and from there looked back at the Dazaifu headquarters. There was an *ukareme* named Kojima with the officials seeing the governor off. She was pained by the casual nature of their separation, and lamented the unlikelihood of ever seeing him again. Wiping away her tears, she recited this farewell poem.[8]

As this note to Kojima's *Man'yōshū* poem suggests, *ukareme* sometimes had sexual relations with the high-status men they entertained—a natural outgrowth, according to Fukutō Sanae, of the custom of engaging in sex after feasting at community religious rituals. Some *ukareme* formed long-term socially recognized relationships with their patrons.[9] Although *Wamyōshō* equates *ukareme* and *asobi*, both Fukutō and Sekiguchi Hiroko argue that the two were differentiated by the latter's role as sexual professionals.[10] By the late tenth century, sexual services were routinely provided to male patrons in exchange for payment, a change that coincided with the increasing use of the term *asobi*. *Wamyōshō* signals the inception of this change by listing both *asobi* and *yahochi* in an occupational category that offered illicit sex.

Yahochi are often identified as common prostitutes in contrast to the *asobi*, who were also entertainers.[11] However, *Wamyōshō* clearly considers *yahochi* a subset of *asobi* and draws no substantial distinction between the two. The only other Heian source that mentions *yahochi* to my knowledge—the mid-eleventh-century *Shinsarugakuki*—does not distinguish between them in any way at all. In short, we do not have enough information about the *yahochi* to conclude very much about them.

According to Sekiguchi, the commodification of women's sexual services necessary for prostitution to develop occurred between the eighth and the tenth centuries, the result of a change in family structures from a system with strong maternal rights and individual freedom of choice in marriage to a patriarchal system in which women were controlled by men and monogamy was expected of wives. While eighth-century *ukareme* had dispensed their sexual favors as they pleased, *asobi* of the tenth century and later transformed these favors into services for market.[12] In other words, the difference between *ukareme* and *asobi* lay not so much in their conduct but in the way that conduct was categorized in the wake of changing socioeconomic and marriage patterns.

Asobi are often identified only by personal names, a practice that may indicate a special occupational status. Sekiguchi argues that in using such names, *asobi* followed distinctive conventions that differed from the standard practices of identifying women as so-and-so's daughter or by office, status, or occupation if they served at court.[13] The names used by *asobi* seem to have been stage names: some had a Buddhist flavor (such as Kannon or Nyoi), while others (Nakanokimi or Kakohime) hinted at high birth or status. The special naming convention for *asobi* suggests a position outside both the patriarchal family and ordinary social hierarchies.

Riparian Pleasure Spots

By the end of the tenth century, *asobi* had developed their distinctive practice of using small boats to stage entertainments for men at ports on the Yodo River and its tributary the Kamusaki, ports such as Eguchi, Kamusaki, and Kaya. These ports became favorite settings for courtiers' essays and diary entries that constructed a romanticized view of *asobi* as alluring singers. The courtiers, mostly middle-ranking aristocrats with a penchant for poetry and Chinese learning, developed consistent figures of *asobi* by employing similar tropes and metaphors. In this section of the chapter, I examine the production of an ideal *asobi* by male courtiers and note deviations in the picture—remnants, perhaps, of the beggar/thief category of slightly earlier times. Using this material, it is also possible to tease out a few historical details about the *asobi*'s lives and the way they did business.

An early account of the boat trade appears in *Asobi o miru* (Seeing *asobi*), an essay by Ōe Yukitoki (955–1010) in the collection *Honchō monzui* (Choice literary selections of our realm). The essay relates that when the governor of Iyo was traveling through the provinces along the Inland Sea—the year was probably 996—he reached the river port of Kaya,[14] where it was the popular practice to "show off the charms of women and peddle their love." *Asobi* would wait for customers at the boat anchorage and detain them on their journey down the river:

> The younger women melt men's hearts with rouge and powder and songs and smiles, while the older women give themselves the jobs of carrying the parasols and poling the boats. If there are husbands, they censure their wives because their

> lovers are too few. If there are parents, they wish only that their daughters were fortunate enough to be summoned by many customers. This has become the custom, although no human feeling is involved. Truly, using [the characters for] "vagabond" *(yūkō)* to designate the women takes reality and makes it into their name.
>
> Ah! Although spending the night behind emerald curtains in their crimson boudoirs violates the rituals of marriage, a tryst in a boat on the waves equals a lifetime of delightful encounters. Whenever we travel this road and see such things, we must sigh in regret at such a persistent custom. Why don't we take our hearts that are so fond of making love and embark upon the road to loving wisdom?[15]

In his final assessment of the *asobi,* Yukitoki paraphrases the Confucian *Analects* ("I have not yet seen people pursue virtue as avidly as they pursue carnal love").[16] Thus while he acknowledges the appeal of the *asobi,* he concludes with a strong tone of disapproval rarely found in later Heian sources.

When the courtier-literatus Fujiwara Akihira (989–1066) depicts a fictional *asobi* in *Shinsarugakuki* (Record of the new monkey music), his lusty account of Heian-kyō street life, he concentrates on the pleasures that she offers, ending with a mild lament that seems almost perfunctory:

> The sixteenth daughter [of a palace official] is the *chōja* [leader] of a group of *asobi* and *yahochi,* a woman who delights in making love at Eguchi and Kawashiri. She is experienced in the wanton pleasures of Kawakami and transmits the brazen customs of Sakamoto.[17] In the daytime she carries a huge parasol and offers her body to customers of high and low estate, and at night she drums the side of her boat and tenders her heart to travelers. Her vigor in soliciting lovers, her knowledge of all the sexual positions, the merits of her lute strings and buds of wheat, and her mastery of the dragon's flutter and tiger's tread techniques—all are her endowments. Not only that, she has the voice of a bird in Amida's paradise, as well as the face of an angel. Although people praise the songs of Miyagi and Kokarasu and the voices of Yakushi and Naruto,[18] compared to hers they are no competition, and set beside hers they are inconsiderable. How can she fail to bewitch any man's eyes or melt any fellow's heart? Alas! Even though she may spend her youth selling her body, how will she pass her remaining days when her beauty fades?[19]

The *Shinsarugakuki* account refers directly to the *asobi*'s lovemaking prowess, leaving no doubt that it was sex as well as entertainment that attracted male

aristocrats such as Akihira. His graphic description employed euphemisms from *Ishinhō,* a late-tenth-century medical text based on Chinese models: lute strings and buds of wheat refer to the female genitals, and the dragon's flutter and tiger's tread allude to two standard positions for intercourse.[20]

In an exchange of letters with a friend, Akihira presents himself as a patron of *asobi* and recalls his encounters with them at Uji, another well-known location of a Heian pleasure district. Akihira's description of his excursion to Uji begins with a picture of color and movement—maples turned scarlet along the bank of the roiling Uji River—built in large part on allusions to Chinese sources. He then continues: "One or two boatsful of *asobi,* floating among the reeds, sang *imayō* [popular songs] for us. I must say that this was pleasure beyond all expectations." Thus to the general picture of *asobi* as alluring entertainers and sexual professionals, Akihira adds one more signature item: the singing of *imayō.* Popular—literally, modern—songs that ranged from direct quotations of sutra verses to vignettes of street life, *imayō* were becoming the rage at court. It was probably *imayō* that attracted noble patronage in the first place and thus generated an image of *asobi* as genteel entertainers of aristocratic men.

Akihira then goes on to invite his correspondent, a minor counselor *(shōnagon)* surnamed Minamoto, to pay a visit to Eguchi:

> One bright moonlit night, a band of several of us want to head toward Kaya and take our pleasure with *asobi* in the vicinity of Eguchi. How about it? A single lifetime is not so long—it passes in a blink. In one evening of delight, we'll forget that we must grow old.
>
> People's hearts are not alike, any more than their faces. Won't those who have no liking for such things surely sneer at our experience? Don't leak this dream to others!

Akihira's correspondent had apparently never visited the *asobi,* but in his reply he makes a firm vow to do so. He writes:

> Should I join the festivities at Eguchi on some bright moonlit night? Wise men of past and present hardly passed such things by. Who should ridicule us for it? It's the blessing of a lifetime. Let's hop on a boat right away. What shall I give the *asobi* in payment? One or two fans to wear at their waists—I've made up my mind to join you.[21]

Women as well as men enjoyed the performances of *asobi,* as indicated by this entry in *Sarashina nikki,* a diary kept by the daughter of a provincial governor and completed sometime between 1058 and 1064:

> Late on the night that we stayed at Takahama [on the Yodo River], I heard the sound of a skiff being poled through the darkness. Someone said that *asobi* were approaching. Everyone perked up and we had the women pull alongside us. A torch glowing in the distance revealed the *asobi,* wearing simple unlined robes with trailing sleeves and concealing their faces behind their fans as they sang. It was very touching.[22]

By far the most detailed account of Heian *asobi* is Ōe Masafusa's essay *Yūjoki.* A scholar and an accomplished poet in both Chinese and Japanese, Masafusa is probably best known for his collections of *ōjōden,* Buddhist tales of rebirth in paradise, but he also wrote vivid descriptions of Heian street life and popular customs.[23] *Yūjoki* is thought to date from the last years of his life.[24] As an intimate adviser to Go-Sanjō Tennō (r. 1068–1072), Masafusa must have regarded the *asobi* with a court official's eye, but he also was no doubt well acquainted with the enjoyment they provided to aristocrats of the highest station. Although Masafusa cites Yukitoki's essay and considered Akihira his mentor, in *Yūjoki* he incorporates neither the concluding exhortation of *Asobi o miru* nor the milder lament of *Shinsarugakuki.* Instead, he offers a romanticized view of the *asobi* as providers of pleasure for the highest Heian elites:[25]

> Heading westward one day's journey down the Uji River from the port of Yodo in Yamashiro, one reaches the place called Kaya. All those who travel back and forth [between the capital and the western provinces] along the Sanyō, Saikai, and Nankai highways must follow this route.[26] The river winds north, then south, twisting around villages and between dwellings, until it turns toward Kawachi. This spot is called Eguchi. The Bureau of Medicine's Ajifu pastures and the Housekeeping Bureau's Ōba estate are located nearby.
>
> Upon reaching Settsu province,[27] one arrives at places such as Kamusaki and Kashima, where gates are lined up and doors are arranged in rows, leaving no space between dwellings. There, female entertainers have banded together; they pole their skiffs out to meet incoming boats and solicit men to share their beds. Their voices halt the clouds floating through the valleys, and their tones drift with

the wind blowing over the water. Passersby cannot help but forget their families. The ripples spray like flowers among the reeds along the shore, and the boats of old fishermen and peddlers line up stem to stern, almost as if there's no water in between.[28] This is certainly the premier pleasure spot in the realm.

Eguchi has chosen Kannon as its head. The others include Nakanokimi, Koma, Shirome, and Tonomori. Kashima has chosen Miyashiro as its mistress,[29] and the others are Nyoi, Kōro, Kujaku, and Tachimai. Kamusaki has chosen Kakohime as its leader. Others include Koso, Miyako, Rokumei, and Shōmi. They are all reincarnations of Kushira [the black cuckoo of India, which has a splendid voice] or Sotoori-hime [a famous beauty who appears in the *Kokin wakashū* preface].

From the highest nobility down to the hoi polloi, the women invite all to their bamboo-matted chambers and bestow favors upon them. Some men make these women their wives and mistresses and love them until death. Even wise men and princes are not exempt.

To the south lies Sumiyoshi shrine and to the west, Hirota. The *asobi* go there to pray for lovers. Hyaku Dayū, whom they especially worship, is their guardian deity.[30] If one were carved for each customer, the numbers would stretch to the hundreds and thousands.

The *asobi* skillfully seduce men's hearts, just as in times of old. In the Chōhō era [999–1004], Higashi Sanjō-in [961–1001; Fujiwara Senshi, Enyū's queen-consort] made a pilgrimage to Sumiyoshi and Tennōji. At that time the Tonsured Prime Minister [Fujiwara Michinaga, 966–1027] made love to Shō Kannon. In the Chōgen era [1028–1036], Jōtōmon-in [988–1074; Fujiwara Shōshi, the consort of Ichijō Tennō] also made her devotions there, and at that time [one of her fellow pilgrims] the Uji Prime Minister [Fujiwara Yorimichi, 990–1074] favored Nakanokimi. In the Enkyū era [1069–1074], the retired monarch Go-Sanjō honored the same shrine and temple with a visit, and Komainu, Kōshi, and their companions came alongside his boat.[31] People called the *asobi* immortals[32]—these were the most extraordinary events of the age.

According to old stories, when courtiers and men of elegance traveled from the capital to the vicinity of Kaya in order to take pleasure with *asobi,* they favored women at Eguchi. People traveling on the river from western Japan, from provincial governors on down, are said to have favored women at Kamusaki. This is because everyone stopped at the first place he reached.

Payment for the women's services is known as *danshu.* When it comes time to distribute the earnings, the women lose all sense of shame and become incredibly quarrelsome. The arguments that ensue, both major and minor, turn into a real battle. One solution is to cut lengths of unpatterned silk into short pieces, or to divide rice into smaller measures, just as Chin Bei[33] divided up the meat.

When serving women from some of the great houses board the boats plying the river, it's called "filling in at the last minute"[34] or "going out to entertain." They can earn a small amount—some extra for the day. The way the women tie up their hair is called "spreading out fabric."[35] Taking their parasols on board, everyone sets out half-moon emblems.[36] Even though one can read the essay by the scholar Gō [Ōe Yukitoki], I thought I'd set down some additional details here.

A multilayered account, *Yūjoki* presents the *asobi* as elegant performing artists who traded in both sex and entertainment. Perhaps, as Barbara Ruch has argued, they might be compared to the ancient Greek hetairai, social and sexual companions to wealthy men.[37] The *asobi* used music for seduction, and the seductiveness of the singers must have added to the enchantment of their art. Since court ladies as well as men enjoyed these performances, however, encounters between nobles and *asobi* involved far more than sexual pleasure.

By naming famous patrons, Masafusa binds the *asobi* pleasure districts to paradigmatic aristocrats of the recent past; by laying out a course for travelers, he creates a guide for present and future journeys. Masafusa's vivid description suggests that he too was a patron of *asobi,* and he offers no moral or social criticism of the women as seducers or courtesans. Only a peek at their private quarters shows them to be greedy and quarrelsome. In public, though, they provide entertainment fit for regents and sovereigns but remain accessible to ordinary men.

A number of other Heian sources detail the relationship between courtiers and *asobi,* confirming and augmenting Masafusa's observations. Sometimes the courtiers invited *asobi* to their own villas. According to the tenth-century *Yamato monogatari* (Tales of Yamato), Shirome—called an *ukareme* in this source and an *asobi* in others—was summoned before the retired sovereign Uda (r. 887–897) and commanded to produce a poem.[38] This poem so impressed Uda that he expressed his admiration and showered her with gifts.[39] In 988, when the regent Fujiwara Kaneie (920–990) gave a banquet to celebrate the construction of his new mansion at Nijō in the capital, a group of *asobi* from Kaya joined the festivities and was rewarded with forty rolls of silk and sixty *koku* of rice.[40] In 1105, Fujiwara Tadazane (1078–1162)—soon to assume the post of regent—was "secretly" entertained in his home by a pair of *asobi.*[41] More often, however, courtier diaries and other sources depict the visits of aristocrats to the pleasure districts—beginning in 1000 with that of Higashi Sanjō-in and Michinaga (cited by Masafusa)[42] and continuing at least until the late thirteenth century.[43]

While accounts in such sources are in general less descriptive—and certainly less overblown—than Akihira's fiction or the essays by Yukitoki and Masafusa, they contain valuable information about the patrons of *asobi,* the types and amounts of payment, and the way *asobi* conducted their business. These sources indicate that most Heian *asobi* were far from *Wamyōshō*'s "beggars and thieves." It is not necessary to establish the literal truth of each account to conclude that *asobi* provided a significant source of entertainment, sexual and otherwise, for elite men of the court.

Pilgrimage and Pleasure

The Yodo basin pleasure districts lay along a busy route that linked the capital with important religious sites such as Sumiyoshi, Hirota and Kumano shrines, Shitennōji, and the Shingon complex at Mt. Kōya. The vicinities of other pilgrimage sites such as Byōdōin at Uji were also locations of a thriving *asobi* trade. In choosing such locations, *asobi* showed themselves to be astute entrepreneurs who took advantage of a profit-making opportunity. Although there was some conflict between religious requirements for abstinence and sexual contact with *asobi,* in general courtiers negotiated a skillful path between the two.

In the Edo period (1603–1867), pilgrims to shrines and temples frequently combined religious devotions with entertainment, including visits to brothels and sexual relationships with other pilgrims. According to James H. Foard, pilgrims found themselves outside the restrictive structures of community and family: "The road itself was the marginal space in which structures broke down. . . . The pleasure and even licentiousness of pilgrims were part of this liberation from structure."[44] More generally, the connection between piety and pleasure can be found in examinations of the amusement districts that developed at the gates of temples, such as Sensōji in the Asakusa district of Edo.[45]

Aristocratic pilgrimage exploded during the twelfth century, as retired sovereigns and their consorts, regents, court ladies, and lesser court officials formed grand processions to favored sacred sites.[46] As in the Edo era, pilgrims made certain to enjoy themselves along the road, taking advantage of liminal circumstances to free themselves from social restrictions. While male Heian courtiers can hardly be called sexually deprived, courtship in the polite society of the capital involved a complex set of rituals and obligations. On a journey, men could shed some of these restrictions in favor of freer, more playful sexual relationships with payment the only obligation.

In the case of commoner pilgrimage of the Edo period, the other side of the temporary collapse of structure was the formation of a sense of communitas, a feeling of equality and fellowship, among pilgrims of disparate status and provenance. Heian pilgrims of the highest station, however, used pilgrimage to express their own cultural superiority and political power. In a study of imperial progressions to the shrines at Kumano, David Moerman argues that "pilgrimage served to enforce rather than dissolve social distinctions; it represented not the negation of power and force but its very articulation."[47] One of the ways courtiers displayed both largesse and cultural superiority was through generous patronage of entertainers such as the *asobi.* Heian aristocrats, in other words, not only took advantage of liminality but also seized the opportunity to enhance their own cultural capital by publicly distributing lavish rewards.

Other accounts confirm the *Yūjoki* claim that *asobi* entertained Higashi Sanjō-in, Fujiwara Michinaga, and Jōtōmon-in when they were on pilgrimages to Shitennōji and Sumiyoshi. According to *Nihon kiryaku,* after the party including Higashi Sanjō-in and Michinaga worshipped at the sacred sites, they stopped at Eguchi, rewarding the *asobi* who entertained them with one hundred and fifty *koku* of rice, respectively. Other court ladies offered unspecified gifts.[48] In another example, Minamoto Tsuneyori (d. 1039) notes in his diary *Sakeiki* that in the ninth month of 1031, Jōtōmon-in and other nobles preparing for a pilgrimage to Shitennōji and Sumiyoshi requisitioned rolls of silk for Eguchi *asobi* who would entertain them along the way.[49] The eleventh-century chronicle *Eiga monogatari* records the same visit. According to that source, the *asobi* who approached the courtiers' boat carried parasols decorated with figures of moons—perhaps the half-moon emblems mentioned by Masafusa—and wore ornaments of mother-of-pearl and gold or silver lacquer. In addition to their visual splendor, the sound of their singing voices joined with that of the waves in the reeds to create an enticing aural moment.[50] Both elegant attire and skilled musical performances enhanced the *asobi*'s appeal.

These sources indicate that *asobi* had been granted *suisan,* the privilege of approaching noblemen uninvited.[51] Although the entertainment was usually welcomed, sometimes it was deemed inappropriate. For example, when the Regent Fujiwara Yorimichi embarked on a pilgrimage to Mt. Kōya in 1048, *asobi* from the Yodo basin pleasure districts unsuccessfully solicited the patronage of his party: "Some *asobi* from Eguchi and Kamusaki asked permission to approach us. Telling them they could entertain us on our return, we admonished them all and sent them on their way."[52] The *asobi* may have been turned back to preserve the pilgrims' ritual purity on their way to a sacred site. Some days later, however, groups of *asobi* waited to greet the returning pilgrims:

> *Asobi* from Eguchi and Kamusaki lined up their parasols, competing to pay their respects and beckoning everyone. [Others][53] flaunted their beauty and sought to join the rows of those greeting us. The young women, singing praises to the buddhas and bodhisattvas, fussed with their clothing and waited eagerly to receive our favor.[54] As we passed beneath Yamazaki bridge, we prepared two hundred skeins of silk thread (from [Yorimichi's?] storehouse) and two hundred *koku* of rice (from Harima and Iyo) and sent these to the *asobi.* (Whether of high or low rank, each *asobi* received the same portion.) Two or three higher-ranking *asobi* (Kandō, Yūemon, and Akogi) were also given padded silk robes *(kosode).*[55]

While the account of Yorimichi's pilgrimage indicates that aristocratic pilgrims preferred to patronize *asobi* after visiting sacred sites, when ritual purity was no longer required, two twelfth-century courtier diaries suggest that worship and pleasure were often closely integrated. *Denryaku,* Fujiwara Tadazane's diary, relates a visit to Byōdōin in the ninth month of 1104, and *Chōshūki,* the diary of Minamoto Morotoki (1075–1136), records a pilgrimage to Hirota shrine in Settsu province in the ninth month of 1119.[56] *Asobi* entertained both sets of pilgrims—including aristocratic women on the journeys—while they were en route to a sacred site. *Chōshūki* shows *asobi* singing *imayō* and using small skiffs to approach the travelers' boats, just as described by Yukitoki, Akihira, and Masafusa.

As recorded in *Denryaku,* Tadazane set out on his journey in heavy rains on the eighteenth day of the month, accompanied by the dowager queen-consort, Fujiwara Kanshi (1036–1121), and his own grandmother, Minamoto Yoshiko (d. 1114). Later that day they were joined by Tadazane's young daughter Taishi

(1095–1155). Others in the party included male courtiers and attendants and two or three court ladies. After the party made an initial visit to the Byōdōin, "around the hour of the dog [7–9 p.m.], five or six *asobi* arrived, and they stayed until dawn. We had these *asobi* serve us in small huts nearby."

The party lodged somewhere along the Uji River. Thunderstorms prevented them from engaging in any outside activity the next day. According to Tadazane, the men spent their time drinking and having fun while the ladies watched. Perhaps *asobi* were present, but Tadazane does not mention them. They reappear in the entry of 9/21, after the party had returned in the evening from visiting the temple: "A group of *asobi* was summoned to entertain us, and one or two of the men gave them gifts of unlined silk garments." On 9/23, some additional court ladies arrived; according to an interlinear note, the women provided gifts of raw silk robes for the *asobi*. During these few days, members of the group spent their time visiting the temple, entertaining themselves with the *asobi*, and pursuing other unspecified amusements in Uji. On 9/25, however, Tadazane notes: "When we undertook penance, the *asobi* went home." Tadazane's account reveals that there was little conflict between pilgrimage and pleasure on this occasion. The pilgrims mixed visits to Byōdōin with *asobi* entertainment, and only at the end did they seem to focus exclusively on their religious aim.

The *Denryaku* account alludes to the sexual role of *asobi* but does not discuss it openly. In contrast, Minamoto Morotoki's diary *Chōshūki* explicitly discusses the sexual services provided by *asobi* to the men accompanying Shōshi (1101–1145), primary consort of the reigning sovereign Toba, on a pilgrimage to Hirota and Nishinomiya shrines. Morotoki, a high official in Shōshi's palace, was joined by several of his relatives: his three sons, his brother Moroyori, his brother-in-law Fujiwara Nagazane (1075–1133), and his cousin Minamoto Akimasa,[57] as well as by at least one Buddhist cleric, a man of the rank of monk-administrator *(sōzu)*. The party departed the capital before dawn on 9/3. Later that day:

> As we were passing the bend in the river,[58] Kumano and Hiwagimi of Eguchi followed us in the same skiff, raising two parasols in a single vessel and offering melodies of *imayō*. When our boats were slowly passing by Kamusaki, Kinju (the *chōja* [of the pleasure district there]), Kosai, Otoguro, and Tsuru [later: Wazuru][59] approached in four skiffs to meet us. In each of the five skiffs was a candidate for

> the amorous attentions of the governor of Iyo [Nagazane]. As we were sporting around in the water for a while, a light rain began to fall, eventually becoming heavy and turning back the court ladies' boat.

At this point missing characters make it hard to translate the text with any certainty. It appears, however, that the *asobi* invited everyone to the home of one of their colleagues:

> With the *asobi* in tow, we all headed for Kozen's [or Hizen's] house, where we stayed up half the night singing and carousing. As dawn approached we retired to our lodgings. The counselor of state [Moroyori] chose Kumano, the governor of Iyo picked Kinju, and the provisional captain [Akimasa] chose Kosai. Fundamentally having no taste for such things, I retreated to my room and went to sleep.

Sexual intercourse with the *asobi* must have taken place very quickly, since Morotoki reports that the courtiers departed at the hour of the rabbit—between 5 and 7 a.m. A party heading in the opposite direction informed them of a storm at sea, and so they decided to abandon the water route and use the highway to Harima instead. The rain along the way was so heavy that everyone got thoroughly soaked, even Morotoki with his umbrella and straw raincoat. Later that afternoon they arrived at Hirota shrine, mentioned in Masafusa's account as one of two shrines where *asobi* from Eguchi and Kamusaki prayed for customers. The group made offerings to the shrine and the monk among them led a Buddhist service, after which they sought lodgings for the night. They divided themselves among several lodgings; the governor of Iyo stayed at the home of a female shaman at Hirota.

After another day at the shrine, the party headed back to the capital, once more passing by the Yodo basin pleasure districts. The entry dated 9/6 reads:

> We left Kamusaki, and at Takahama we summoned six *asobi* to receive their gifts. The *chōja* Kinju received three robes and an unlined silk garment, while Kumano, Eguchi [name of *asobi*], and Iya [or Ise] also received three robes each. Hiwa[gimi] from Eguchi and Wazuru each received one. In addition, I heard that the governor of Iyo gave them some rice. While we were on the road, Nagatani, Maue, and Hirata estates (the latter is a holding of Byōdōin) sent wine and fish.[60]
>
> As we were passing by Eguchi a group of *asobi* approached us. The *chōja* Sonson [or Sonboshi] . . . [the rest of the sentence is missing].[61] Kumano [of Eguchi] was already on the boat. In preparation for a banquet, a letter of transfer *(yuzuribumi)*

> was composed, and we secured Sonboshi's [Sonson's] seal and gave the document to Kumano.[62] We then entrusted the gifts [for the Eguchi *asobi*] to Sonboshi. In addition, we gave fans to Toto and Sonboshi.[63] The details taken care of, we took Kumano and Iya along with us, lodging at the estate of the Hachiman shrine's administrator, Kōshō, who prepared for us a banquet of unusual delicacies.[64]
>
> The party returned to the capital the following day.

Denryaku and *Chōshūki* avoid Masafusa's hyperbole, instead giving straightforward accounts of entertainment for hire. The most important of men—for example, the soon-to-be regent Tadazane—were publicly entertained by *asobi.* At least in the case of the *Chōshūki* party, sexual services were an integral part of *asobi* entertainment for the men. Even the abstinent Morotoki suggests that choosing whether or not to have sexual relations with *asobi* was merely a matter of personal taste, and he offers no negative judgment of his kin for doing so.

While *Denryaku* and *Chōshūki* suggest that courtiers were attracted to *asobi* by their singing as much as by their sexual favors, *Taiki,* the diary of Fujiwara Yorinaga (1120–1156), offers a different perspective on this issue. On 1148/3/18, Yorinaga arrived at Shitennōji, intending to worship at the temple. He wrote:

> That evening, I summoned the dancer Kimikata, wanting to penetrate him. But in a dream, I realized that tomorrow I was to enter the main hall at the temple. Since violating *(okasu)* even a man would render me impure, I did not penetrate him. What an extraordinary dream!

After his visit to the temple the next day, Yorinaga boarded a boat and headed toward the ocean. On the way, a group of *asobi* approached them, and they anchored near Kashima. On 3/21 the party moved on, stopping for the night at Hashiramoto:

> That evening, I secretly invited an *asobi* on board the boat, and penetrated her.
>
> 3/22: I sent back the *asobi,* giving her some rice and some other gifts as well.[65]

Unconcerned with *imayō,* Yorinaga states his intentions bluntly and clearly. The *asobi* in this case acts as a prostitute, not as an entertainer—an interesting contrast, incidentally, with the man Yorinaga had summoned on the first night at Shitennōji, who is initially identified as a dancer. The absence of any mention of actual music or dancing in either case makes the encounter with the *asobi* raw and explicitly sexual and that with the male dancer potentially so, perhaps contributing to Yorinaga's reluctance to violate ritual purity at the boundary of Shitennōji.

Kugutsu and *Shirabyōshi*

Ōe Masafusa's essay *Kairaishiki* (An account of *kugutsu*), a companion piece to *Yūjoki,* describes *kugutsu* women, another type of late-Heian sexual entertainer often confused with *asobi.* Masafusa draws sharp distinctions between the two, although he characterizes both as singers of *imayō* and providers of sexual services. The contrast between the two essays shows how issues of class and culture colored the way male aristocrats viewed two similar entertainment professions. The *kugutsu* in *Kairaishiki* are described as a nomadic tribe —including men as well as women—whose customs set them apart from ordinary Japanese. Here *Kairaishiki* is translated in its entirety:[66]

> The *kugutsu* have no fixed abodes and no permanent households. They live in animal-hair tents and drift from place to place in pursuit of food and water, just like the northern barbarians.[67] All the men are skilled in archery on horseback and make their living by hunting. They twirl pairs of swords, juggle as many as seven balls, make wooden puppets dance, and stage wrestling competitions between puppets made of peachwood. The way they make these puppets act like living people resembles feats performed by Chinese magicians.[68] They transform sand and pebbles into gold coins and change grass and twigs into birds and animals. Indeed, their hands are quicker than a person's eyes!
>
> The women paint narrow curved eyebrows on their faces, use powder to make false teardrops on their cheeks, saunter in a flirtatious manner, and smile as if their decayed teeth hurt them. They adorn themselves with rouge and powder, sing seductive songs, and play voluptuous music, thereby pursuing sexual pleasure. Their parents and their husbands do not admonish them. They frequently entertain travelers, but they do not hesitate to spend a whole night of pleasure [with a single man]. Since their many lovers indulge them with valuables such as embroidered and brocade clothing, golden hair ornaments, and boxes decorated with gold, the women can't help but treasure these things.
>
> The *kugutsu* do not cultivate a single rice field or harvest the leaves from a single

mulberry branch. Thus they are not under the control of provincial authorities, and none of them is settled. Instead, they are nothing but gypsies, who neither recognize the court nor fear local officials. Because they pay no taxes, they live their entire lives as they please. In the evenings they worship Hyaku Kami,[69] beating drums, dancing, and making an uproar to pray for help in obtaining good fortune.

The finest and most esteemed bands come from the eastern provinces of Mino, Mikawa, and Ōmi; coming next are bands from Harima in the Sanyō district and from Tajima in the San'in. Those in Kyushu come last. The *kugutsu* I can name are Komi, Nippyaku, Sanzensai, Banzai, Kokimi, Magokimi. . . .

When [the famous singer] Kanga made the dust move with a powerful voice that shook the rafters, the audience soaked the dangling cords of their caps with tears and Kanga was unable to take an intermission.[70] One cannot count all the genres—*imayō, furukawayō, ashigara, kataoroshi, saibara, kurotoriko, tauta, kamiuta, saouta, tsujiuta, mako, fuzoku, zushi,* and *beppō*.[71] Indeed, this is the finest music on earth. Who can help but be moved by it?

Several points in this essay distinguish *asobi* and *kugutsu* women. *Kairaishiki* embeds discussion of the women in an ethnographic description of a social group that includes both men and women and is fundamentally different from ordinary Japanese. *Kugutsu* are hunters, not farmers; itinerants, not settled residents; they live in tents, not houses. These characteristics make them seem foreign, and they are explicitly compared to nomads who lived along China's northern border. Perhaps, however, Masafusa was also thinking about the Emishi of northern Japan. Moreover, it is only after depicting *kugutsu* women as sexual entertainers that Masafusa turns to their role as performers, a reversal of the order in *Yūjoki*. Unlike the *asobi, kugutsu* women lure men by voluptuous gaits, seductive smiles, and cosmetics, rather than by melodic voices. While Masafusa distinguishes *asobi* and *kugutsu,* other sources present them both as banquet entertainers, singers of *imayō,* and sexual professionals.[72]

By the end of the Heian period, *asobi* and *kugutsu* were joined by a new type of female entertainer, the *shirabyōshi,* who not only sang *imayō* but also pioneered a spectacular dance form using swords and scabbards and initially performed in male dress. According to Jacqueline Pigeot, *shirabyōshi* added dance to the repertoire of female performers, who had previously entertained only by singing.[73] Like *asobi* and *kugutsu, shirabyōshi* attracted the patronage and sexual attentions of elite men; the *shirabyōshi* Giō and Hotoke, favored and then rejected by Taira Kiyomori in *The Tale of the Heike,*[74] became a literary object lesson in the perils of such relationships for women in the entertainment profession.

In the Kamakura period, the retired sovereign Go-Toba (1180–1239; r. 1183–1198) was particularly fond of *shirabyōshi* dancing, inviting performers to entertain him at his palace or when he went out on excursions.[75] Several *shirabyōshi* became Go-Toba's concubines. One pretext for the Jōkyū uprising of 1221, in fact, was bakufu anger at the retired sovereign when he took the rights to income from two estates from their warrior holders and gave them to his *shirabyōshi* concubine Kamegiku.[76] The very popularity of *shirabyōshi* was accompanied by changes in the situation of *asobi.* According to an entry dated 1202/6/2 in the poet Fujiwara Teika's diary *Meigetsuki:* "Today, *shirabyōshi* were hired. It is said that they arrived wearing entirely new costumes. This time, *asobi* were not given clothing."[77] This passage suggests that *shirabyōshi* were treated more favorably than *asobi;* indeed, their dances seem to have replaced the singing of *imayō* as the rage at court.[78]

Warrior elites of the Kamakura age joined men of the court as patrons of sexual entertainers—for example, *asobi* and *shirabyōshi* entertained Kamakura dignitaries, including shoguns and their retainers. In 1187 the *asobi chōja* at an inn in Shinano province traveled to Kamakura to press a lawsuit. While she was there she sang *eikyoku* for the future shogun Minamoto Yoritomo and several close retainers.[79] When some warriors were traveling through the province of Tōtōmi in 1190, several *asobi* gathered at their lodgings and entertained them, receiving numerous gifts; and in 1202, shogunal vassals *(gokenin)* on a pilgrimage stopped at an inn in Sagami province, summoning a group of *yūkun (asobi)* to perform. Although *asobi* continued to utilize the familiar boat trade—entertaining the shogunal party from their skiffs at a Sagami port in 1229—the Kamakura period often found them at inns as well.[80] Warrior patronage no doubt contributed to the geographic expansion of the sex trade, and the Yodo basin pleasure districts began to fade in favor of other locales, seeming to disappear entirely by the late fourteenth century. When the shogun Ashikaga Yoshiakira visited Eguchi in 1364, he recalled a poem about an Eguchi *chōja* by the famous Heian poet Saigyō but made no note of the presence of any *asobi.*[81]

What Can We Know?

Courtiers' diaries and essays no doubt reveal far more about those who wrote them than about sexual entertainers themselves; still, a number of details about the women's lives can be mined from such sources. According to these accounts, *asobi* specialized in travelers at harbor and on the road. In addition to the ports along the Yodo River and its feeders, *asobi* gathered in Uji near the capital, Sakamoto at the foot of Mt. Hiei, and Muro, a port on the Inland Sea.[82] Such venues differ from the urban locations of prostitution in medieval Europe. In her study of prostitution in medieval Languedoc, Leah L. Otis argues that "only in towns is the demand for sexual services large enough to justify the existence of a professional category to satisfy it."[83] That was not the case in Heian Japan. Although *asobi* sometimes visited Heian-kyō—for example, when Tadazane or Kaneie invited them to their mansions—the silence of Heian sources suggests that if many were based in the capital, they took second place to those at ports and on the road.

Two accounts in *Sarashina nikki* indicate that even in the mid-Heian period, *asobi* might also be found in provincial locales far from the capital or any substantial body of water. One passage relates the author's experiences as a young girl returning with her father to the capital from Kazusa province, where he had served as provincial governor. Crossing Mt. Ashigara in Sagami province, the governor's party encountered three *asobi:*

> We crossed Mt. Ashigara, a dark and frightening expanse four or five *li* across. After traveling for a while, we reached the foot of the mountain, passing through a forest so overgrown that we could barely see the sky. It was really terrifying. We lodged there, fearing we would lose our way in the gloom of the moonless dark night.
>
> Just then three *asobi* appeared out of nowhere. One seemed to be about fifty years old, the second around twenty, and the third about fourteen or fifteen. They stopped in front of our encampment and set up a large parasol, and our boys lit some torches so that we could see them better. They claimed to be the descendants of Kohata of ancient times.[84] Their long hair swept gracefully across their foreheads and their faces were pale and not at all coarse or dirty—they were pleasing enough to be maidservants in a courtier's house. Everyone felt some sympathy for them. They sang some delightful songs for us, their incomparable voices soaring to

> the sky. It made us all feel terribly melancholy, and as we drew close to them in fascination, someone said, "The *asobi* in the western provinces can't compare to you." They replied in a splendid song, "If you compare us to the ones at Naniwa . . ."
>
> They were not at all displeasing in appearance, and their singing voices had no match. When we watched them walk off and disappear into the terrifying mountains we all wept, thinking we had not heard enough. Naive as I was, I retreated to the hut, feeling sadder than ever.[85]

A later entry finds the author in Mino province, where she and her party once again encounter a band of *asobi:* "We crossed the border into Mino province at Sunomata and arrived at a place called Nogami. A band of *asobi* came out to entertain us, and sang the whole night long, making us feel nostalgic about our experience at Ashigara."[86]

Sarashina nikki demonstrates that *asobi* could be found far from the capital and its environs. The three women at Ashigara may have moved from place to place to practice their trade, while the Nogami *asobi* probably performed regularly at rest-station inns *(shuku)* along the highway, entertaining customers who traveled back and forth to Heian-kyō. Heavy traffic between the capital and even distant provinces—parties that transported tax goods, carried official messages, and assumed or retired from appointments—probably offered opportunities for *asobi,* no less than the better-known pilgrimage travel along the rivers of the Kinai.[87] While the patrons of eastern *asobi* may not have been as exalted as Michinaga, they no doubt supplied a solid base of support for a thriving business.

Various locales were chosen for *asobi* to entertain or to have sexual relations with male patrons: inns, the patrons' own homes or boats, or the dwellings of the *asobi* themselves. In *Chōshūki,* for example, the visitors to Kamusaki stayed up all night making merry at an *asobi*'s dwelling, then took the women back to an inn for sexual intercourse.[88] I have seen no clear reference to the institution of the brothel before the mid-Kamakura period, when an *Azuma kagami* entry dated 1241 relates that a band of warriors spent an evening carousing at a house of sexual pleasure *(irogonomi no ie)* on a main street in the shogunal capital of Kamakura.[89]

The audience for *asobi* included other women as well as men, but women rarely recorded their observations of the pleasure districts. In *Sarashina nikki,* the female diarist found *asobi* quite appealing and looked back with nostalgia on her first encounter with them. On the other hand, Murasaki Shikibu has her fictional Prince Genji reject the advances of *asobi* on the grounds that the women were fickle.[90] There is not enough evidence, however, to argue that gender made any difference in the way someone regarded *asobi.* Accounts of pilgrimages that passed through the pleasure districts indicate that court women not only willingly watched *asobi* performances but also lavishly rewarded them with gifts. Women as well as men must have welcomed the opportunity to demonstrate their largesse publicly; and the erotic lyrics and seductive behavior of *asobi,* far from being considered "unsuitable" for female consumption, may have helped to lubricate delicate social relationships. No doubt the pleasure districts served complex functions as sites for social exchange, not only between male patrons and *asobi,* but also among various elite men and their female peers at court.

Not surprisingly, *asobi* concentrated their efforts on those most likely to reward them with fine clothing and other valuables. Patrons ranged from the very highest in status—retired emperors and regents—but also, according to Masafusa, included men below the provincial governor level. These were probably district officials or lesser functionaries in provincial headquarters. There seem to have been no set prices for the services of *asobi,* but compensation was probably considered a patron's obligation. While patrons may have regarded their compensation as quite generous, we often do not know how many women had to share the rice and textiles given to their band, and Masafusa hints that sometimes there was hardly enough to go around.

The commercial essence of the transaction was masked by the term most commonly used for payment—*tentō* (rewards to singers and dancers).[91] Thus the accounts not only preserved the illusion of a willing exchange based on mutual desire rather than a marketed service but also cast noble patrons as dispensers of largesse. Even Yorinaga, so blunt about the sexual nature of his encounter with the *asobi,* referred to his payment as *tentō.* One source, however, uses the designation *reiroku* as well as *tentō;*[92] the term *roku* is often used for court officials' salaries, leading Fukutō Sanae to surmise that in this case the *asobi* may have had responsibility for a public function.[93] In both cases, however, the sexual services of *asobi* were commodified services available for purchase, with "gifts" of rice or textiles performing the function of currency.

How autonomous were *asobi* organizations? Men are visible in Heian sources as patrons, but not as pimps, and the sources suggest that *asobi* were organized and led by the women themselves. When Masafusa refers to the leaders of *asobi* organizations, he uses the terms *hajime, mune,* and *chōja.* These may have the same meaning, although *hajime* can indicate an ancestor or founder and *mune* can be a festival official, leading Toyonaga Satomi to argue that the names suggest a ritual function.[94] Most other sources refer to *asobi* leaders as *chōja,* a term also employed for heads of male occupational groups. Masafusa implies that the *asobi* chose their leaders from among themselves, but *chōja* may have been the wealthiest or best-connected women in the *asobi* organization. In her discussion of *Chōshūki,* Toyonaga points out that when gifts were apportioned, the Kamusaki *chōja* Kinju was distinguished from the others.[95] Heian- and Kamakura-period sources also suggest that some *chōja* may have been born into prominent families or had powerful associates. In Akihira's fictional account, the *asobi chōja* is the daughter of a lieutenant of the guards. *Azuma kagami* identifies Ōi, a *chōja* at the inn of Aohaka in Mino province, as the mistress of the warrior leader Minamoto Yoshitomo and the daughter of a middle-level official whose family's fortunes declined after they supported the losing side in the Hōgen War of 1156.[96]

It is difficult to know how powerful the *chōja* were or how much control they had over their subordinates. Two different interpretations of a passage in *Chōshūki* raise this issue. I have translated this passage, which unfortunately contains several unreadable characters, as follows:

> The *chōja* Sonson [or Sonboshi] . . . [the rest of the sentence is missing]. Kumano [of Eguchi] was already on the boat. In preparation for a banquet, a letter of transfer *(yuzuribumi)* was composed, and we secured Sonboshi's [Sonson's] seal and gave the document to Kumano.

Narahara Junko, however, fills in the lacunae to produce a different interpretation: "The hereditary position of *chōja* was transmitted to Kumano." In Narahara's reading, the *yuzuribumi* was not a letter of permission to attend a banquet but a document transmitting the *chōja* position from mother to daughter. "Sonboshi" (literally, descendant-mother-child) becomes an indication of generational continuity rather than a name.[97] This interpretation follows that of Takigawa Masajirō, which characterizes the *chōja* position as a *shiki,* an officially recognized right to position or income.[98] Indeed, *yuzuribumi* generally means a document that passes on property or rights from one person to another. However, Narahara's interpretation requires us to ignore the context in which the letter of transfer was issued—clearly it was in connection with an off-site banquet, and the passage explicitly states that Kumano and Iya accompanied the men to the Hachiman administrator's estate. Furthermore, there is no indication in any material I have seen that the *chōja* position was regarded as a *shiki*.

In my reading, which agrees with that of Toyonaga Satomi,[99] the *yuzuribumi* was a letter of permission from the Eguchi *chōja* Sonboshi allowing Kumano and Iya, two *asobi* under her jurisdiction, to leave their regular work location and accompany their patrons to a party elsewhere. In other words, when *asobi* wanted to leave the pleasure district to entertain at a patron's residence, the *chōja*'s written approval was required.[100] The document indicates that the *chōja* was a woman of authority and perhaps some education—she may very well have been able to read the documents she was asked to approve. The term *yuzuribumi,* in fact, suggests that the services of Kumano and Iya, if not their persons, were considered the property of the *chōja.* The Eguchi *chōja,* moreover, took charge of the gifts given the other *asobi* in her group—whether this means she claimed ownership and distributed them as she pleased or simply took them for safekeeping.

The suggestion that the position of *chōja* may have been passed on from mother to daughter, however, is supported by other evidence that *asobi* formed matrilineal groups. In some cases, such as that of Ōi, the *chōja*'s biological daughter worked as an *asobi* under her mother's supervision.[101] Adoption and fictive kinship ties may have also been used to recruit women into the profession and control their labor. Very little is known about the recruitment process, but perhaps the *asobi* profession was an option for women of some status who fell through the cracks of the family system. Such women no doubt were numerous: since men's liaisons were limited only by their income and their desire, there must have been many abandoned spouses, lovers, and children.[102] Women in such circumstances, as well as those disadvantaged by a husband's death or a father's political failure, had few viable options for making a living. Some may have used their skills at music, poetry, and clever conversation to join *asobi* organizations. With a few such women in key positions, young girls could have been recruited or even purchased from the entire female population, placed in fictive kinship relationships with their sponsors, and trained in performance as well as in sexual techniques. Yukitoki's essay blames parents for the improper activities of the *asobi,* hinting that mothers or fathers sometimes sold their daughters into the profession.

Did most *asobi* have lifetime careers, or could a woman move easily in or out of the profession? The trio observed by the author of *Sarashina nikki* included one who was about fifty years old and another of fourteen or fifteen, suggesting that *asobi* sometimes began work not long after puberty and remained in the profession for a good portion of their lives.[103] According to Masafusa, on the other hand, part-timers such as maids from provincial mansions sometimes swelled the *asobi* ranks—an indication that boundaries between *asobi* and the rest of the female population were permeable or even nonexistent. It was possible, moreover, for an *asobi* to leave the profession by establishing a long-term relationship, sometimes with a high-status man.

Courtier essays and diaries reveal only glimpses into the lives of *asobi,* seen primarily from the viewpoint of male patrons in a considerably higher social position than the women. Questions that might be asked about women in a modern version of the sex trade—about disease, abortion, pregnancies, or the fate of male children—are impossible to answer from Heian and Kamakura sources. And except for a few extant *imayō* lyrics, which I will examine shortly, we have no way of knowing how sexual entertainers felt about their own lives.

Sexual Entertainers and Popular Culture

As singers and composers of popular genres such as *imayō* and *saibara,* female entertainers played a particularly important role in the Japanese performing tradition. No doubt that is why they delighted such different individuals as Fujiwara Akihira, the retired sovereign Go-Shirakawa, and the Kamakura warrior chief Minamoto Yoritomo. Perhaps even more than the sex trade, musical performance linked all categories of female entertainers in the contemporary imagination, often making it hard to draw firm distinctions between *asobi* and other performers such as the *kugutsu.*

Asobi, kugutsu, and *shirabyōshi* entertained patrons with songs that ranged in tone from pious to bawdy: *imayō* include verses from the sutras, and one *saibara* lyric lists colloquial terms for a woman's genitals.[104] Pageant was also a part of the entertainment package. When a group of *asobi* entertained the shogun Minamoto Sanetomo and his guests in 1212, the women all dressed up as children, wearing garments with patterns of maple leaves and chrysanthemums as they paraded in front of the men.[105]

In terms of artistic production, however, the most important contribution of female entertainers was *imayō.* The musical form shaped the way in which the women were portrayed in Heian and early Kamakura sources. Probably sung at first among ordinary people, *imayō* became popular among the late-Heian aristocracy. *Imayō* were sung to the beat of a small drum, but little is known of their melodies or rhythms.[106] Many of the lyrics were collected in the late-twelfth-century anthology *Ryōjin hishō* (Songs to make the dust dance), however, edited by the retired sovereign Go-Shirakawa.[107] Along with *imayō* music and performing techniques, the lyrics were taught to Go-Shirakawa by *kugutsu* such as Otomae, who came from the inn of Aohaka in Mino.[108]

The lyrics in *Ryōjin hishō* address a variety of topics. The extant sections lean heavily toward Buddhist themes—this may be due partly to Go-Shirakawa's piety and partly to accidents of text preservation. Clearly, it was considered neither odd nor blasphemous for *kugutsu* or *asobi* to sing praises to the Buddha. Quite a few of the lyrics, however, concern the daily life of the common people, and some may refer directly to the lives of the women who sang the songs. For example, the protagonist of this lyric is probably some kind of female entertainer:

> Tokenoboru came down from the capital,
> built herself a house to live in at Shimae.
> But "he" abandoned her without a second thought.
> No matter how she prays—Hyaku Dayū—
> without your miracle,
> she's headed back for the capital of flowers.[109]

While the lyrics of *Ryōjin hishō* sometimes reflect a woman's anger at an unreliable man who abandoned her, it is more difficult to find signs of resistance to an exploitative system of sexual exchange. If the women felt exploited—and we cannot be sure that they did—it would hardly have been good business to complain at banquets where they were paid to entertain. As entertainers, *asobi* and *kugutsu* no doubt sang the songs that aristocratic men favored, and even in *imayō* their voices were muted and their complaints disguised. However, the following two lyrics, which show a small helpless creature treated cruelly, might be interpreted as complaints about a patron's sexual brutality:[110]

In the depths of the Yodo River
the young sweetfish writhes,
bitten from behind by the cormorant—
how pitiful![111]

Dance, dance, snail!
If you don't dance,
I'll have colts and calves kick you
and trample you to pieces.
But if you dance exquisitely,
you can play in my flower garden.[112]

Female entertainers played an important role in bringing the culture of the street to the aristocracy and, later, to the military elite. The significance of this interaction for the Japanese artistic world has been discussed in detail elsewhere.[113] Perhaps the very success of these women—their proximity to centers of power, their ability to form liaisons with elite men, their growing visibility as they expanded their areas of operation—contributed to the doubts and fears that became an important thread within the male discourse on female entertainers in the sex trade.

Names and Categories

Much of the evidence cited so far suggests that in Heian times and later, the term *asobi* was a professional designation. Essayists and diarists used the term somewhat consistently to refer to women who traded in sex and entertainment. The women too referred to themselves as *asobi*. The following *Ryōjin hishō* lyric describes a figure that would have been familiar to Masafusa:

Here's what an *asobi* favors:
her skills, her drum, her little boat,
the woman who holds her parasol,
the woman who poles her boat—

and Hyaku Dayū:
she prays to him for the love of men.[114]

In short, "*asobi*" formed a category that was understood in much the same way by a number of Heian observers, and this understanding has been passed on to us today. Consistent accounts, however, do not necessarily indicate objectively factual portrayals (if such can be said to exist). In fact, consistencies in both observations and value judgments can be explained, at least in part, by the common practice of alluding to the work of one's predecessors and by the similar experiences and social background of essayists and diarists, almost all of them aristocratic men. As Jacqueline Pigeot has noted, certain themes in essays and poems, such as itinerancy, water imagery, and associations with fisherfolk, contributed to the construction of the sexual entertainer as a poetic subject.[115] Terry Kawashima has made much the same point, especially concerning the construction of aging entertainers as lonely, pathetic old women. She suggests that the common images found in Chinese-style poems *(kanshi)* as well as in *kanbun* essays by Masafusa and Yukitoki indicate the wide circulation of such tropes in the late Heian period.[116]

A closer look at the sources indicates considerable variation within a broad definitional area. While *asobi* (but not necessarily *kugutsu*) are generally portrayed as genteel and sophisticated entertainers, occasional glitches in the picture suggest some slippage between ideal and reality, even in the minds of patrons and admirers. Masafusa peeks into their private quarters and shows them squabbling behind the scenes. Yorinaga, concerned only with sexual pleasure, ignores the *asobi*'s function as entertainers. Other accounts suggest that patronizing the pleasure quarters was embarrassing *(Unshū shōsoku)* or improper *(Asobi o miru)*.

The earliest known source on *asobi, Wamyōshō,* indicates that by the mid-tenth century *asobi* had emerged as a recognized social category with both occupational and status characteristics. Yet these characteristics differ from those of *asobi* depicted just a half-century later. Absent from *Wamyōshō* are the boat trade and *imayō.* Absent from later depictions is the "beggar and thief" rubric that associates *asobi* with pirates and robbers. It seems unlikely that men such as Fujiwara Tadazane would have patronized the *Wamyōshō asobi,* any more than they would have invited robber gangs to a banquet.

There are several possible explanations for the difference. Perhaps there were simply disparities in taste and judgment between *Wamyōshō* compiler Minamoto Shitagō and other observers. Or the *asobi* profession may have changed in the years that separate *Wamyōshō* from the next known account, the far less negative essay by Ōe Yukitoki. Or—which seems most likely to me—the term *asobi* may have actually embraced women who engaged in a variety of activities related to sex and entertainment; the most imaginative and artistic of them won aristocratic patronage toward the end of the tenth century and thus a place in recorded history. In that case, references in later sources to *asobi* who simply traded sex for payment might not be the result of actual historical change but, instead, an indication that "*asobi*" always had been a broad and variable category.

The professional sexual culture of Heian and early Kamakura Japan embraced several types and styles of activity. Its players had common characteristics, making them sometimes hard to distinguish. Moreover, not all those called by a single name conducted their business in the same way. In the case of *asobi,* Toyonaga Satomi points to class differences between *chōja* and others.[117] Regional variations add to the difficulty of firmly defining the term *asobi.* According to Amino Yoshihiko, while *asobi* of western Japan conducted their trade at ports or on the water, those of eastern Japan were for the most part based inland.[118] Examples include those encountered by the *Sarashina* diarist in Sagami and Mino. Eastern *asobi* based at inns along the highway were easily conflated with *kugutsu* women, who also worked at inns, sang *imayō* at banquets, and exchanged sexual favors for payment.[119] Such confusion, which continues in modern scholarship, underscores the difficulties of naming and classification in studies of the classical and medieval ages. Differences in both terms and their definitions render impossible a one-to-one correspondence between name and phenomenon. Most evidence, however, points clearly to a thriving entertainment trade, based in part on sophisticated artistry, in part on the provision of sexual services.

Little is known of sexual entertainers—whether or not they are called *asobi*—who catered to nonelite men, but Watanabe Shōgo finds evidence for lower-class prostitution in several *Ryōjin hishō* lyrics. For example, he cites the following jibe at a low-status provincial retainer:

> Yesterday he came from the east without his wife—
> he'll trade his indigo undercloak for a woman.[120]

Watanabe maintains that the west side of the capital, which suffered considerable deterioration in late Heian times, was one location for lower-class prostitution, offering the following *imayō* lyric as evidence:

> If you go to the west capital
> I've heard you'll find sparrows,
> and cuckoos with blackened mouths.
> It's a world of desire, so
> its fame reverberates but
> the echoes don't reach me.[121]

A tale in the early-thirteenth-century tale collection *Uji shūi monogatari* (Collection of tales from Uji) suggests that lower-class prostitutes entertained men in the capital. In the story, a man has sexual intercourse with a woman called a *keisei* at a festival-viewing stand along a main street.[122] The term *keisei*—literally, castle-toppler—became common as a pejorative for prostitute in the later Kamakura and Muromachi periods, and the semipublic venue that the couple had chosen suggests that the woman was a streetwalker. Prior to the thirteenth century, however, most sources focus on women who entertained and provided sexual services for courtier and warrior elites. This would not have been the case, I believe, if elite men had been seriously concerned with the regulation of sexual entertainment or with its moral and social consequences for the general populace.

Any stigma suffered by sexual entertainers was lightly and inconsistently applied until the middle of the thirteenth century, when socioeconomic forces related to the maintenance of order and the distribution of property helped to redefine both orthodox and transgressive sexual relationships. In the next chapter, I will explore the way in which male elites—courtiers, warriors, and clergy—constructed such concepts.

2 Defining Transgression

NEITHER MAKING THEIR bodies publicly available nor accepting compensation in exchange for sexual services automatically stigmatized women in the sex trade in the relatively tolerant sexual climate of Heian Japan. Yet from late Heian times, changing marital and other socio-economic patterns began to constrict the range of permissible sexual activities for unmarried women, wives, and widows. Few explicit parallels were drawn between sexual professionals and women in general who violated societal norms, but the construction of a sexually virtuous woman with identifiable behavioral characteristics helped to set apart those in the sex trade. Even so, there was no sharp contrast between "whore" and "honest woman" as one might have found in contemporary Christian European societies.

Many of the changes in marriage and sexual norms were subtle and not completely in place, even by the late Kamakura period. The disadvantages of sharing a husband in a polygynous system continued to be offset, at least among some segments of society, by uxorilocal marriage or female inheritance rights. Virginity was not yet expected of unmarried women. Throughout most of the period, wives could often count on bequests from their natal families, and their ability to bequeath property gave them leverage over their children. Widows could remarry, although eventually this cost them certain property rights.[1] Policies of the Kamakura bakufu, beginning in the 1230s and continuing throughout the thirteenth and fourteenth centuries, marked the watershed of change from relative freedom to restriction for women, but not all these policies were effective right away, nor were they applied uniformly across all classes of society. On the other hand, preexisting social attitudes or policies condoned rape, excused male but not female promiscuity, and defined the crime of adultery as an affair between a married woman and another man—married men being largely free to do as they pleased. There had long been ambiguous and inconsistent approaches toward female sexual choice and freedom, dating at least from early historic times.

In short, no clear picture of a sexually transgressive woman emerges even by the end of the Kamakura period; but such a picture was under construction, shaped by dynamic forces such as changes in kinship, marriage, inheritance, and property holding, as well as shifting religious approaches to female sexuality. This chapter focuses on societal norms in areas other than professional sexual entertainment, including adultery, female desire and promiscuity, and sexual relations between women and Buddhist clergy. The very ambiguity that marked these norms also characterized attitudes toward sexual professionals. Over time, judgments of female sexual behavior in general became more restrictive, contributing, I would argue, toward increasingly negative evaluations of sexual entertainment.

After a brief overview of kinship and marriage patterns as examined by other scholars, I turn to two types of evidence on which I base my own arguments: the first is law codes and legal decisions; the second is collections of didactic tales known as *setsuwa*. Each offers a somewhat different perspective on sexual norms, sometimes leading scholars to privilege one source (as more factual) over another. *Setsuwa* and other fictional sources are widely used by historians of classical and medieval Japan. One reason is the paucity of documentary sources, especially those illuminating the lives of ordinary people. It can be argued, however, that tales do far more than fill in missing evidence—that because they had to "ring true" to the reader, in the words of Barbara Ruch,[2] they reflect actual social conditions and standards. To a certain extent I find this a valid argument. However, the didactic nature of many *setsuwa* tales suggests that they were often used to construct social norms rather than simply reflect them.

Law codes, on the other hand, are sometimes dismissed as pro forma regulations that were rarely enforced and were therefore insignificant in comparison to the customary practices related in sources such as *setsuwa*—the latter being regarded as reflections of historical fact.[3] Since a number of Kamakura-period court cases involved legal regulations of sexual behavior, however, I believe that this view is flawed. Moreover, even unenforced laws could help to produce social norms. Both laws and *setsuwa* could function as tools of social engineering employed by elites to construct models of orthodoxy and transgression. Interactions with custom and the demands of various elites contributed to this process. In this chapter I examine the treatment of sexual behavior defined as transgressive in *setsuwa* and law codes in both Heian and Kamakura times. Although my work focuses on women, it is impossible to assess sexual norms without considering men's behavior as well. Such issues as the power of sexual desire, relations involving nominally celibate Buddhist clergy, premarital sex and promiscuity, adultery, and widow remarriage are dealt with here.

Kinship and Marriage

Over the course of many centuries, the organization of kinship and lineage in Japan was transformed from a bilateral to a patrilineal structure, and marriage —once a fluid and unstable arrangement with several residence options—became firmly defined as a patrilocal institution in which a bride was incorporated into her husband's lineage. This institution was the *ie,* a patrilineal stem family with continuity over a number of generations. In the *ie,* the rights of women to inherit and bequeath property, to choose their own sexual partners, and to exit an unsatisfactory marriage were severely circumscribed. It is hard to say exactly when we might begin to call the system of kinship and marriage "patriarchal," since elements of patriarchy—exclusion of women from official positions, restrictions on female property rights, the control of female sexual activity by husbands and fathers, to name a few—emerged at different historical points. Some developments in family organization, such as the formation of more-or-less stable conjugal unions, probably occurred first among the highest elites in the early Heian period and gradually spread downward to upper-level cultivators by late Heian or Kamakura times. There may have been geographic variations as well.[4] Such variations, along with our incomplete knowledge of family organization among nonelites and in peripheral regions, make it extremely hard to set a "watershed" period for the inception of patriarchy.[5]

Many scholars argue that, as far back as one can trace lineage patterns in Japanese historical records, descent was reckoned bilaterally: in other words, an individual traced ancestry through both the father's and mother's lineage, and names, property, and family membership could be passed on through either one. Evidence for bilateral lineage comes in part from kinship naming conventions: unlike patrilineal societies such as China, the same terms were used for equivalent relatives on the mother's and the father's side. Individuals sometimes claimed membership in both their father's and their mother's lineage organizations *(uji)* or chose one over the other for political reasons.[6]

Nevertheless, there was a long-term trend toward tracing descent through the male line. In fact, principles of patrilineal descent began to make inroads very early: an inscription on a sword, probably dated 471, traces an individual's ancestry through the male line to an ancestor eight generations in the past who had established the family's service to the sovereign. According to Yoshie Akiko, the inscription indicates that patrilineal principles were recognized at least within elites; nevertheless it was still common for most people to trace their ancestry through both parents.[7] The eighth-century *ritsuryō* codes also emphasized patrilineal descent and inheritance, but throughout most of society bilateral principles gave way very slowly. The ability to count on one's kin—and to inherit property from them—gave women a degree of independence that they would eventually lose.

In the Nara and Heian periods, marriage did not mean that a woman ceased being a member of her natal family and became part of her husband's. Residence patterns varied; as Sumi Tōyō points out, residence could depend on circumstance in a bilateral system without rigid kin groups.[8] Marriages often began when a man visited a woman in her parents' home. Sometimes the visiting arrangement continued for several years, but often a couple established their own separate household after children were born. This household was sometimes located in the same residential compound as that of the wife's or the husband's parents. The couple rarely if ever lived under the same roof as the husband's parents, however, since it violated custom for a wife to share a hearth with her mother-in-law or sister-in-law. Nara-period marriages were poorly defined and unstable: there was no set ritual to legitimate a marriage, and separation and divorce were common. A woman might have children with each of several husbands.[9] In the Heian period, conjugal relationships became more stable, but residence patterns still varied and many liaisons ended in divorce.

Among Heian elites, the variety of residence patterns may be understood as a response to the practice of polygyny. A man might live with his primary wife, the spouse of highest status, and pay visits to the others; or he might live separately from all his wives, visiting each when he chose. Literary sources depict complex residence patterns on various levels of society: the famous Prince Genji visited his high-status primary wife, who remained in her father's home, but took his beloved Murasaki, of lower social status, into his own home. Genji even set up a residential compound where several of his women lived, an arrangement probably patterned after the women's quarters in the sovereign's palace rather than after actual living arrangements among the aristocracy. The second wife of the lieutenant of the guards in *Shinsarugakuki* is described as the manager of his household; his other two wives probably lived elsewhere, although the text does not say so explicitly. A tale in the twelfth-century *setsuwa* collection *Konjaku monogatarishū* (Tales of times now past) depicts a man of Tanba province who had two wives living in houses side by side; he visited—or lived with—each of them as he chose.[10]

Several scholars have combed this collection for evidence of marriage residence patterns among commoners. Takamure Itsue, for instance, found many tales in which a husband lived with his wife's parents, but none of the opposite case; and more than twice as many tales in which a married couple set up housekeeping in the wife's home than in the husband's.[11] Others have disputed her methodology and calculations, but most would agree at least that *Konjaku,* along with other works of literature, provides evidence of the social acceptability of varied residence patterns in late Heian times.

During the Kamakura period, pressures in favor of virilocal marriage (and patrilineal descent patterns) increased, but society remained based on bilateral kinship, and marriages, some of them uxorilocal, were not always lifetime unions.[12] Divorce and remarriage were frequent, and although legal proclamations sometimes distinguished between "wives" and "concubines," there was no clear distinction between the two in terms of the status of their children. Court disputes among heirs, some of which are discussed in this chapter, often pitted the child of one wife against that of another; there is little sense that one child was more worthy of an inheritance because of the status of his or her mother.

It would still be some time before the patrilocal, patrilineal *ie*—which required the transfer of the wife's person to her husband's home and lineage and mandated control over her sexual activities to assure that her children were legitimately those of the *ie*—became the norm throughout Japanese society. In late Heian and Kamakura times, nevertheless, women were increasingly subjected to behavioral restrictions and censured for activities and relationships they had once pursued with little blame. This was the case despite the yet fuzzy definition of sexual orthodoxy. If orthodoxy remained poorly defined, however, various types of transgression were so labeled very early, a topic to which I now turn.

Sexual Violation in Early Japanese History

In her comprehensive study of marriage and sexual relations in early Japanese history, Sekiguchi Hiroko uses sources such as the *Nihon shoki* and *Shoku nihongi* to identify sexual taboos as well as penalties for breaking them in the eighth century and earlier. According to her findings, certain forms of incest, sexual relations between men and female ritualists or Buddhist nuns, relations between ordinary commoners and low-status persons, relations with the ruler's spouse or intended spouse, and rape were all forbidden.[13]

The term most commonly used for sexual violation is 奸 or 姦, usually pronounced *kan* in combination with other characters but also read *midare, midasu,* and *okasu*. Both characters can refer to various types of wickedness and mischief, not limited to improper sexual relations, and all imply disorder. Another term for sexual violation is 淫 (pronounced *in*). In Heian materials, this is sometimes used to indicate licentiousness, rather than a specific offense, and is often applied to women.

Entries from the eighth-century chronicle *Nihon shoki* show that both men and women could be punished for sexual violations. Perhaps the most extreme penalty for a woman was that imposed on a Paekche princess who had an affair with another man despite the Japanese ruler's intent to "favor" her: she was burned alive by the ruler's retainers.[14] Men too were executed for sexual violations, and one, accused of relations with a *saigū* (royal priestess at Ise shrine), was even killed by his own father. The unfortunate *saigū* hung herself though later the two were proved innocent.[15] Sekiguchi argues that female ritualists were expected to maintain celibacy, whether they were *saigū* or ordinary shrine shamans, but suggests that punishments were fairly mild for the latter and their male sexual partners.[16]

As Sekiguchi points out quite forcefully, the most serious violations were those that offended royal authority. Specifically mentioned are sexual relations with a woman chosen as a consort by the ruler, and Sekiguchi notes that the requirement of monogamy for women developed first in the case of the ruler's spouses. Relations with *uneme,* women sent to serve in the palace by provincial chieftains as a sign of submission to the ruler, were also severely punished. The emphasis on royal authority is hardly startling: most of the sources Sekiguchi cites were commissioned by the court during the eighth century, when the throne was at its height of power and the centralizing impulse was strong. The sources reflect the concept of the ruler's absolute right to the bodies of women designated for him, a concept that of course might not have been realized in practice. Ordinary men did not have that right, however, and Sekiguchi argues that in this early period, when marriages could be easily formed and dissolved at the will of the partners, wives were not prohibited from having sexual relations with other men.[17] Women were expected to be neither chaste wives nor virgin brides.

Law codes issued in the eighth century present a somewhat different picture from the general situation described here, suggesting a gap between actual practice and models of good behavior promoted by the *ritsuryō* state. When the Yōrō law code was issued by the central government in 720, its provisions on sexual relationships reflected a Chinese patriarchal model. Sekiguchi notes that in Tang China, socially recognized marriage required that the patriarch of both the man's and the woman's family consent to the match and that the principals perform set premarital rituals. Except for concubinage and relations between a master and his female servant, all other male-female sexual relationships were forbidden and could be punished.[18] Consequently, the Yōrō code prescribed penalties for premarital intercourse, adultery, and rape.

The original text of laws on consensual fornication or adultery *(wakan)* and rape *(gōkan)* has been lost, but it is quoted in *Hossō shiyōshō* (Essentials of legal scholarship), a legal commentary dating from late Heian or early Kamakura times:

> The miscellaneous section of the penal code provides that in case of consensual illicit relations, the guilty parties will be sentenced to a year of penal servitude, but if the woman is married, the sentence is two years. The penalty in both situations will be increased one degree in the case of rape. Moreover, the article specifies that if the relationship is consensual, woman and man are considered equally culpable. The woman is not considered guilty if she has been raped.
>
> In other words, the punishment for raping an unmarried woman is a year and a half of penal servitude. If the woman is married, the punishment is two and a half years. In the case of consensual relations, the woman is as guilty as the man.[19]

We may assume that *wakan* was any consensual relationship not defined as legitimate marriage in another section of the code, which specifically mandated a match approved by both parties' close relatives or, if there were none, by the parties themselves.[20] The legal code defined *wakan* as an offense, whether involving an unmarried or a married woman; the marital status of the man does not seem worth mentioning, since presumably the penalty would not vary.

We do not know how often the laws on fornication and adultery were enforced in the Nara and Heian periods, especially in light of the fuzzy definition of marriage and the casual attitudes toward male promiscuity, including sexual violence against women, expressed in literary sources. In one example cited by Sekiguchi that postdates the code, in 799 a palace attendant was flogged for raping a nun;[21] the punishment differed from that prescribed, although the clerical status of the victim may have been a "special circumstance." In less drastic circumstances, the law seems to have been applied quite leniently: according to *Ryō no gige,* a commentary on the code dated 833, a couple guilty of fornication—having sexual relations without the proper ceremony—were automatically pardoned if their families later announced their marriage.[22] Later the Yōrō code provided a partial model for similar statutes issued by the Kamakura bakufu in the thirteenth century.

Legal regulation, of course, was only one method of shaping social norms, which were also influenced by customary attitudes and practices and by elite propaganda directed at all segments of society. Evidence of both customary practices and propaganda can be found in *setsuwa* collections, which contain many tales of marriage, courtship, and sexual relationships. Several important collections are examined here: *Nihon ryōiki,* compiled by the monk Kyōkai in the early ninth century; *Konjaku monogatarishū,* probably compiled by a monk or monks in the 1120s; *Uji shūi monogatari,* compiled by an unknown person in the early thirteenth century; *Kokon chomonjū,* compiled by the lay courtier Tachibana Narisue in 1254; and *Shasekishū,* completed in 1283 by the monk Mujū Ichien. Perceptions of sexual behavior vary not only throughout the genre but even within a single collection.[23] Some tales appear in more than one collection, and in some cases differences in the versions suggest a temporal change in concepts of sexual orthodoxy. The most striking differences, however, occur between the early and late Heian periods, perhaps reflecting the growing consolidation of the conjugal relationship.[24]

Whether monks or laymen, *setsuwa* compilers seem to have aimed at a broad audience: the protagonists of the tales came from nearly all social classes, and stories were taken from many different sources (sometimes earlier *setsuwa* collections) or perhaps were invented by the compiler. Some tales treat their didactic mission lightly; others hammer it firmly home. At times the need to entertain appears paramount; at other times the compiler doggedly illustrates a Buddhist teaching or a moral precept. While some tales may have reflected preexisting norms, others appear to promote new ones. Thus it is necessary to inquire into the purposes that might have been served by portraying sexual relationships and behavior in certain ways. I begin with an examination of sexual desire as depicted in *setsuwa*.

Lusty Men, Lascivious Women, and the (Almost) Missing Virgin

In a seminal study of the discourse on gender and the body in *Konjaku monogatarishū,* Hitomi Tonomura points out significant asymmetries in the treatment of male and female sexual bodies. In particular, she argues that "uncontrollable lust and the freedom to satisfy it" were attributed to men and that women, empowered to entice men, were deemed responsible for keeping both their own and men's sexuality under control.[25] Such a construct was common but not uncontested. However convenient it may have been for individual elite men, it threatened broader elite interests: those of Buddhist institutions based on a nominally celibate clergy and those of government authorities responsible for keeping the peace. *Setsuwa* tales demonstrated the unfortunate consequences of unbridled lust for men as well as for women and portrayed some male sexual activities as transgressive, just as did codes of law. The tales were probably aimed at establishing behavioral norms, especially among the clergy.

However, the overwhelming power and danger of sexual desire, which renders even practiced ascetics helpless, is a common theme in both Heian- and Kamakura-period collections. Women are occasionally cast as witting temptresses, but male lust sometimes overwhelms both an unwilling man and a reluctant woman, or women are overcome by their own passions. Lust thus appears as a force of nature rather than an impulse of human agency. Many tales preach avoidance for clergy, caution for laymen—whose progress toward enlightenment was endangered by desire—and self-concealment for women. But the fact that monks are often portrayed in the throes of desire suggests that clerical celibacy was the most pressing issue. As Bernard Faure has pointed out, breaches of celibacy were often tolerated;[26] nonetheless, they were seen as undesirable and many in the Buddhist establishment took great pains to prevent them. For example, in 1212 the monk Jōkei stipulated that nuns should not be permitted to live near his temple, Kaijūsenji, on the grounds that monks should avoid contact with all women.[27]

Two tales from *Uji shūi monogatari* suggest the lengths to which monks were expected to go to avoid contact with women. In one, the disciple of the Indian holy man Upagupta is crossing a river when a woman appears and is suddenly knocked down by the current. When she calls for help, the disciple at first ignores her but finally feels so sorry for her that he takes her hands and helps her cross the river. Overcome by sexual desire, the disciple persuades her to accompany him to a secluded place, then forces open her legs and begins to rape her. At that moment she appears in her true form, that of Upagupta, who proceeds to upbraid his disciple and use the incident as a device to lead him toward enlightenment.[28] In another tale, a boy studying the *Lotus Sutra* encounters a woman on horseback who asks him to lead her horse. He refuses to help her, even when the horse rears up and throws the woman to the ground. The woman, it turns out, is the bodhisattva Monju, testing the boy's resolve to avoid the slightest intimacy with women.[29]

The following tale, from *Konjaku monogatarishū,* examines the power of sexual desire in a relationship between a Buddhist monk and a young unmarried woman:

> In a time now past, there lived a certain governor of Ōmi province who had a wealthy family and many children, including a daughter.
>
> She was still young and quite beautiful, with long hair and a pleasing disposition. Thus her parents loved her dearly and cared for her without even a moment's neglect. Even though highborn princes and nobles tried to visit her night after night without ceasing, her father the governor—without regard to his status—wanted to give her to the sovereign and refused to take any of her suitors as a son-in-law.[30] When the daughter became possessed by a spirit that haunted her day after day, the parents grieved and cared for her, wearing themselves out saying prayers for her cure and persevering even without a sign that she was getting better. At last they heard of a holy man named Jōzō Daitoku, whose unparalleled skill at working miracles resembled that of the Buddha. Because of this, the whole world held him in the highest esteem.
>
> The governor thought, "I'll have Jōzō recite spells to cure my daughter's illness." In response to the governor's respectful invitation, Jōzō arrived at the mansion.

Overjoyed, the governor had the holy man recite the healing spells, upon which the possessing spirit revealed itself immediately and the daughter was cured. The parents urged Jōzō, "Please stay a little longer and recite more prayers," to which he consented. However, a chance glimpse of the daughter suddenly aroused his sexual desire for her and he could no longer think of anything else. It turned out that the young woman returned his feelings, and they began to make love every day, whenever the opportunity arose.

Even though the couple tried to keep their affair hidden, word got out and finally their relationship became public knowledge. When people began to criticize him, Jōzō became embarrassed and eventually stopped visiting the governor's home. Thinking, "I've gotten such a bad reputation that I can't show my face in public," he disappeared from view, quite ashamed of himself.

He secluded himself deep in the mountains at Kurama to pursue an ascetic regimen. Perhaps because of some deep attachments from a former life, images of the governor's daughter kept appearing in his mind. Since his heart was filled with longing for her, his devotions seemed meaningless.

One day when he arose after a nap, he found a letter by his side. His lone companion, a disciple who had accompanied him to the mountains, did not know where the letter had come from. When Jōzō opened the letter, he realized that it was in the hand of the one who had occupied his thoughts. Thinking this very strange, he read:

Would that he
who vanished into
Mt. Kurama's darkness
search for the road
that returns him to me.

Jōzō had a very weird feeling when he read the letter, wondering whom she had asked to carry the letter and how it had arrived. It was all very strange, he felt, deciding to forget her and devote himself to his religious practices. But he could not resist his desire for the woman. That evening he secretly returned to the capital and went to her home. When he called "Hello!" at the door, someone let him in. Learning he had arrived, the young woman stealthily invited him into her room. Before the night was up he returned to Kurama.

Still in the throes of desire, Jōzō secretly sent a poem to the young woman's home:

Those feelings for you that
I thought I had finally forgotten
were painfully aroused
by the voice of the nightingale.[31]

She replied:

Well! You forgot me.
How painful that
only the nightingale's voice
reminded you of me.

And he answered:

If I have forgotten
one who made me suffer,
why do you hate
one who has done you no wrong?

Such exchanges continued for some time, and eventually everyone came to know about their relationship. Consequently the young woman disappeared from view, disowned by her parents—even though they had nurtured her so carefully, prevented princes or nobles visiting at night, and groomed her to become a royal consort.

This shows that a woman's heart is truly detestable. Even though we may say that Jōzō made every effort to seduce her, if the young woman had not responded to his advances, they could not have consummated their affair. Thus people said, "When a woman follows her own wishes, she makes a mess of her life." I've recorded this story just as it was told to me.[32]

The concluding moral is missing from an earlier version of this story in the tenth-century poem-tale *Yamato monogatari,*[33] suggesting that the *Konjaku* compiler may have been breaking new ground in defining transgressive elements in the daughter's behavior.

Both the *Konjaku* tale and its tenth-century predecessor seem more concerned about public opinion of an errant monk than about the monk's spiritual welfare, let alone that of the daughter. The authority of the Buddhist clergy depended in part on their separation from ordinary life. Sexual activity with women (unlike that with boys, which was often tacitly accepted) inconveniently produced children and entangled a man in family ties. Public knowledge of a monk's illicit sexual relations with a woman endangered monastic authority, all the more so when that authority depended on special powers of healing and magic thought to derive from severe asceticism. Jōzō's error lay more in the fact that his breach of celibacy became public than in the breach itself. In general, however, he is treated far more sympathetically than the governor's daughter. Despite the fact that it was he who had initiated the affair, she is made to take the blame for it.

In this story the overwhelming power of male desire is written off as a result of karma from one of the monk's former lives. The mysterious means by which Jōzō receives his lover's first letter also points to an underlying karmic cause. The daughter, on the other hand, is supplied with no such excuse; her part in the affair is blamed on her willfulness and her "detestable" woman's heart, both attributes of her current existence. The tale, it seems to me, has several intended results: to protect Buddhist authority by absolving the monk from any personal responsibility for his acts; to warn monks against drawing near a woman, even unintentionally or with the purest of motives; and to caution women themselves against the potent mix of uncontrollable male lust and their own desires. Yet female premarital sexual activity is not in itself portrayed as transgressive; the problem is the status of Jōzō as a monk.

Concern for the preservation of monastic celibacy shapes the depiction of other *setsuwa* monks in addition to Jōzō, as illustrated by another *Konjaku* tale. The beautiful Somedono, consort of a ninth-century sovereign of Japan, was possessed by an especially persistent evil spirit. When all attempts to exorcise the spirit failed, the sovereign turned to a famous holy man who had secluded himself at Mt. Kongō, some distance from the capital. Many years of ascetic practice had enabled the holy man to perform miracles, and thus he was successful in expelling the spirit from Somedono's body. Her grateful father, the regent, invited the holy man to stay on at court.

> One summer day, when Somedono was wearing only an unlined kimono, the wind blew open the curtains on the screen in her chamber, and the holy man glimpsed her through the opening. Seeing her aroused a sensation that he had never felt before. The glimpse of her elegant and beautiful body deluded the holy man and caused him great distress, and he developed a powerful sexual desire for her.
>
> The situation was completely impossible, but he was so agitated that it seemed his breast was on fire, and he could not endure his desire for even a moment. Finally he completely lost his senses and, seeking a time when no one else was

> around, he pushed aside Somedono's screen and seized her around the waist as she lay sleeping.

Despite her resistance and the outcries of her maids, the holy man overcame Somedono and raped her. He was seized and imprisoned, but when he made the terrifying threat to die and be reborn as an *oni* (demon) that could "become intimate with Somedono as he pleased," he was released and sent back to Mt. Kongō. Still unable to suppress his desire, he managed to starve himself to death. He was immediately reborn as an *oni*.

> He was about eight feet tall, with a shiny black skin that looked as if it had been lacquered. His eyes flashed like blades, and his gaping mouth revealed teeth like daggers and fangs protruding from his upper and lower jaws.

This terrifying creature returned to the palace, burst into Somedono's chambers, and forced himself upon her. Not only did he possess her body, but he seemed to possess her mind as well, and people could hear her sounds of delight behind the screen as the two engaged in intercourse. The sovereign engaged venerable monks to conduct prayer services to defeat the *oni* but succeeded only in obtaining a brief respite. The *oni* continued to return to Somedono's quarters, even raping her in front of her own husband. He and her father, the most powerful political figure in the nation, were unable to prevent the continued violations. The moral of this story is "It is strictly forbidden to approach a monk."[34]

While the compiler sharply admonishes the governor's daughter for willingly making love to Jōzō, Somedono merely provides an opportunity to caution women against unwittingly tempting monks. Yet even though she is guilty of no intentional act, Somedono's fate seems far more horrendous than that of the governor's daughter. The pattern of this story, more frequently than that of the governor's daughter, is repeated in other *setsuwa* tales, which present both woman and man as victims: the woman of rape, the man of his own desire. It was often chance—in Somedono's case, the wind blowing open her curtains—that gave men the intimate glimpse that stimulated their passion.

The rapist is very rarely criticized,[35] but a tale in the thirteenth-century collection *Kokon chomonjū* presents rape as an act worthy of censure, perhaps because the victim is a nun. However, the compiler still provides an excuse for the man: "Perhaps they had made vows to one another in a past life. . . . A demon must have invaded and transformed the man's heart, and as long as he could see the nun, he could not make himself leave her alone and return home."[36] The victim, on the other hand, blames herself for the incident and goes into permanent hiding.

In an article on Indian Buddhist *avadāna* literature—a genre similar to *setsuwa*—Andy Rotman considers the theory that certain objects, such as Buddhist images, arouse immediate faith *(prasāda)* and a compulsion to perform meritorious deeds such as donating to Buddhist temples.[37] The result of the mechanism of automatic arousal need not be a deed of merit: in two tales discussed in this article, sages react in a similar fashion to "objects" who happen to be divine nymphs—the men ejaculate spontaneously. Comparing such compulsions with the automatic sexual arousal attributed in some quarters to pornography, Rotman argues that they were thought to be independent of the subject's state of mind. Following Pierre Bourdieu, Rotman suggests that portraying socially constructed behavior as natural and innate betrays a political agenda; he speculates that the monastic community may have used *avadāna* tales about *prasāda* to encourage pilgrimage and donations.[38]

Rotman's insights might also be applied to the characterization of male sexual desire seen in the tales of Somedono or the raped nun. The logic of a mechanism by which observation generates immediate and unconsidered action may very well have been passed on to Buddhist-influenced literature in Japan, especially *setsuwa*. Such construction of male desire as a natural force absolved the man of wrongdoing, but only rarely—as in the case of the Ōmi governor's daughter—turned the female victim into an instigator or a partner in crime. Often, as in the case of Somedono, the construction of male desire denied the woman agency and made her into an object similar in function to those that aroused *prasāda* (or to the nymphs). If no one was to blame, however, no one could be trusted. Even the most practiced ascetics were susceptible, and even the most unlikely women could arouse sexual desire. The men in *setsuwa* and other Japanese sources rarely stopped at premature ejaculation, however, but proceeded to seduction or rape. In other words, monks could become *oni*, violating monastic celibacy and endangering the authority of Buddhist establishments.

Setsuwa tales repeatedly caution women to avoid rape by avoiding opportunities for men to rape them. To modern eyes these cautions may seem not only absurd—the ascetic-cum-*oni* spotted Somedono in her own chambers—but also an effort to demonize a woman simply for existing. In some tales, women are depicted as careless creatures who invite their own rape: one foolishly accompanies an ascetic into a wooded area of the mountains, another visits a temple attended only by a servant girl, and a third relaxes her guard in front of a trusted servant, who abducts her.[39] Yet there is rarely any moral condemnation of rape victims, who are usually presented as enticement rather than enticers. Although this can be characterized as a variation of "blaming the victim," the raped women are considered far less culpable than someone like the Ōmi governor's daughter, who willingly complied with a monk's efforts to seduce her.

We have seen that male desire was commonly depicted as an irresistible force caused by a chance glimpse of a woman or by that old fallback, karma from a past life. What of female desire? Selfishly following her passions "made a mess" of the life of the Ōmi governor's daughter. Licentiousness—actively pursuing sexual relationships with many men—could make a mess of a woman's next life as well. An early example, from the ninth-century *Nihon ryōiki,* indicates that even in a milieu of relative female sexual independence, licentious behavior on the part of women was disparaged—not, however, because of an inherent moral issue but because of the practical results of such behavior.

In this story, the dharma master Jakurin has a dream in which he meets a woman with painfully swollen breasts, pus leaking from their nipples. She identifies herself as a woman from Echizen who abandoned her children to hunger so that she could make love to many men. Condemned to suffer in hell, she asks Jakurin to seek out one of her children and ask his forgiveness. The son joins with his siblings to make Buddhist images and copy sutras, dedicating the merit of their acts to their mother's release from suffering.[40] Another *Ryōiki* tale relates the fate of a male crow and the hatchlings he has fathered, abandoned by their mother for another mate. The death of the male and the offspring is attributed to the female crow's wickedness.[41] It is worth noting, however, that these *Ryōiki* tales, compiled at a time when the ties between mothers and children were far stronger than those between husband and wife,[42] focused on the suffering of abandoned children rather than on that of the deceived husband. Neglect, not promiscuity, is the true sin of both the woman of Echizen and the female crow.

Late Heian and Kamakura sources, however, sometimes condemn female promiscuity in and of itself. For example, the mid-thirteenth-century *Kokon chomonjū* describes the last moments of a woman who "had a lascivious heart and reveled in sexual pleasures":

> When she fell ill and neared the end of her life, she was encouraged to chant the *nenbutsu* but did not do so. Instead, she grasped the things hanging from the rack behind her pillow and tossed them back and forth with her hands until she breathed her last. She was buried in the vicinity of Hōshōji.
>
> More than twenty years passed. When her grave was opened for reburial around 1253, nothing was found inside. When people dug deeper, something shiny that resembled an oily yellow liquid bubbled out of the excavated ground, congealing after it was ladled out. Once the hole was dug to a depth of about five *shaku*,[43] there was no more liquid to be found. Using a hoe, people poked around what appeared to be the coffin. When they failed to dig up anything, they groped with their hands and discovered a tiny fragment of the woman's skull. Since following the way of sexual pleasure mired her in transgression, she suffered retribution even after her death. The remains of the woman's mother were disinterred for reburial at the same time. It is said that even though she had died many years before her daughter, her body had not decayed but remained just as it was at death.[44]

Nothing is said of the mother's life; but in the religious imagination, purity and asceticism tended to preserve the integrity of corpses. In contrast, sexual desire dehumanized the daughter, turning her into a disgusting substance. This was an especially potent and uncontrolled form of desire, completely possessing the woman's being and causing her to reject the salvific *nenbutsu*. The compiler Narisue seems to be censuring excess rather than desire itself.

Like holy men, even nuns and female ascetics were susceptible to sexual desire, as demonstrated by the following two episodes—the first from *Konjaku monogatarishū*, the second from *Kokon chomonjū:*

> In a time now past, there was a temple in Kyoto's Higashiyama district called Chōrakuji, where a monk was following Buddhist ascetic practices. He journeyed deep into the mountains to gather flowers to present to the Buddha, and the sun set as he was roaming across the peaks and valleys. He settled down for the night beneath a tree.
>
> Around ten at night, he heard the faint sounds of a fine voice chanting the *Lotus Sutra* coming from somewhere nearby. "Strange!" he thought, and listened the

whole night through. "There was no one around in the daytime. This must be a wizard or something." But he still thought it unusual, and as he listened reverently, dawn approached. He then set out to find the location of the voice. After walking for a while he saw what appeared to be a small mound. "What can this be?" he wondered, as everything became visible in the light of morning. Before him was a rock covered with moss and brambles. "Where on earth did that voice reading the sutra come from?" he wondered in amazement. "There must be a wizard sitting on the rock and reciting the sutra." As he was solemnly and respectfully gazing at the rock, it suddenly seemed to move, becoming a little higher. "How strange!" he thought, watching the rock seem to transform itself into a human being who stood up and ran away. He realized that it was a female ascetic of about sixty years of age. When he followed her, the brambles thrust themselves in his way and cut him all over.

This frightened the monk but he asked, "What could this possibly be?" Weeping, the woman ascetic answered, "I have passed many years in this place, and I have never felt the stirrings of sexual desire. Now, however, when you appeared, I thought, 'It's a man!' and sadly I regained my original human form. There is nothing so wretched as the human body. Now, after passing so many years in the form of a rock, it seems I have reverted to what I was before." Weeping and lamenting, she fled into the mountains.

When the monk returned to Chōrakuji he told the story to his disciples, who passed it on to the world.

Hearing this tale makes one realize that if such a thing can happen to even a nun suspended in meditation, how much more can befall an ordinary woman mired in transgression![45]

The *Kokon* tale (no. 552) reads as follows:

In the southern capital there lived a nun who had never had sexual relations with a man. Finally she fell ill, never having been touched by any scandal, and people expected miraculous phenomena at her deathbed. When she reached a crisis in her illness, she invited a monk to attend her and guide her dying prayers. He encouraged her to recite the *nenbutsu,* but instead she cried out, "It's coming, that devil, that cock!"[46] and breathed her last. She must have uttered such words at the end of her life because, even though she had been enlightened by Buddhist teachings, such thoughts still clung to her heart. One's good or bad karma depends on the things that control one's heart. One ought to pay careful attention to this matter.[47]

Nuns like the protagonists of these two tales were expected to remain celibate, but what of unmarried laywomen? According to Wakita Haruko, the increased emphasis on guaranteeing paternal lineage in the late Heian and Kamakura periods led to an emphasis on female chastity.[48] Wakita supports her argument with two *Konjaku* tales. According to the first tale, a woman is condemned to hell for two sins, leaving a sermon early and having sexual intercourse with a man or men *(nan'in).* Happily, she is rescued by her faith in Jizō Bodhisattva. In the subsequent tale, conversely, a woman escapes hell because she died a virgin—she had never engaged in *nan'in.*[49] The use of the term *nan'in* in these obviously paired stories suggests that it was sexual intercourse itself, not simply a socially disapproved relationship, that consigned a woman to hell. These tales suggest some effort to construct male-female sexual relations as transgressive in and of themselves.

This appears, however, to have been a minority view. Female chastity and even celibacy may have been an ideal, but most Japanese sources suggest that premarital sex for women was of little actual concern. An episode in *Uji shūi monogatari,* for example, introduces a woman who has several lovers.[50] The fact is mentioned casually and the compiler does not dwell on it, suggesting that it was a routine situation. Female promiscuity, however, could invite public embarrassment, as Wakita points out. For example, according to an episode recorded in *Toshiyori kudenshū* (by Minamoto Toshiyori, 1055–1129), village women who attended the Ōmi Chikuma Myōjin festival had to present as many earthen kettles to the kami as men with whom they'd had sexual intercourse. Since the women were under oath to tell the truth to the kami, those who had had relations with too many men would attempt to avoid shame by making one big kettle and hiding the smaller ones inside.[51] In comparison with some medieval Christian societies, which branded, imprisoned, or banished women who had had premarital sex, this shaming ritual seems a relatively light punishment. Yet another view of female promiscuity appears in *Goshūi ōjōden,* a collection of tales about rebirth in paradise compiled between 1137 and 1139. A woman of Mutsu province has sexual relations with many men, refusing no one. After she grows old, she explains that she accepted everyone out of compassion, in imitation of a bodhisattva, and that she did so without sexual desire in her heart. In this tale the woman's intent is deemed more important than her actual deeds: upon her death, she is welcomed into paradise by golden figures of buddhas filling the sky.[52]

One reason for low expectations of chastity was the fuzziness of the line between marriage and nonmarriage. In some *setsuwa* tales, coitus apparently makes a couple into husband *(otto)* and wife *(tsuma),* without any apparent recourse to formal engagements or ceremonies. Hitomi Tonomura points out that in one *Konjaku* tale, a raped wife's husband becomes her "former *otto,*" implying that the rapist has become her new *otto.*[53] Under such conditions, female premarital virginity would have had little meaning.

Setsuwa tales by no means always depicted either male or female sexual desire in negative terms. Some tales treat the subject with humor; others show desire blossoming into mutual love. *Kokon chomonjū,* Tale 551, takes an encounter that might be regarded as a serious moral transgression and presents it, with humor, almost as an affirmation of desire—even between a monk and a nun:

> Not long ago, there was a nun who had lived her whole life as a virgin. She was still in her prime, her countenance and bearing were beautiful and appealing, and she lived in comfortable circumstances. Once when she was visiting a temple, a certain monk saw her, and he realized that he was helpless before her irresistible beauty. Lost in the throes of desire, he made note of where she lived and returned home. Afterwards he was unable to put her out of his mind, and spent several days in an agitated state. Since there was no way he could overcome his feelings, impelled by a desire that none could imagine he paid a visit to the nun's house.

The monk, being quite feminine in appearance, disguised himself as a nun and knocked at the woman's door. Claiming to be a widow without means of support, he asked to be taken into her service. Without hesitation, the nun agreed to employ him. He worked diligently as a servant for a year and commended himself to his employer who, still thinking he was a woman, invited him to sleep beneath her robes in winter because the evenings were so cold. Although this aroused his desire even more, he held himself in check for yet another year.

From the beginning of the new year, his mistress the nun devoted herself to special *nenbutsu* services in her private chapel, secluding herself for seven days. On the eighth day she emerged from the chapel exhausted and fell asleep in her servant's presence. Deciding that it was time to bring matters to their conclusion, he forced apart the legs of the sleeping nun and penetrated her. Shocked and bewildered, she jerked away from him and fled into the chapel. While he was lamenting, the monk suddenly heard the sound of a bell ringing over and over again from the other side of the chapel wall. Just as he was about to conclude that his efforts had resulted in disaster, he heard the nun cry out, "Where are you?"—apparently not in too bad temper. Overjoyed the monk answered, "I'm right here," and she emerged from the chapel to find him. When he saw her, he mounted her and took his pleasure with her over and over again as he had hoped to do for several years.

> When he asked her, "Why did you push me out the first time and run into the chapel?" she answered, "Because I thought, why should I enjoy such a good thing all by myself? I thought I'd give a portion to the Buddha, so I ran inside to ring the bell for him." Ever afterward the two were inseparable, becoming husband and wife.[54]

Thus even a collection attributed to a single compiler is inconsistent in its treatment of both sexual transgression and female and male desire. In *Kokon chomonjū,* Tale 551, the rape of a nun is recast as the stereotypical tale of a rape victim enjoying her own violation. The woman's own sexual desire is affirmed, unlike that of the woman who turned into a disgusting yellow liquid in Tale 330 or the nun in Tale 552 who also refused to chant the *nenbutsu.* The obsessive nature of sexual desire distinguishes these two tales from no. 551: dying, both women reject the *nenbutsu,* while the nun thinks first to share her pleasure with the Buddha. It is tempting to imagine that the compiler purposely paired Tales 551 and 552 to suggest his own ambiguous views of female passion. The man's passion, too, receives an unconventional treatment in Tale 551: on the one hand he cannot resist pursuing the nun, but on the other hand he endures two years of close contact with her before he consummates his desire. Irresistibility, it seems, is a matter of definition.

Unfaithful Wives, Embarrassed Lovers, and Murder

Rather than defining any specific act as a violation in and of itself, *setsuwa* episodes tend to focus on excess and context. Stories that do concern a specific act such as adultery pay far less attention to the moral failings of the protagonists than to mistaken identities, affairs discovered by chance, and clever schemes for humiliating transgressors. Such circumstances are sometimes treated comically, targeting lovers, unfaithful wives, or unsuspecting husbands for ridicule. However, censure is largely reserved for adulterous couples who commit the additional crime of murdering the husband or trying to do so.

In one such tale a yin-yang master warns the husband that he is about to become a victim, and the husband is able to avoid being slaughtered. The wife is divorced and the would-be murderer, a retainer of her lover, is arrested; nothing is said about the fate of the lover himself, who conspired with the wife to arrange the murder. The compiler uses the tale to caution husbands against trusting even wives of long standing.[55] In an earlier version of this tale, dating from the late ninth or early tenth century, the wife's moral failings are ignored and commentary focuses on the cleverness of the yin-yang master.[56] In another tale, when the husband decides to stay married to his would-be murderer, the compiler declares his act "truly beyond comprehension."[57] In yet another tale, a wife who succeeds in killing her husband is discovered, tortured, and jailed through the extraordinary perspicacity of the sovereign Daigo (r. 897–930):

> Long ago, in the Engi era, Daigo Tennō was in his bedroom in the palace one evening. Suddenly he called for an official of the Secretariat. When the official arrived, Daigo ordered: "I heard a woman weeping somewhere to the southeast of here. Go quickly and find out about it." Having received the monarch's command, the official called for the guards, lit a torch, and searched throughout the residential palace, but he did not find a weeping woman.
>
> When the night grew so dark that one could not even make out people's faces, the official returned and reported the details to the sovereign, who ordered: "Look more thoroughly." Again, when the official searched the various offices to the southeast of the residential palace, he did not hear a sound. Once more he returned to report his failure, and the sovereign ordered him to search outside the palace compound. The official immediately called for a horse from the palace stables and mounted it, preceded by the guardsmen carrying torches and accompanied by many men. He thoroughly searched the capital to the southeast of the palace, but everything was quiet and he could not hear anyone's voice—much less the sound of a woman weeping. Finally, he reached the neighborhood of Kujō Horikawa....

> "All was quiet in the city, and there were no sounds of a woman weeping," the official had the guards report to the sovereign. "Then I found such a woman in a small house at Kujō Horikawa." The guardsmen returned with the following royal order: "You should seize that woman and bring her here without fail. She is weeping because she is plotting something in her heart."
>
> When the official arrested her, she told him: "My house is polluted. A thief broke in tonight, and my husband has already been killed. His corpse is still in the house." She raised her voice and wailed without ceasing. However, because the sovereign had ordered it, the guardsmen seized the woman and brought her to the gate of the residential palace, reporting from outside [to avoid transmitting pollution]. The Kebiishi (police) were summoned and they took the woman into custody. Daigo Tennō said, "This woman has committed a serious crime. Thus she hid her true feelings and outwardly wept and lamented. She should be brought to judgment immediately and punished," and the Kebiishi took the woman away.
>
> When the next day dawned the interrogation began. For some time it was impossible to make a decision, but the woman collapsed under torture and confessed. To everyone's surprise, it seemed that she had taken a lover and murdered her husband. Then she wept so that everyone could hear her lamenting her husband's death. In the end, the woman was unable to conceal the truth. When the officials of the Kebiishi obtained the results, they reported to the sovereign, who said: "Indeed. When I heard that the sound of that woman weeping differed from what was in her heart, I demanded an investigation. Find her lover at once and arrest him." The lover was seized and imprisoned along with the woman.
>
> Everyone who heard about this said, "One should not let down one's guard against wives like that, who seem basically evil at heart." Of the sovereign, they said with respect, "He is no ordinary person," as they handed down the story.[58]

Even in a single collection, and even for a crime so heinous as plotting to kill a husband, retribution differs for the wife from tale to tale. The fate of the woman in the foregoing tale, in fact, probably hinges both on her successful accomplishment of the crime and on her deceitful attempt to conceal it. The real purpose of the story, of course, is to illustrate the sovereign's extraordinary wisdom.

Murder is a common element in *setsuwa* tales of adultery. A number of episodes tell of a husband discovering his wife with her lover or mistakenly thinking he has done so. One way the husband takes retribution is to try to kill the lover, but unlike later times in actual history the wife is never killed—although she might be punished in other ways.[59] Here are two examples:

Konjaku monogatarishū:

Some time ago in the capital there lived a monk who, although he had some flaws, was somewhat of a celebrity. Because people often invited him to perform services, he traveled all around.

One time, the monk received a request from a respectable household. He set out gladly, but was unable to hire a carriage, so he decided to go on foot. He took along his formal robes, but since the household was some distance away he thought he might soil them on the walk. So he put on ordinary robes and took a flat parasol, and packed his formal robes in a sack. "I'll borrow a small house near my appointment to change my clothes," he thought as he walked along.

Coming upon such a house, he called "Hello!" and asked if he could use it. The mistress of the house, a young woman, said, "Please come in right away," and he entered the house. Straw mats were laid out in a small room that seemed to be a guest room. The monk, wearing a cap, entered the room with the intention of changing into his formal robes.

In fact, the young wife of the house had a monk as a lover. Her true husband, a jack of all trades in an aristocratic household, had pretended to go out but was hiding in a neighbor's house in the hopes of spying on the two of them. When he saw the monk, who knew nothing of all this, the husband thought he had caught his wife's lover and dashed into the house without a moment's hesitation. The monk happened to look up, and saw an enraged young man flying into the house from the street outside. The man turned to his wife and said, "You bitch! Deceiving me this way!"

Before she could explain the actual situation, the husband drew his sword, rushed at the monk, seized him, and aimed at his chest. Astonished, the monk raised his hands and cried, "What is this?" But he could not muster the strength to ward off the sword, so the husband ran him through, and he collapsed on his back. The wife exclaimed, "How disgraceful!" and tried to pull the sword out, but it was no use. After the stabbing, the husband dashed out of the house and fled, but at last the monk's young attendant crept into the street and called out, "A murderer is escaping," and the husband was seized.

The monk lived for a while after having been stabbed, but eventually he died.

Someone from a nearby house had hauled the killer off to the police. The wife too was taken into custody. The husband was interrogated and sentenced to prison.

Three people's lives were destroyed for no good reason at all. This must have been the result of karma from their previous existences. Thus people, whether of high or low estate, should never even for a moment enter the houses of those they do not know, without a reason. Things such as this may happen unexpectedly. This tale has been told as a caution to prevent such things.[60]

Kokon chomonjū:

When Minamoto Yoshiie was young, he had an affair with a certain *hōshi*'s wife.[61] The woman lived in the vicinity of Nijō Inokuma. A splendid mansion had been constructed on the lot, with a moat in front of it and brambles planted alongside. Since the *hōshi* was a pugnacious fellow, he was prepared for invaders. Taking note of his opportunity while the *hōshi* was away from home, Yoshiie would draw his carriage alongside the moat in the depth of night. The woman would open the door of the house, raising the bamboo blinds, and Yoshiie would leap from the back of the carriage. Although the moat was exceptionally wide, Yoshiie would vault it nimbly, unlike an ordinary man. After many such occurrences, the *hōshi* heard about the affair. When he grilled his wife, she confessed. "Then this man came in here regularly whenever I was gone," the *hōshi* said, and the wife could not escape admitting the truth.

The *hōshi* raised the lattice on the upper floor of the mansion. Intending to cut off Yoshiie's usual place of entry, he stood up a heavy *go* table like a shield to trip Yoshiie. Then he drew out his sword and waited. According to plan, when Yoshiie's carriage was allowed to approach, the woman came out as usual. But Yoshiie leaped over the moat like a bird on the wing, drawing his short sword as he flew, and cleanly sliced a few inches from the corner of the *go* table. The *hōshi*, thinking this was certainly no ordinary human being, turned tail and ran in helplessness and terror. When questioned later, he referred to his rival as Hachiman Tarō Yoshiie and seemed all the more intimidated.[62]

It is not clear whether tales of vengeance such as these reflect a socially accepted custom or simply offered the compiler a chance to illustrate certain points while telling a juicy story. Of course husbands sometimes did try to kill lovers, according to evidence other than that of *setsuwa:* in 1024, a Kōfukuji provisioner complained that an aggrieved husband had sent a thief to murder him;[63] in 1200, an officer of the guards killed a provincial governor for having violated his wife "in broad daylight."[64] In both cases, however, the husband's right to kill the lover was challenged, especially in the incident of 1200, in which the lover outranked the husband.

Of course, social rank and relationships of power conditioned attitudes toward extramarital affairs. An entry dated 1142 in Fujiwara Yorinaga's diary *Taiki* tells of the affair of a low-ranking married attendant and Yorinaga's father Tadazane. The woman's husband was also an attendant of insignificant status, while Tadazane was the former regent. When a daughter was born, the woman named Tadazane as the father. He acknowledged the child, despite doubts that were eventually resolved by divination.[65] In relating the story, which focuses on the question of paternity, Yorinaga does not criticize the woman, nor does he mention what happened to her afterward. Tadazane's willingness to acknowledge the affair suggests there was no stigma involved for him. Her husband certainly did not try to kill Tadazane, an act that would have been unthinkable because of the great difference in rank between them.

In the incident of 1200 just cited, a low-ranked warrior was punished for killing the courtier who raped his wife. According to the warrior chronicle *Azuma kagami,* the former governor of Wakasa "violated" the wife of Yoshida Chikakiyo of the Right Equestrian Bureau "in broad daylight" on a public street in the capital. Chikakiyo, on his way home from duty at bakufu headquarters, seized his sword, hunted the culprit down, and killed him. Attempts to capture Chikakiyo and hand him over to the Kebiishi failed, and the culprit fled, apparently to the eastern provinces. At this point civilian officials turned to the bakufu for help, and "man wanted" posters were circulated throughout the east. Chikakiyo was eventually captured and imprisoned.

As Hitomi Tonomura notes, the serious issue in this case was not rape but a murder committed publicly.[66] Hōjō Yasutoki, later a shogunal regent, judged the murder a serious crime. Not only had it occurred in broad daylight, but because a low-ranked retainer had killed a noble with the privilege of royal audience, the social order had been violated. Yasutoki recommended the death penalty.[67] The sympathy of the *Azuma kagami* chronicler is clearly with the rapist/murder victim, even though he violated the woman in the same "broad daylight" in which he was murdered. Public sympathy was also with the rapist, apparently considered quite handsome: "After he was cut down, the garment he was wearing fell open at his throat, laying bare his chest. A huge crowd gathered. It is said that everyone wiped away tears of regret."[68] In this incident, the issue was complicated not only by the public nature of both rape and murder but above all by the class difference between the murderer and his victim.[69] At a time when the fledgling bakufu was attempting to win the court's cooperation, the murder of a courtier by a low-ranking warrior—no matter how severe the provocation—would have been seen as a serious threat to social order.

A third example of the role of rank and power is a *Kokon chomonjū* episode that tells of a married woman who reluctantly accepts the attentions of the sovereign Go-Saga. The woman's attempts to escape Go-Saga's summons are portrayed with sympathy, but in the end both she and her husband agree that she has no choice. The husband is given a promotion and praised by the compiler for understanding the true relationship between ruler and subject:

> We may say that lord and retainer are like fish and water. Those above must not lord it over those below or make them suffer for no purpose, and those below must not envy and resent those above or violate the hierarchical order. In China, King Zhuang of Chu was merciful enough to excuse the retainer who pulled off his consort's robe,[70] and the wise second emperor of the Tang dynasty [r. 627–649] sent one of his favorites to a retainer because she had been promised to him. One may hear many similar examples from ancient times in our own realm—such as the gracious behavior of Go-Saga Tennō and the understanding of the captain who allowed his wife to visit the sovereign. Both should surely be transmitted to future generations as excellent examples of noble actions. It has been said from ancient times that nothing can come between lord and retainer and that their relationship must be based on mutual understanding and sympathy. This is thought to be the way of nature.[71]

The Bakufu Acts

Adulterous affairs were socially disruptive, partly because the peace was threatened by angry husbands who tried to kill lovers, partly because the paternity of children had become an issue affecting the inheritance of property. In her discussion of the respect accorded to women as mothers in the medieval age, Wakita Haruko argues that female chastity was a key to establishing patrilineal succession in the male-dominated family.[72] Although I do not agree with Wakita that this issue mandated female chastity and premarital virginity, it did help to shape the concept of female sexual orthodoxy and transgression. In the realm of law, in fact, adultery was closely tied to issues of inheritance and other forms of the distribution of property.

Although *Hossō shiyōshō* indicates that the *ritsuryō* regulations on fornication, adultery, and rape were known at least in legal circles in late Heian and early Kamakura times, civilian authorities seemed little concerned with illicit sexual unions. An entry of 1212 in *Meigetsuki* (Record of the full moon) relates that when a husband filed suit against his wife's lover, the retired sovereign refused to hear the case.[73] Guilty parties may have been punished by their own families, as in the twelfth-century tale *Torikaebaya monogatari* (The changelings) in which an adulterous wife is temporarily disinherited by her father.[74] Takamure Itsue cites several historical examples in which sexual transgression or its violent consequences were handled by a culprit's family.[75] According to *Hyakurenshō* items dated 1175 and 1176, a man was assassinated by two former lovers of his married paramour, one of whom was her wet nurse's husband and the other, her brother-in-law. The former was arrested by the police, but the brother-in-law was seized by his own family and sent off to exile on Sado Island.[76] In 1226, according to *Meigetsuki,* a father killed his two children and discarded their corpses in the street because they had had incestous sexual relations.[77] In these instances, "private punishment" seems to have been socially sanctioned retribution.

Another issue these examples raise is the extent to which illicit sexual behavior took place within the confines of families. Stepmothers and stepsons seem to have been a particularly volatile combination. An incident dated 1225 recorded in *Meigetsuki* tells of the wife of an official of the Yin-Yang Bureau who took many lovers "from courtiers on down." One night when her husband was away, the woman was visited by a palace official. Her stepson—who, not at all incidentally, was rumored to be the woman's lover as well—attacked the palace official but failed to kill him and ended up losing his topknot in the process. The woman was seized by authorities of the bakufu office at Rokuhara, but she managed to plead and bribe her way out of trouble and was released.[78] Takamure Itsue cites this incident as another example of family punishment,[79] but it seems rather an instance of jealousy and revenge.

What these steamy tales of dueling lovers reveal, of course, is the high social cost of personal vengeance. Although the civilian government was reluctant to act in many cases, it was probably the disorder resulting from illicit affairs that inspired the Kamakura bakufu to regulate private sexual behavior within the warrior class. An episode dated 1209 in *Azuma kagami* provides a good example of the problems faced by the bakufu. The entry depicts two warrior bands on the verge of battle over an affair between one Okashima Kiminari and his neighbor's wife:

> Around dusk, a young wife suddenly entered Kiminari's gate. One must say that, faintly visible in the moonlight, she was perilously beautiful. For some unknown reason, she aroused Kiminari's desire. In any case, they have already spent some nights together. This is a motive for murder.[80]

Sexual rivalry had escalated into armed conflict, endangering public order. What may have resulted at worst in a simple murder in *Konjaku* times was exacerbated in the Kamakura age by bellicose warriors all too eager to find an excuse to fight. The bakufu's bumbling efforts to keep the peace—the woman was ordered home, but both husband and lover prepared for battle—must have underlined the need to control potentially incendiary sexual activities such as adultery. Since the early bakufu's legitimacy rested in large part on its ability to control other warriors, such problems were of paramount importance.

When the bakufu issued its Jōei code *(Goseibai shikimoku)* in 1232, several provisions governing sexual activity were included. While the laws contained prohibitions similar to those of five hundred years earlier, penalties differed substantially. Clause 34 in the code reads as follows:

> *The penalty for clandestine sexual relations* (bikkai) *with another man's wife*
> Those who have sexual relations with another man's wife—whether consensual adultery or rape—shall have half their property confiscated and must cease service to the bakufu. Those without holdings shall be banished to a distant place. The woman's property shall also be confiscated to the same extent, or she shall be exiled.
>
> Regarding roadside abductions, however, a Kamakura retainer *(gokenin)* who kidnaps a woman shall be barred from service for one hundred days. Lesser retainers *(rōjū)* and below shall have one half of their hair and sideburns shaved off, as was done in the time of the Utaishō's lineage.[81] If the offender is a cleric, however, any punishment should be applied according to circumstance.[82]

The law was extended in 1253 to cover local land overseers and cultivators *(myōshu* and *hyakushō),* who were punished by fines.[83] Unless abduction was involved, sexual relations involving unmarried women or widows were not prohibited, even if the woman had been coerced.

Why was a raped wife punished? Since the main purpose of bakufu law was to preserve peace and order, adultery was prohibited primarily because betrayed warrior husbands could generate armed conflict on a substantial scale.[84] However, bakufu lawmakers also needed to keep false accusations based on political rivalry to a minimum—something they did not always accomplish successfully. In the case of rape, the law discouraged charges of a crime that was difficult to prove, while providing a loophole for the much more easily proved crime of abduction—an offense that was often tantamount to rape and involved a public violation of order besides. In an abduction, the female victim was not automatically penalized, but the man was punished much less severely than in the case of adultery. No reason was given for the lighter punishment, but it may have been connected to the assumption—sometimes expressed in *setsuwa*—that a woman in public without protection invited her own rape. The laws of the bakufu showed little concern for morality or fairness to individuals. But I doubt that the bakufu had a particularly misogynist agenda or was systematically concerned with establishing male control over the bodies of women, even though eventually its laws produced that very effect. It should be emphasized, however, that laws punished men as well as women for sexual transgression, and court cases which enforced these laws were aimed at depriving men as well as women of their property.

The bakufu did not have legal jurisdiction over the entire realm. Estates directly controlled by civilian authorities were subject to regulations issued by those authorities. Since this meant in effect that jurisdiction was balkanized, there must have been a patchwork of regulations concerning sexual as well as other offenses. One example is found in an order issued in 1263 by the Jingikan (Bureau of Shrines, an arm of the central government) to Hirota shrine. Since the late Heian period, the holdings of shrines directly under Jingikan control had been treated as personal holdings by the bureau directors, the Shirakawa family. The situation has been compared to that of ordinary estates, with the Shirakawa functioning as overlords *(ryōke)* and shrine priests as onsite custodians *(azukaridokoro).*[85]

The item titled "violating another man's wife" provides for a one-*kan* cash fine for each party in the case of consensual adultery. If the violation was a rape, the man would be fined two *kan* and the woman would not be charged; however, if the woman had seduced the man, she would bear the entire fine and the man would be exempted.[86] Hitomi Tonomura points out that this law, like the Yōrō code, "positioned rape as a subcategory of *kan*—that is, 'violation'—and maintained the philosophical and functional distinction between rape, or *gōkan* (illicit and coercive violation), and adultery, or *wakan* (illicit and consensual violation)."[87]

The penalties were not to be invoked unless someone filed a complaint —presumably the woman's husband although court cases in other contexts demonstrate that accusations of adultery or rape were sometimes made by other interested parties. Fines for adultery or rape originally totaled three *kan*, and one purpose of the Jingikan order, which covered a number of criminal violations, was to lighten punishments in general. This clause states, however, that if the two-*kan* fine did not satisfy the husband, the old penalty should be invoked. Kasamatsu Hiroshi suggests that the original fine may have been based on village practice that the Jingikan found impossible to ignore.[88] If that interpretation is correct, the document provides a rare glimpse at local customs concerning sexual violation as well as a comparison between warrior and civilian law.

It is not entirely clear how thoroughly the bakufu laws were enforced. Kamakura's probable motivations—to preserve the peace and distribute property in an orderly manner—no doubt influenced the way penalties were applied.[89] In a well-known argument, the legal scholar Katsumata Shizuo, relying on *setsuwa* evidence, maintains that the clause on adultery was rarely enforced and that, instead, a deceived husband had de facto permission to kill his wife's lover if the two were caught in the act under certain circumstances: if the adultery took place at home, if the offending couple were caught in the act, and if revenge took place on the spot.[90] (In Katsumata's examples, the husband does not consider killing the wife.) In arguing that the bakufu law was rarely enforced, however, Katsumata overlooks the fact that many cases of adultery did not quite fit such unambiguous circumstances.

Katsumata illustrates his position with tales from *Shasekishū* (Sand and pebbles), a late-Kamakura collection. In one tale, a husband who catches his wife and her lover in the act of adultery agrees not to kill the other man as long as the latter consents to an exchange of wives, servants, and belongings—an advantageous outcome for the husband, since the lover is much the richer of the two.[91] In the second episode, a suspicious husband hides himself above the ceiling in his wife's quarters, intending to catch her lover in an adulterous act and kill him. Instead he loses his footing and falls to the floor, at which point the lover rescues him and nurses him back to health. "I've heard that since they were both gentle in nature, they forgave one another and became good friends."[92] According to Katsumata, the stories' surprise endings hinge on the assumption that the husband would have been justified in killing the lover. Nevertheless, as I discuss later in this chapter, there is considerable evidence that the law was applied as written. First, however, I wish to explore the terminology used for sexual transgression in the Heian and Kamakura periods.

Clandestine Intimacies

The term used in *Taiki* for Tadazane's adulterous affair is *mittsū,* literally "clandestine intimacy" or "clandestine penetration." Though absent from *Konjaku,*[93] the term was actually in use quite early: in an episode in the *Nihon shoki,* an emissary sent by the sovereign to investigate potential consorts ends up having clandestine affairs—*mittsū*—with the women himself.[94] *"Mittsū"* appears with increasing frequency in sources from the thirteenth century and later. It is often translated as adultery, but in an *Azuma kagami* entry dated 1202 it refers to an affair involving an unmarried woman.[95] There is not enough evidence to support a definitive conclusion, but an alternate term *bikkai* (clandestine attachment or affection), which appears in Kamakura law codes and legal decisions, may have been an attempt to construct a legal expression for illicit sexual activity in contrast to the less formal *mittsū.*

Mittsū and *bikkai* were only two of several terms employed in the Heian and Kamakura periods to denote illicit affairs. The accompanying table lists the vocabulary of sexual transgression as it appeared in a number of sources. As the table shows, there were several different terms that could be applied to adultery, but these terms sometimes also signified relationships that we would call fornication. In other words, while the marital status of the woman was a crucial factor in legal prohibitions against adultery, it does not appear to be quite so important in the vocabulary of transgression. Rather, the vocabulary, which often employs characters meaning "clandestine," emphasizes the secret

Vocabulary of Transgression

Source	Date	Term	Refers To
HI 495	1024	*kataraitoru* (to seduce)	adultery
Konjaku	1120s	*maotoko* (in-between man); *mippu* (secret spouse)	adultery
Taiki	1142	*mittsū* (clandestine intimacy/ penetration)	adultery
Azuma kagami	1200	*tsuma o okasu* (to violate a wife)	adultery
Azuma kagami	1202	*mittsū*	secret affair involving unmarried woman
Azuma kagami	1209	*mittsū*	adultery
Meigetsuki	1212	*mippu*	adultery
Meigetsuki	1225	*tsūzu* (to penetrate)	commit adultery
Meigetsuki	1226	*akugyō* (wicked act)	brother-sister incest
Jōei code	1232	*tanin no tsuma o bikkai* (clandestine attachment to another man's wife)	adultery involving a married woman (specified); term may be broader
Jōei code	1232	*wakan* (consensual violation)	consensual illicit relations
Jōei code	1232	*gōkan* (coerced violation)	rape
Tsuikahō	1239	*mitsugi* (secret affair)	widow's clandestine sexual relations
Azuma kagami	1241	*bikkai*	adultery
Shin seibai shikimoku	1242	*sekkai* (clandestine meeting)	clandestine adultery and fornication (unmarried women mentioned)
KI 6266	1243	*bikkai*	adultery

Vocabulary of Transgression *(continued)*

Source	Date	Term	Refers To
Azuma kagami	1244	*mittsū*	adultery
Tsuikahō	1253	*tanin no tsuma o bikkai*	see Jōei code (1232)
Kokon, no. 339	1254	*bikkai*	adultery
KI 8732, 8733 (see Chap. 3)	1261	*mittsū*	adultery or fornication (woman's marital status not specified)
KI 9285	1265	*hisoka ni aitotsugu* (to have secret sexual relations)	a woman's premarital relations with two men
KI 11167	1272	*kaihō* (sexual embrace); *totsugu* (to marry, have intercourse)	adultery between stepmother and stepson
Tsuikahō	1286	*mitsugi*	widow's clandestine sexual relations
KI 29167	1325	*maotoko; hoka no otto o totsugu* (to have intercourse with a man other than one's husband)	adultery
Hyakurenshō	late Kamakura	*mittsū*	adultery

Note: For characters, see the Glossary.

nature of several types of unorthodox relationships: with widows and unmarried women as well as with wives.

Hitomi Tonomura suggests that the use of *mittsū* indicates "a clear-cut and operative concept of adultery that presupposes the husband's claim to his wife's body," a concept which belonged to more strongly patrilocal times than the age of *Konjaku*.[96] Based on both its early occurrence and its occasional broader use, I suggest that *mittsū* indicates, rather, affairs conducted out of the public eye and thus out of public control. The use of characters indicating secrecy—not only in *mittsū* but in other terms for illicit relations—suggests that the clandestine nature of these relations was a major factor in perceiving them as transgressive. While monastic authorities may have preferred monks like Jōzō to keep their affairs secret to avoid undermining the authority of the clergy, lay authorities seem far more concerned with controlling sexual relationships in general; the best way to do this, perhaps, was to assure that all relationships were openly conducted.

The most common application of terms such as *mittsū* or *bikkai* is for extramarital sexual relationships involving a married woman. Despite Katsumata's claim that adultery was rarely punished in the manner prescribed by the Jōei code, several instances in which the law was enforced may be found in Kamakura-period materials.[97] For instance, an *Azuma kagami* entry dated 1241 notes that a bakufu retainer had been dismissed from duty and his holdings were forfeit because he had committed adultery with another retainer's wife.[98] In another case dated 1243, an officer of the guards was convicted of adultery with his brother's wife and his confiscated property was handed over to the accuser, his uncle.[99] The accused were not always convicted, however: in 1244, a wife and her alleged lover proved themselves innocent of adultery by confining themselves in a shrine and swearing their innocence to the deity on the pain of dire punishment. As a result, the woman was permitted to keep her property, a holding she had been given by her husband prior to their divorce on grounds now shown to be spurious.[100]

In 1272, a dispute over landholdings between an uncle and nephew revolved in part around accusations that both of them, as well as the nephew's father, had committed adultery with one or more of his stepmothers—or, in one case, step-grandmother. At issue was a holding *(myō)* in Iyo province, originally belonging to a man of the Kawano family identified only by the Buddhist name he took upon retirement, Kyōren. Kyōren's sons Michitoki and Michitsugu quarreled over the property;[101] according to Michitoki's representative, the holding had been divided between them through a compromise agreement *(wayo)*. However, Michitsugu's son Michiyoshi claimed that Kyōren had actually disowned Michitoki because he had committed adultery with one of Kyōren's spouses and that Michitsugu had allotted him some land out of kindness. (See the accompanying chart.)

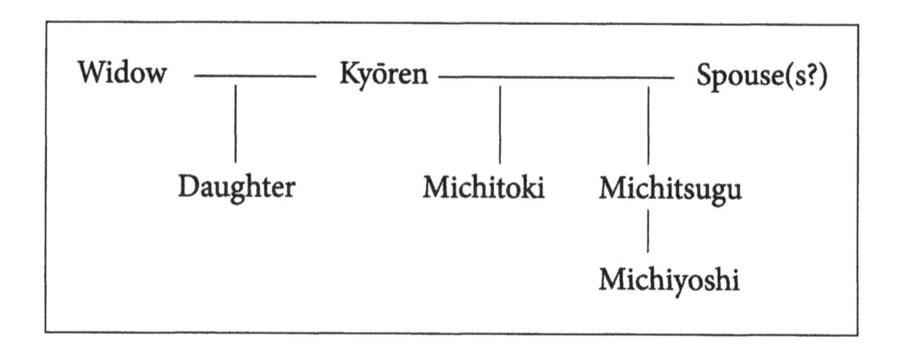

Michitoki's representative then countered with a double-barreled accusation: Michitsugu had committed adultery with Kyōren's widow and his concubine, and Michiyoshi had had sexual relations with both his own stepmother and the widow, his step-grandmother. The dispute also involved another holding entrusted to Kyōren's widow during her lifetime but, after her death, passed on to their daughter. This holding also was claimed by Michitoki, whose representative argued that "the nun [widow] took Michitsugu and Michiyoshi and had them make love to her" and had therefore married at least one of them. Since bakufu law required that widows who remarried relinquish property given them by their husbands,[102] Michitoki argued that his stepmother's holding should have been forfeit prior to her death. The bakufu deferred a decision on this matter until further investigations were conducted. The judges, Hōjō Tokimune and Taira Masamura, seemed to be leaning toward Michitoki, claiming that Michiyoshi had presented no evidence that he had not had sexual relations with Kyōren's widow—the burden of proof in this case being on the accused.[103]

Ironically, bakufu efforts to keep order by mandating a public and nonlethal punishment for adultery opened the way to increased litigation based on possibly counterfeit claims. In the cases of 1243 and 1244, the plaintiff stood to benefit from the conviction; and either party in the 1272 case would have profited if the other had been found guilty. In fact, plaintiffs were often relatives of defendants, and property disputes within families were quite common in the Kamakura age.[104] Such circumstances, along with the nonjudgmental language of most of the complaints and bakufu decisions, suggest that the main issue was property rather than sexual transgression.

In a case decided in 1325, however, the language changed: adultery was

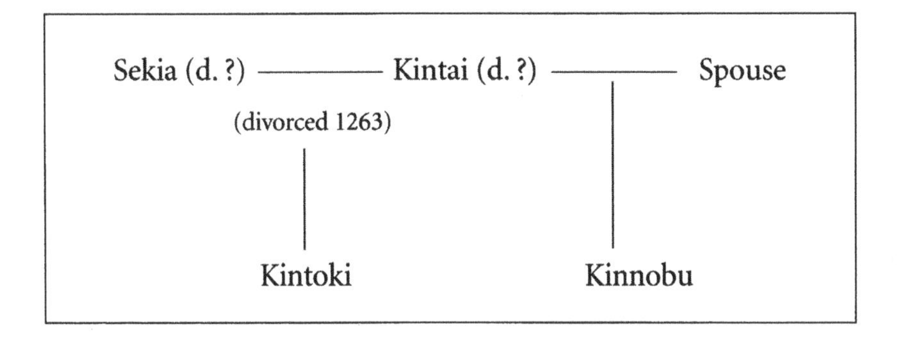

characterized as a source of ignominy for an unfaithful wife and a cause of humiliation for her deceived husband, suggesting the beginnings of the construction of a transgressive identity for adulterous wives that transcended the property issue.

Events in the case, a dispute between two half-brothers over property that originally had belonged to their father, stretched across many years. In 1263, Ajimu Kintai divorced his wife Sekia, deeding her property as part of the divorce settlement; while still living, she passed the property on to their son Kintoki. In 1278, Kintai reclaimed the property and deeded it to another son, Sekia's stepson Kinnobu. (See the accompanying chart.) In support of his legitimate right to the property, Kinnobu submitted a document dated 1298 that bore Kintai's name. According to the document:

> Remaining behind when [Kintai] went to Kamakura [in service to the bakufu], Kintoki's mother took the yin-yang master Etchū Hōshi as a lover. Because she made a bad name for herself, she was banished from the holding altogether. Kintoki too committed a lewd act. Although this was unfilial because he was Kintai's son, he was pardoned because he had enlisted in the service of Lord Hiraoka.

Kinnobu used this document to claim that Kintai had divorced his wife for a serious fault, and thus he was justified in taking the property from her heir Kintoki and giving it to Kinnobu himself.[105] Kintoki's "lewd act" is not identified, but later the document implies that he had committed incest with Sekia: "Kintoki has a deep filial obligation to his mother, and his lewd act is unpardonable." Thus Kinnobu not only attempted to cast Sekia as a transgressor but accused his half-brother of a serious crime that violated the most basic principles of filial piety.

In arguing that this document was a forgery, Kintoki accused his half-brother of "exposing their dead father to shame" by publicly accusing his wife of infidelity. The issue was complicated, moreover, by the fact that Sekia had had relations with at least two men after her divorce; Kintoki claimed that the relationship with Etchū Hōshi also occurred after she had separated from Kintai. The court defined at least one of these relationships as "remarriage," justifying the confiscation of the property Sekia had given to Kintoki. Moreover, the bakufu supported Kinnobu's claim on the grounds of Sekia's transgression, approving Kintai's decision to revoke the transfer of property to her because she had "made a bad name for herself."[106]

In this late-Kamakura case, adultery had been clearly delineated, criminalized, assigned specific consequences, and named a disgrace for both the adulterous wife and her husband. The lover seems to have suffered no consequences—perhaps he had died—but the wife's property rights were revoked posthumously. Another factor in the bakufu court's calculations was widow remarriage, which was intimately related to concepts of *mittsū.* Widow remarriage—and its effect on property distribution—tested the way bakufu courts dealt with evidence of sexual transgression and led to the beginnings of a definition of marriage as a patrilocal arrangement.

Widow Remarriage, Property, and Clandestine Sexual Relations

In the discourse on sexual transgression in Kamakura Japan, terms containing the character *mitsu* (clandestine) often referred to sexual relationships between a man and a woman married to someone else—one relationship that we might call adultery—but they could also have the broader meaning of an illicit affair not sanctioned by society.[107] Unmarried women and widows could become involved in "secret" relationships that were not punishable under bakufu law. Widows could also remarry, at the pain of losing property given them by their husbands.

While widow remarriage seems to have been common, it was not necessarily socially sanctioned, even in the more tolerant late Heian period. A *Konjaku* story tells of a young widow who refused to remarry, even though she was urged to do so by her parents. She pointed out a pair of swallows nesting at their house and asked her parents to kill the male and mark the female.

Only if the female returned with another mate the next year would she remarry. Of course the female swallow returned alone, justifying the woman's argument—and by extension that of the compiler—that widow chastity is a matter of nature.[108]

In requiring that remarried widows relinquish property originally belonging to a deceased husband, the bakufu was attempting to establish and protect patrilineal inheritance patterns.[109] The Jōei code justified this confiscation in terms redolent of both Buddhist and Confucian morality:

> If widows are to retain property given to them by their husbands, they should abandon other concerns and seek the salvation of their dead husbands in the afterlife. Those who ignore the law in this regard are not without blame: widows who immediately abandon chastity and remarry must return the property given them [by their husbands] to their late husbands' children. If there are no such children, the property will be disposed of in another way.[110]

Just like accusations of adultery, accusations of widow remarriage were probably often false, since the plaintiff was frequently allotted the confiscated property. Disputes over property often arose between widows and their stepchildren, and the latter would sometimes claim that their stepmothers had remarried.[111] In the case decided in 1272, described earlier, one issue was widow remarriage. While Kawano Michitoki argued that the property of his nephew Michiyoshi should be confiscated because of adultery, he also claimed that the widow's property should have been forfeited because she had married either Michiyoshi or his father—or perhaps both.

Widows were not forbidden to have sexual relations; but how could the bakufu distinguish such relations from remarriage? Officials in 1239 decided that a widow's "secret relationship"—*mitsugi*—would not automatically result in property confiscation. Only when a widow handled the daily affairs and dealt with the property of a husband's household was she considered remarried.[112] In other words, marriage was defined as a patrilocal arrangement in which the woman left her own family and joined her husband's. This definition was difficult to apply in the case of 1272, and this may be one reason why the bakufu postponed a decision on the issue of widow remarriage in that instance. However, in 1286 the bakufu reversed its decision of 1239, rescinding its demand for proof of patrilocal arrangements and accepting public knowledge of sexual relations as evidence of widow remarriage.[113] Seno Seiichirō suggests that many remarried widows may have tried to avoid property confiscation by claiming to be involved, instead, in "secret" sexual relationships.[114] If there was any shame in such an affair, it could be trumped by economic considerations.

Although patrilocal patterns were strengthened among the warrior class during the Kamakura period, the age was a transitional one with complex bilateral modes of succession and descent. Defining legitimate marriage as patrilocal would seem to have clear advantages for warrior families attempting to keep holdings intact and under control of a single family head;[115] but in reality, marriage patterns were still so complex that a single definition would not do. Ironically, limiting the definition of widow remarriage to a patrilocal arrangement may have worked against the goal of consolidation, since women were handed a device with which to deny their remarriage and retain their holdings. Even though the bakufu eventually abandoned the definition, it was operative for forty-six years, during which time it no doubt contributed to a firmer sense of orthodox and heterodox sexual relationships.

Orthodoxy and Transgression

No clear figure of a transgressive woman emerges from either *setsuwa* tales, on the one hand, or laws and legal decisions on the other. In neither case do we find an effort to essentialize particular modes of female sexual activity and define them as transgressions. Context and ill-defined excess seem to determine whether or not a particular act is censured in a *setsuwa* tale. And despite laws criminalizing adultery, vague concepts of both marriage and *mittsū* made identifying transgression a slippery business. Nonetheless bakufu legislation and enforcement contributed to definitions of sexual orthodoxy and suggested that marriage and sexual relationships ought to be subject to control by authorities. Figures of both "virtuous" and transgressive women began to take shape, each helping to define the other.

For the most part both men and women were punished for sexual transgressions. But in Kamakura as well as Heian times, uncontrollable sexual desire provided an excuse for the man but rarely for the woman. Sometimes even the unwitting arousal of male desire resulted in punishment for the female victim. Whatever the bakufu's motivation, the Jōei code provisions on rape became a case in point. Later, even a woman who had been abducted could be penalized. A commentary on the code cites a late-thirteenth- or fourteenth-century court case in which a monk was charged with attempting to rape a woman walking alone at night. After a hearing, he was released: "He had not committed a crime. Although he had lust in his heart, that was to be expected." The unfortunate woman was jailed, however, because she had invited her own rape by taking a walk late at night.[116] The "carelessness" that had invoked admonitions of caution in *setsuwa* tales was now characterized as a criminal act.

Both *setsuwa* and law codes reflect the needs of the male elites who produced them. The frequent appearance of Buddhist monks as lovers in *setsuwa* tales of illicit sexual relationships points to a concern with clerical celibacy on the part of their compilers, whether laymen or monks themselves. The bakufu saw adultery as a potential threat to peace and sought means to curb its attendant violence—while individual warriors manipulated the codes to aggrandize themselves by casting stepmothers, half-siblings, or nephews as sexual transgressors. Although some developments stiffened the concept of transgression, other forces seemed to move in the opposite direction. Men of high rank, whether of the civilian or the military elite, continued to insist that the privileges of their rank include unimpeded access to women of a lower class, a motivation that may have contributed toward lingering lenient evaluations of some adulterous affairs. As individuals, moreover, men of all social positions had a stake in promoting the myth that sexual desire was an irresistible force of nature. Forming concepts of orthodoxy and transgression was not a neat linear process, moreover, since the repression of the freedom and sexual power of women denied past practices and structures. The apparent resistance of widows to the governmental promotion of chastity is one case in point. Conflicts in the way sexual relationships were presented in even a single *setsuwa* collection also suggest that it was difficult to settle upon one orthodox set of relationships between men and women or indeed upon one orthodox mode of sexual behavior. Actively tempting men or giving in too readily to an inappropriate lover's blandishments, however, were generally negatively coded, a factor that links the Ōmi governor's daughter, the woman who turned into yellow liquid, and the accused adulteress Sekia. This also suggests that trades such as sexual entertainment, in which women purposely enticed men, were candidates for stigma despite their overall public acceptance among Heian aristocrats.

Sexual professionals engendered far less concern in *setsuwa* and law than did unfaithful wives, but two Kamakura-period documents indicate that negative attitudes toward sexual entertainment and sanctions against adultery were sometimes conjoined. According to the provincial law code *Shinseibai shikimoku,* issued in 1242 by the military overseer *(shugo)* of Bungo province: "Except for designated women, to entice wives and unmarried women into secret liaisons is a basis for disorder and must cease."[117] The order is aimed at go-betweens called *nakadachi* who arranged illicit affairs. Since go-betweens *(nakadachi* or *nakōdo)* were linked with prostitution in other sources, the "designated women" may be identified as sexual professionals.[118] The intent of the order is twofold: to prevent "respectable" wives and daughters from having extramarital relations and to draw a line between such women and professionals, for whom such relations were not considered illicit.

The other pertinent document is a bakufu edict of 1267 regulating the distribution of property owned by *gokenin,* which set forth restrictions on the rights of widows or divorced women to property given them by their husbands. The edict was issued together with two others that limited the transfer of land rights held by *gokenin* through mortgage, sale, or compromise settlement *(wayo).* Although the other two edicts were repealed three years later, the restrictions on widows and divorced women remained in force.[119] According to the edict, those women who were the daughters of other *gokenin* could retain the property even in the case of divorce, as long as they were judged "blameless" in the matter—meaning, most likely, that they had not been convicted of adultery; they had to cede the property to their husbands' families only if they remarried. The same privilege, however, was not automatically granted to several other categories of divorced women: "daughters of non-*gokenin* families, as well as *kugutsu, shirabyōshi,* and all women of base origin" who had "enticed" their spouses into granting them property.[120] The main intent of this edict, which also exempts "chaste widows" from any requirement to return property, was doubtless to keep holdings out of the hands of potential bakufu rivals who might marry the divorced women—hence its inclusion in a package attempting to limit the dissipation of *gokenin* holdings. Singling out *kugutsu* and *shirabyōshi* and classifying them as "base women," however, indicates that in their case the reason for limiting their inheritance rights was their sexually potent occupation and its low social status. The remark that these women had "enticed" their spouses into giving them property suggests that the bakufu viewed them as seducers rather than legitimate spouses. As transgressors, the women were classified as the equivalent of adulterous wives and denied property rights on this basis.

These two documents are very different in nature: one marks out an exclusive sphere of activity for sexual professionals; the other classifies them as transgressive individuals who cannot be accorded the rights of ordinary women. Both, however, depend on definitions of illegitimate sexual behavior that were crafted to apply to all women. These definitions were not the only factor in stigmatizing sexual entertainers and casting them as prostitutes, but they played a significant role in the process.

Sacred Sex or Sexual Pollution?
Asobi, Shamans, and Bodhisattvas

To the south lies Sumiyoshi shrine and to the west, Hirota. The *asobi* go there to pray for lovers. Hyaku Dayū, whom they especially worship, is their guardian deity. If one were carved for each customer, the numbers would stretch to the hundreds and thousands. — Ōe Masafusa, *Yūjoki*

You and I
speaking words from another world
longed to make love
as drums and breasts throbbed in rhythm.
— caption for a picture of an elderly female shaman, *Tōhokuin shokunin utaawase*[1]

MANY SCHOLARS HAVE ARGUED that sexual entertainment in premodern Japan cannot be understood entirely as a secular, everyday phenomenon. *Asobi* have been considered not only as entertainers or prostitutes but also as shamans (or their heirs) and as exemplars—witting or no—of Buddhist teachings. Some scholars characterize sexual intercourse with *asobi* as a sacred act, and many argue that, in some way or other, *asobi* belonged to the realm of the sacred. A weaker but still discernible thread in the discourse on sexual entertainment characterizes it and its practitioners as ritually defiled. This chapter considers issues of purity and defilement in relation to the sex trade, beginning with common propositions that equate female shamans and sexual entertainers or propose an evolutionary tie between the two.

Sexual Relations and States of Ritual Purity

Anthropologists studying Japan posit three possible states related to ritual purity: the sacred *(hare),* the ordinary *(ke),* and the polluted *(kegare).*[2] Temples, shrines, and holy images were obviously regarded as sacred, and it was necessary to preserve extraordinary purity around the person of the sovereign. On the other hand, death, blood, and childbirth generally fell into the polluted category. Daily productive activities were regarded as "ordinary,"[3] but they might embrace the sacred—for example, harvest festivals were a "sacred" finale to an "ordinary" agricultural season. However, particular phenomena or classes of persons sometimes moved from one state to another, and the intensity of pollution associated with a particular act might change with time or circumstance. On the surface sacrality and pollution seem to be polar opposites, but both may also be seen as "extra-ordinary" in opposition to *ke* and thus may actually overlap. Such a possibility is proposed, for example, by Yamaguchi Masao, who argues that the sovereign and the aristocracy, on the one hand, and low-status people ("craftsmen, entertainers, diviners, gravediggers, and minor priests"), on the other, occupied similar positions as "outsiders" vis-à-vis ordinary Japanese society.[4]

Defining states of sacrality or pollution was the job of the religious systems that also played a major role in defining sexual orthodoxy and transgression. Inconsistent evaluations of the sexual are often attributed to differences between early Japan's two major sets of religious beliefs and practices, Buddhism and the collection of largely indigenous folk-based cults later called Shintō: it is often said that Buddhism saw the sexual as dangerous while indigenous beliefs affirmed it.[5] Indeed, much folk religion had a strong phallic character: the celebration of fecundity embraced all life-giving forces, from the cultivation of rice to human sexuality. Buddhist teachings, on the other hand, saw all desires, including sexual passion and the desire for children, as potent obstacles to the pursuit of enlightenment and salvation. In actual practice, however, there is no clear dichotomy between Buddhist attitudes toward the sexual and those found in indigenous beliefs and practices. Despite a general affirmation of sexual activity, indigenous systems fostered taboos on when, where, and with whom one might have intercourse; and Buddhist authorities wasted little effort in fact on regulating lay sexual activity. Moreover, both institutionally and in lay practice, it is hard to distinguish Buddhism from indigenous religion; they influenced one another and shared space and ideology, and themes from both were often intertwined in the same stories.

Sexual relations may be viewed through the *hare–ke–kegare* lens. Certain activities—relations involving the indigenous deities called kami, for example—were regarded as sacred and hence extraordinary. Human sexual relations, or those of anthropomorphized kami, played a large part in early religious beliefs. Perhaps the best-known example is the story of Izanagi and Izanami, the kami pair whose mating produced the islands of Japan as well as the female kami Amaterasu, claimed as ancestor by the ruling clan. The systematic linkage of the Izanagi-Izanami story with the history of the ruling house appears in the eighth-century chronicles *Kojiki* and *Nihon shoki* and justifies the sovereign's position by rooting it in the very birth of the land that he or she ruled.[6] Thus sexual relations between kami provided a cosmic basis for kingship.

Human beings sometimes participated in the sexual relations of the kami world: legends in provincial gazetteers called *fudoki,* also dating from the eighth century, told of intercourse between male kami and human females. Ritualists who served a kami sometimes claimed to be descended from the offspring of such unions. For example, a *Kojiki* myth tells of a woman who had intercourse with the serpent-kami of Mt. Miwa and gave birth to his son. The child founded the Miwa clan that took charge of worshipping the kami.[7] Another example is the story of Tamayori-hime, who found an arrow floating in the river where she was bathing. After she took the arrow home and inserted it in her bedding, she became pregnant with, it turned out, the son of the kami of thunder. In this case it was not her descendants but those of her older brother who became ritualists to that kami.[8] *Fudoki* legends also indicate that at festival time human couples engaged freely in sexual intercourse to activate the kami's sacred power.[9] Such activities were often a communal experience that took place openly at shrines and mountain sanctuaries, a public act ratified by the community.[10]

The assignment of phenomena to the realm of *hare, ke,* or *kegare* was historically conditioned, changing, and contested. Heian-period sources indicate that in some cases the sacred sexual activities that had once taken place at shrines had shifted to urban streets, becoming a form of secularized play. One urban street festival is described in nearly identical passages in the histories *Honchō seiki* (938/9/2) and *Fusō ryakki* (939/9/2), possibly taken from an earlier common source:

> These days, people have carved deities out of wood and installed them opposite one another at street corners in the east and west capital. In general, these figures look like courtiers.[11] Their heads are crowned with official-looking caps *(kanmuri),* with cords dangling beside their sideburns.[12] The red lacquer applied to their bodies makes it look as if they are wearing crimson robes—quite out of the ordinary.

> Each one differs in appearance. At the same places, people have carved female figurines and placed them facing the males. Each figurine has genitals painted and carved below the abdomen. Bowls are set on tables placed in front of the figurines. The young folks pay uproarious homage to the sexual intercourse ["performed" by these figurines], either draping them with sacred strips of paper or presenting them with flowers and incense.[13] These figurines are called "kami of the crossroads" *[chimata no kami = dōsojin]* or *goryō* [spirits of the dead]. We're not yet sure what fortune they bring, but sometimes people regard them with wonder.[14]

Another mid-Heian source gives an example of ritualized sexual intercourse originally designed to please the kami that had become the object of jokes and ridicule. A letter in Fujiwara Akihira's collection *Unshū shōsoku* describes a performance at the Inari shrine festival in Heian-kyō that reflects ancient festival rites of sexual intercourse. Along with another courtier, the correspondent, an adviser to the Council of State surnamed Tomo (Ban), paid a clandestine visit to the popular festival. After noting the participants' riotous behavior and extravagant dress, Adviser Tomo went on to say:

> There was some carnival entertainment, in which the actors pretended to be husband and wife. One, modeling himself after a feeble old man, became the husband; the other took the role of a young woman as the wife. They began by exchanging flirtatious words and later went so far as to have sexual intercourse. All the townsmen and women who saw this bellowed in laughter until it split their guts. It was pretty vulgar stuff.[15]

Fukutō Sanae proposes that this event was a variation on a spring planting ritual in which an elderly couple had (or feigned) sexual intercourse to assure a good harvest.[16] In this case, a rite that had once belonged to the sacred realm had bled through to the everyday world, the streets of the capital, even while retaining some sacral elements as part of a shrine festival. Any effort to define professional sexual entertainment as sacred or polluted requires consideration of the shifting historical context that this changed ritual so powerfully represents.

Asobi and Female Shamans

In analyses of the premodern Japanese sex trade conducted over the last century, sexual entertainers have been far more often linked with the sacred than with the polluted. In particular, scholars have focused on the relationship between female shamans (called *kamunagi* or *miko*) and *asobi,* as well as that between female shamans and prostitutes of any type. Arguments are based in part on literary evidence such as the two selections quoted at the beginning of the chapter—one from Masafusa's late-Heian-period essay, the other from a late-Kamakura picture scroll. The discussion has given rise to three major conclusions: first, once shamans lost their positions at shrines and became wanderers *(arukimiko),* they routinely turned to prostitution—a conclusion so commonplace that it is sometimes cited as a given;[17] second, *asobi* originated as shamans; and third, *asobi* actually were shamans, either because they practiced shamanic arts or because their trade in sexual services replicated the performance of female shamans as "wives" of the kami they served. Although the implications of the conclusions differ, they are often presented together and a number of scholars accept one or more.

The sources on which these arguments are based are fragmentary and conflicting. They include material such as legends and poems, which may not reflect objective reality but do give a sense of the possible and plausible. A number of scholars have milked these sources and interpreted them in various and—in my view—imaginative ways. After analyzing some of these interpretations, I will suggest some alternative ways to understand the evidence on which they are based.

Theories linking female shamans and sexual entertainment took shape in the first half of the twentieth century. Folklore scholar Yanagita Kunio argued that female entertainers, including *ukareme, asobi,* and *kugutsu,* were originally a type of shaman; using puppets such as Hyaku Dayū/Hyaku Kami figurines mentioned in *Yūjoki* and *Kairaishiki,* they introduced the veneration of roadside kami to the populace. Yanagita focused on religious elements and parallels in the entertainment of *asobi* and *kugutsu,* and he clearly regarded the trade in sex as a secondary supplement to their religious function.[18] Orikuchi Shinobu, on the other hand, traced the "origins of *asobi*" to women who introduced young men to sexual intercourse; some of these women, he argued, lived at shrines while others were ordinary villagers. Thus he concluded that the shaman-origin theory was an oversimplification and only partially valid.[19]

Arguing from another perspective, Nakayama Tarō maintained that certain female shamans turned to prostitution or were forced into the profession. In his two major works that examine this theme, Nakayama suggests several paths by which shamans evolved into sexual professionals. For instance, he claims that *ukareme*—whom he characterizes as prostitutes—were remnants of the ancient shamanic Asobibe, an occupational group that conducted rituals to summon back the spirits of dead rulers. As ancient beliefs weakened and social conditions changed, other types of shamans—some attached to particular shrines and seen as wives of the kami venerated there—were expelled from their positions and turned to prostitution to make a living.[20] To support his arguments, Nakayama cites linguistic similarities between terms for shamans and for prostitutes; the proximity of many pleasure districts to shrines; and the participation of prostitutes in various shrine festivals. While much of this evidence comes from the Edo period or even later, Nakayama also uses several Heian-period sources. For example, he argues that the inclusion of male and female shamans along with *asobi* in the "beggars and thieves" category in *Wamyōshō* suggests the sexual aspects of the shamans' profession. Nakayama also refers to a passage from *Shōmonki* in which a woman identified as a banquet entertainer serves as an oracle who predicts that the rebel Taira Masakado will be Japan's next ruler.[21] Poems in *Ryōjin hishō* that depict female shamans as the subjects and objects of sexual desire are also used to support the arguments of Nakayama and several other scholars who equate female shamans and *asobi*.[22]

More recently scholars have crafted some intriguing expansions and reconfigurations of shaman-origin theories. In a more detailed argument than that of Nakayama, Gorai Shigeru also traces the origins of *ukareme* to the Asobibe and similar ritualist organizations. Such groups eventually lost their ritual function, for reasons Gorai does not venture to specify; one possibility is that with the popularity of Buddhist funerals and cremation among elites, summoning the dead had become an empty rite. In any case, Gorai argues that some female ritualists became *arukimiko,* continuing in a fundamentally shamanic profession, while others became *ukareme,* progenitors of both *asobi* and *shirabyōshi.* Sometimes, Gorai speculates, male and female ritualists stayed together, forming special entertainers' groups known as *kugutsu.* Gorai also argues that the swords and spears used in *shirabyōshi* dances resemble the weapons in pacification rituals conducted by the Asobibe. It is reasonable to suppose that remnants of the Asobibe continued shamanic rituals in somewhat different form, but Gorai offers no firm evidence linking them to *ukareme* and other female entertainers.

Gorai argues convincingly, however, that *asobi* and *kugutsu* performed rituals to invoke the help of the kami. *Yūjoki,* Ōe Masafusa's twelfth-century essay on the *asobi,* cites the women's devotion to Hyaku Dayū. In the passage quoted at the beginning of this chapter, *Yūjoki* notes that Hyaku Dayū figurines were carved for the women at Sumiyoshi and Hirota shrines. Masafusa identifies a similar deity in *Kairaishiki,* his account of the *kugutsu:* "In the evenings [the *kugutsu*] worship Hyaku Kami, beating drums, dancing, and making an uproar to pray for help in obtaining good fortune." Both *asobi* and *kugutsu,* in Gorai's view, performed shamanic rituals to guarantee their own prosperity. He points out that wandering shamans used wooden figurines in their rituals that may have been similar to those mentioned in *Yūjoki.*[23] Perhaps the figurines also resembled the *chimata no kami* mentioned in the *Honchō seiki/Fusō ryakki* passage quoted earlier.

Recently Saeki Junko has argued that female shamans did not "become" *asobi;* rather, *asobi* in fact were shamans. Rather than attempting to trace a process by which female shamans evolved into entertainers and prostitutes, Saeki identifies religious components in *asobi* activities and performances. She points out similarities between the songs *(imayō)* performed by *asobi* and the songs *(kagura)* performed for religious purposes.[24] Saeki also cites legends in which *asobi* attain rebirth in the paradise of Amida Buddha by singing *imayō* or are depicted as manifestations of bodhisattvas,[25] a topic I explore in detail later in this chapter. Saeki does not regard the *asobi* profession as a degeneration of the shaman's function; in fact, she views prostitution as an inherently shamanic act. She concludes that, far from being degenerate shamans, *asobi* were transmitters of sacred life-giving sex. Drawing comparisons with temple prostitution in the ancient Middle East, Saeki argues that shamans were expected to have sexual relations with the kami they served and contends that human males were sometimes substituted (or substituted themselves) for the kami.[26]

All of these theories are intriguing, and none can be disproved; but I think they are based on inconclusive evidence and colored by modern evaluations of the sexual nature of female shamans. For example, Orikuchi Shinobu argues that since a shaman would have sexual relations with a different man each year as substitute for the kami she served, this made her "close to a prostitute" *(baishō no onna).*[27] However, I have found no direct evidence that female shamans as a group may be categorized as sexual professionals, and the circumstantial evidence that does exist is open to interpretation. This differs from the case of *asobi,* who are linked explicitly with the sex trade in Heian and Kamakura sources, their activities described in considerable detail by their patrons and others who observed them. We know where they set up business, how they attracted customers, and how they were paid. While descriptions of *asobi* may very well be unrealistic, different kinds of sources—such as dictionaries, diaries, essays, temple documents, and *setsuwa*—make it clear that the sale of sex was a central feature of their occupation. In contrast, I know of no delighted patrons' recollections of sexual adventures with shaman-prostitutes, no complaints about shamans peddling sex, no stories of repentant shamans abandoning a life of prostitution and seeking the Buddha's mercy—all common features found in accounts of *asobi.* While the absence of such accounts does not mean there were no female shamans who traded in sex, it does suggest that the practice may not have been common enough to attract public notice.

The presumed association with prostitution questions the religious function of shamans, particularly those of low social status. The presumed association with shamans has contributed to a process of mystification by which *asobi*—and sexual relations with them—are accorded a special status at the borders of the everyday world. Because the circumstantial evidence for a shaman-*asobi* connection has been so widely accepted, and because it uncovers crucial elements in the lives of both sets of women, it needs to be examined critically. But first we should know a little more about shamans.

Black Magic Women

Both men and women could be shamans in early Japan, but it is women who seem to have attracted the greatest notice in literary and artistic sources. Powerful female shamans appear in the eighth-century Japanese chronicles, and *haniwa* figurines found in burial mounds from the fifth and sixth centuries depict female shamans with painted faces and artifacts such as bells and small mirrors, which they used to enter a state of trance and invite possession by a kami.[28] Chinese records from the third century and Japanese chronicles compiled in the eighth attest to the power and prestige of female shamans as rulers who governed by transmitting the will of the kami. In villages, too, female shamans in trances spoke with the voices of kami thought to have possessed them. Female shamans could be found in individual households, at shrines, or on the road. By the mid-Heian period, they transmitted not only the words of the kami but also those of dead humans—in other words, they were both oracles and mediums.[29] They were also performers, a natural outgrowth of their sacred song and dance to summon the kami. Picture scrolls from the Heian and Kamakura periods show female shamans at shrines performing *kagura* dances and playing musical instruments such as koto, drums, and bells or riding on horseback or in carriages at shrine festivals. Itinerant *arukimiko* are portrayed outside shrine gates or at the market, telling customers' fortunes.[30] One scroll depicts a female shaman performing a ritual at a parturition hut for the protection of a mother and her newborn.[31]

When they functioned as oracles for the kami, shamans were both powerful and dangerous: a kami's admonition delivered through a shaman's mouth could topple the powerful and arouse crowds to riot. Yamakami Izumo argues that one threat which shamans posed to central authority lay in their pivotal role in the pre-*ritsuryō* religious system that the government tried to co-opt or suppress. When the eighth-century *ritsuryō* polity strengthened central control over shrines and religious rituals, a wedge was driven between official systems of worship and shamanistic practice. Nonetheless, shaman groups continued to function at important shrines such as Usa Hachimangū in northern Kyushu.

As mouthpieces for the kami, shamans sometimes endangered the authorities by relaying oracles that opposed powerful individuals or their policies. Sometimes, too, shamans were accused of casting evil spells for political purposes. Female shamans were active in ninth- and tenth-century *goryōe,* ceremonies to pacify the angry spirits of political losers, and in related protest movements.[32] For example, after Sugawara Michizane died in political exile in 903, the court faced a number of disasters blamed on his angry spirit. In 942, a female shaman named Tajihi Ayako claimed to speak for Michizane and demanded the construction of a shrine to revere his spirit.[33] Female shamans also participated in popular outbreaks of ecstatic singing, dancing, and prophecy, such as the popular uprising of 945 that invoked the name of Shidara no Kami.[34] As Nishiguchi Junko points out, moreover, provincial families might use shamans' oracles successfully to oppose central rulers, as in a quarrel of 804–805 between Isonokami shrine and the court. A female shaman, speaking with the voice of the shrine's kami, blamed the sovereign's fatal illness on the court's appropriation of a shrine treasure. Nishiguchi argues that local Yamato families were behind the oracle, which resulted in the return of the treasure to the shrine.[35] The political danger posed by shamans may explain their inclusion in *Wamyōshō* in an occupational category that included beggars, sneak thieves, robber gangs, pirates, convicts, and, of course, *asobi.*

The subversive potential of shamans was sometimes linked to sexual misbehavior and public disorder. An edict from the throne dated 780 accuses shamans of misleading ignorant and foolish subjects, in part through sexual play or enticement. Other court proclamations issued in the late eighth and early ninth centuries forbade street festivals and public gatherings that mixed men and women in a public setting. In one order, dated 798, licentious behavior is linked with rioting at an evening festival that both men and women celebrated with song, dance, and wine. Yamakami identifies these activities as early *goryōe.*[36] One additional example may be the festival, described in *Honchō seiki,* discussed earlier in this chapter.

I suspect that in the eyes of court authorities, the subversive potential of shamans was enhanced by their involvement in festivals that involved public sexual display, such as those mentioned here. It should be noted, however, that shamans were a broad social group, many of whom served authority rather than challenging it. Symbolically, the bodies of some female shamans were offered to the kami they served and, by implication, to the political apparatus that governed official shrine activities. The proposed relationship between female shamans and *asobi* (or prostitution) is based in part on the implications of such service. Was the symbolic relationship with the kami reified into an actual sexual relationship with a human man or men, and did this process "degrade" the shaman into a prostitute? Did the bodies of *asobi* offer sacred sex outside a ritualized setting? These questions depend on how the relationship between kami and shaman was conceived and, in particular, on what was expected sexually of the shaman.

The Sexuality of Female Shamans

Female shamans are sometimes characterized as "wives" of kami. According to Yamakami Izumo, myths in the *Kojiki, Nihon shoki,* and *fudoki* cast shamans as the sexual partners of *marebitogami,* deities who visited a community during festival time.[37] In this interpretation, the penetration of the shaman's body when possessed by the kami is expressed in terms of sexual penetration. It can be argued that if a shaman were indeed the wife of a kami, that made her unavailable to ordinary men; in other words, she had to remain celibate during her tenure, if not a lifelong virgin—unless, of course, her sexual partners could be seen as surrogates for the kami. In the view of some scholars, a shaman's sexual relationships outside this sacred sphere are transgressive and cast her as a prostitute. Others, such as Orikuchi Shinobu, find intimations of prostitution even within a shaman's sacred sexual activities.

The evidence of both history and legend casts doubt on the claim that shamans were consistently expected to be virgins. The famous shaman-queen Pimiko, who appears in third-century Chinese chronicles as the ruler of the elusive state of Yamatai, is portrayed as a secluded virgin.[38] But the legendary sovereign Jingū, possessed by a kami who ordered her to invade Korea, succeeded her husband on the throne and bore her own successor.[39] Whether or not these cases are historically accurate is beside the point. They suggest that at even the highest levels in early times, celibacy was an option for female shamans but not an obligation.

Yoshie Akiko's research uses shrine records and legendary sources to challenge the standard picture of shamans as sacral virgins. Yoshie's findings indicate that it was ritualized sexual relations between human men and women, not the spiritual power of the woman alone, that were thought to persuade the kami to grant the community a good harvest. The female ritualists known collectively as "Tamayori-hime" were paralleled by male "Tamayori-hiko," who were also empowered to host the kami; the *hiko* and similar male figures were sometimes depicted as brothers of the *hime,* but sometimes as their lovers. Furthermore, while some women might spend their whole lives serving a kami, this did not necessarily prevent them from having sexual relations with men. At Kamo shrine in the early Heian period, for example, the requirement of celibacy applied to the court-appointed princess-priestess; but a lesser Kamo shaman from a lower-ranked ritualist family was permitted to marry and continue in her position.[40] Yoshie argues elsewhere that in early times female ritualists *(monoimi),* later identified as wives of the kami, were shrine officials responsible for various duties and contends that "the figure of the virginal woman *[miko]* was a product of later ideas about female impurity."[41]

On the other hand, Sekiguchi Hiroko cites a Council of State order dated 801 which indicates that the sexual violation of a *monoimi* was a ritual offense. The order lists various such offenses and the fines for each of them. Offenses were classified as huge, big, medium, and small, and a guilty party was required to provide suitable materials for a ceremony to purge the offense. Sexually violating a female ritualist was considered a medium offense, along with neglecting designated festivals, assaulting certain shrine attendants, having contact with impure things, and visiting the ill or mourners on designated festival days. The transgressor was fined twenty-two items, including weapons, foodstuffs, and wine. The heaviest offenses—such as visiting the ill on the day of the realm's most important festival, the Daijōsai conducted upon the ruler's enthronement—were assessed larger quantities: six swords and six deer hides instead of one each, for example, and additional items, including a horse. As Sekiguchi points out, the fine for violating a female ritualist was relatively light, and no further penalties were levied—in contrast to the severe punishments for those who violated women in direct service to the ruler.[42] The source may indicate a pro forma prohibition that was often ignored without serious consequences for the woman or her sexual partner. Another possibility—since only the man was punished—is that the violation was rape rather than consensual sexual intercourse.

Both Saeki Junko and Yamakami Izumo use another early Heian source to argue that a female shaman's role as "wife of the kami" sometimes involved not celibacy but sexual relations with a shrine priest as a substitute for her kami-husband.[43] A Council of State order dated Enryaku 17 (798)/10/11 castigates the priest of Izumo shrine for having overindulged himself with attendants at the shrine on the pretext of performing his sacred duties:

> The chief ritualist *(kuni no miyatsuko)* of Izumo province is forbidden to accumulate daughters of local landholders as his concubines in conjunction with sacred matters.
>
> The minister of the left has presented the following edict from the throne:
>
> "We have been informed recently that the current ritualist of the province has been concurrently appointed priest [of Izumo Taisha] and that on the day that he assumed his new duties, he abandoned his legitimate wife, then took a number of taxpayers' daughters as his sexual partners, claiming that they were attendants *[uneme]* at the shrine. He had sexual relations with them and made them into his concubines. He does not know any limits. Completely without authority to do so, he has promoted licentious behavior in conjunction with sacred matters. The way

> of the kami may benefit the world, but in this case it seems that it does not. From now on, [such behavior] is forbidden. Moreover, it is forbidden to associate sacred affairs with sexual relations with concubines."
>
> [The Council of State order continues.] Let the provincial governor record names, seal the register, and select one woman among them—not a large number—by tortoiseshell divination. If anyone violates this command he shall be punished accordingly. This also applies to the priest of Munakata shrine in Chikuzen province.[44]

According to Yamakami, the Izumo priest's relationship with the shrine attendants represented the ancient shamanic practice in which the shaman's body became the vessel *(yorishiro)* for a kami's spirit. Comparing the Izumo incident to the legend of Mt. Miwa, in which a female shaman became the wife of a male kami and bore his child, Yamakami characterizes the Izumo incident as an example of the transformation of female shamans into *asobi.* He argues that the women must have consented to sexual relations with the priest, either as a way to make a living or because they accepted him as surrogate for the kami.[45]

The Council of State's decision—to allow the ritualist one woman instead of a hundred—suggests that the priest indeed may have exploited an ancient sexual ritual which the council reluctantly recognized as legitimate. Taking so many women, however, was seen as an abuse of both sacral prerogatives and secular position, and the power imbalance between a wealthy provincial notable and local taxpaying families appears to have posed a threat to the throne. When Yamakami assumes that the women consented to sexual relations with the priest, he overlooks this imbalance. Rather than suggesting an avenue by which shamans willingly evolved into *asobi,* the source provides a glimpse of what "wife of the kami" may have really meant for female ritualists in the service of a powerful male priest.

Three sources from later in the Heian period provide an opportunity to assess the connection, if any, between female shamans and *asobi.* Although the earliest, *Wamyōshō,* lists both shamans and *asobi* in the "beggars and thieves" category, it does not justify the inclusion of shamans. Nakayama contends that the listing offers a glimpse of the sexual life of the times,[46] but the text itself says nothing about the sexuality of shamans, male or female. Including both *asobi* and shamans in the same occupational category does not mean that the two were equated or that one became the other—any more than it means, for instance, that *asobi* were originally pirates, another occupation in the same category.

One important Heian source that has received little attention in discussions of the relationship between *asobi* and female shamans is Fujiwara Akihira's *Shinsarugakuki,* written in the mid-eleventh century. The text describes the large family of a fictional lieutenant of the guards. In his opening paragraphs, Akihira supplies a general description of street life in the capital—observing, among other sights, "the painted face of a '*kannagi [kamunagi]-asobi.*'"[47] This term might be translated as shrine prostitute or shaman-entertainer; but because it is not commonly used it cannot be defined with any certainty. It does not appear in dictionaries, and even the reading, supplied by *Kodai seiji shakai shisō* editor Ōsone Shōsuke, is not certain. I suggest that it simply means one who performs songs and dances for the kami.

More definitive evidence is found within Akihira's portraits of the women in the lieutenant's family—three wives and sixteen daughters. One daughter is an *asobi,* as discussed in Chapter 1, but another is a shaman:

> The fourth daughter is a shaman *(kamunagi),* skilled in divination, entertaining the kami with *kagura* dances, summoning them by plucking the string of a catalpa bow, and speaking with the voices of the dead. When she dances her sleeves billow like those of wizards at play, and when she sings her tones are dulcet and sublime, like the voice of a bird in the Gokuraku paradise. The atonal sound of her koto reaches down to the kami of earth, while the arhythmic beat of her drum makes foxes prick up their ears. And so men and women from all over the realm follow one after the other to see her, and high and low from near and far crowd around her. Their offerings of rice pile up until there is no place to put them; their paper offerings accumulate until there is no time to count them. As for her husband, he is a scribe in the Right Equestrian Bureau and a neighborhood chief south of Shichijō.[48]

This particular shaman is skillful enough to appeal to kami, to animals, and, perhaps most important, to lay patrons who bring offerings to her—destined either for an unnamed shrine or to profit her personally.

The lieutenant's sixteenth daughter, the *asobi,* is explicitly described both as a peerless chanteuse and as a sexual professional experienced in techniques of making love. (See Chapter 1 for a full translation.) The portraits of the two daughters are linked by their musical skills, especially the comparison of their voices to that of a bird of paradise. Both are described in hyperbolic terms similar to those in the later portrait of *asobi* by Ōe Masafusa, and both are performers, the shaman luring the kami through music and dance, the *asobi* luring customers with the beat of her drum. Yanagita uses this text as an example to argue that shamans transformed performance for the kami's sake into song and dance to delight ordinary humans, and he compares such shamans to *shirabyōshi* who entertained at religious festivals.[49]

Akihira's reference to the offerings accumulated by the fourth daughter suggests that her skills were amply rewarded; although the *asobi* seems to have many customers, nothing whatsoever is said about any goods she receives. While the description of the *asobi*'s sexual activities is quite explicit, Akihira makes no reference to sexual activities on the part of the shaman, except to mention that she is married. Thus we may assume that she is neither a virgin nor even temporarily celibate during her service as a shaman. As Fukutō Sanae points out, moreover, the men in *Shinsarugakuki* are all described in terms of their occupations, but among the women, only the shaman and the *asobi* receive similar treatment.[50] In other words, their contemporaries may have found them similar in that both were working women in a milieu in which women were becoming increasingly dependent on husbands and fathers.

Another source that depicts both *asobi* and shamans is the late-twelfth-century *imayō* collection *Ryōjin hishō.* The lyrics in the collection were originally sung by *asobi* and other female entertainers, who sometimes depict their own lives. Shamans appear in some 20 songs out of a total of 566 in the extant portions of the collection.[51] This does not seem like a very large proportion, but it does suggest that the entertainers, or perhaps their patrons, were intrigued by shamans and their profession.

A number of scholars in addition to Nakayama Tarō have used *Ryōjin hishō* lyrics to equate shamans with *asobi* or to characterize them as prostitutes. For example, Yung-Hee Kim's work on *Ryōjin hishō* associates both shrine shamans and *arukimiko* with prostitution and entertainment.[52] Both Yamakami Izumo and Ōwa Iwao also examine the lyrics in *Ryōjin hishō,* coming to similar conclusions.[53] As Terry Kawashima has pointed out, however, scholars often make unwarranted assumptions about the conditions depicted in *imayō* lyrics and the identification of their speakers.[54] Any attempt to interpret *Ryōjin hishō* lyrics as representations of historical reality must consider the ambiguity of the lyrics themselves, the primary function of *imayō* as entertainment, and retired sovereign Go-Shirakawa's role, as compiler of the text, in selecting the songs to be included.

Some of the lyrics portray shamans at work, dancing, beating drums, or shaking bells. For example:

The shaman on sacred Kinpu mountain
beats her drum and shakes it up and down—
what a sight!
Let's worship at the shrine!
Hear the drum beat and echo!
However she pounds the drum,
the music never stops.

Tōta the shaman who
shakes the bells brightly,
shakes them high above her eyes—
shakes them so they really jangle!
Shaking them below her eyes
is lazy and neglectful,
it's bad fortune and
it makes the kami angry.[55]

In some *Ryōjin hishō* lyrics, shamans are explicitly shown as agents or objects of human sexual desire. These are the poems that have been used by numerous scholars to construct an image of female shamans as prostitutes. For example, the following lyric set at Sumiyoshi shrine is cited by both Nakayama and Ōwa as evidence that shamans engaged in prostitution:

A royal beauty dwells
at the gate to the four shrines of Sumiyoshi.
Who might be her lover, I asked—
he's a gallant from Matsugasaki.[56]

Based on the reference to the lover, Nakayama, Ōwa, and Kim identify the woman in the poem as a shaman-*asobi*.[57] Yamakami, on the other hand, suggests that the woman may be Okinagatarashi-hime (the legendary sovereign Jingū), worshipped as a kami at one of Sumiyoshi's four subshrines. He admits, however, that the Matsugasaki lover is difficult to identify.[58]

Several other lyrics in *Ryōjin hishō* are used to support an erotic image of female shamans. For example, Yung-Hee Kim interprets the following poem as a lament by a *miko*'s would-be lover:

In the south guest room
of Sumiyoshi shrine
the one I desire has locked the door,
and I cannot get it open.[59]

Yamakami suggests that shaman-prostitutes may have gathered in front of shrines or at ports, seducing men who passed by. Ōwa agrees with his interpretation of the following lyric as a shaman-prostitute's appeal to her customer:

If you're a kami
please descend when I dance.
What kind of kami
would be so shy?[60]

Kim interprets the following lyric as a shaman's sexual invitation to a desired lover—playing on the double meaning of the term *iro* as color and sexual desire:

Are you going home from the shrine
without changing colors *(iro)*?
Even the deer who run and sleep in the mountains
change their coats from summer to wintertime.[61]

And according to Kim, this lyric describes a promiscuous shaman:

The bamboo grass at Ōji shrine
flourishes though horses graze there.
Though a husband never comes,
her bed's never empty, she's young so . . .[62]

Another *Ryōjin hishō* lyric used as evidence that shamans engaged in prostitution is the following:

My child, more than ten years old now,
is a shaman roaming from place to place.
When she treads the salt beds of Tago Bay

how the sea-folk must gather,
challenging her truthfulness, teasing her with questions—
how she must suffer![63]

Both Nakayama and Ōwa identify the child as an *arukimiko* who has turned to prostitution.[64] This lyric, however, indicates that the girl was quite young and perhaps had not even reached puberty. There is no suggestion whatsoever that she is a prostitute; her suffering is blamed not on sexual exploitation but rather on ridicule. As Barbara Ruch has pointed out, moreover, the lyric's true focus is the mother, separated from her child and grieving for the girl's hard life.[65]

While the interpretations of this lyric perhaps stretch the farthest to show that shamans were sexual professionals, others are suspect as well. The setting of several lyrics at Sumiyoshi shrine makes it tempting to equate its shamans with *asobi* who, according to Masafusa, frequently worshipped there; but the lyrics themselves do not support such an interpretation. The royal beauty at the shrine is not clearly identified as a shaman—she does, in fact, live *outside* the shrine gate. The person who has locked the Sumiyoshi shrine door to a would-be lover may not be a shaman at all but a pilgrim seeking to avoid—not encourage—the sexual contact that often took place between lay believers visiting shrines.[66] Similar ambiguities mark other sources used to support the shaman-*asobi* equation—for example, the poem from *Tōhokuin shokunin utaawase* quoted at the beginning of the chapter. Ōwa contends that the speaker is an *asobi,*[67] but there is nothing in the source itself that identifies her as a sexual professional.

The lyrics used to support the shaman-*asobi* equation do not depict shamans as professionals who exchanged sex for payment; nor do they suggest that their bodies were publicly available, even in a form of ritual prostitution. Evidence from Heian sources does not prove the equation, and in many cases alternative explanations are plausible or even more probable. Some oracles may have been secular banquet entertainers, such as the one portrayed in *Shōmonki;* but it seems that, by and large, it was musical performance and not the provision of sexual services that was common to Heian-period shamans and *asobi.*

Some Heian sources, such as *Ryōjin hishō,* portray female shamans as subjects and objects of sexual desire. But the argument that they became sexual professionals rests on the propositions—powerfully challenged and characterized as "modern" by Yoshie Akiko—that virginity was valued and that shamans, especially, were expected to be virgins. Thus sexual activity degrades the shaman and suggests that "prostitute" is an appropriate label for her—a conclusion based on later judgments that prostitution itself was degraded. Defining shamans as prostitutes depends first on interpreting their sexual relationships as transgressive and then on applying the label "prostitute" to any sexually transgressive woman. Neither conclusion can be supported, especially in the tolerant milieu of late-Heian Japan. Only when popular lyrics are read through the lens of more recent attitudes toward both professional sexual exchange and the sexuality of female shamans do the shamans depicted in them appear as prostitutes. Certainly it is possible that some shamans, especially those on their own without support from a shrine, made a living in the sex trade. There is no reason to believe that they did so more frequently than any other down-and-out women, however, or that there was some inherent and natural evolution from shaman to *asobi*.

The mirror image of these arguments is the contention, most powerfully expressed by Yanagita Kunio and Saeki Junko, that *asobi* were in essence shamans. Other scholars as well have pointed out that *asobi* frequented Sumiyoshi and Hirota shrines and performed phallic rites to assure themselves customers, that many adopted religious names such as Kannon or Yakushi, that they were sometimes likened to wizards or angels, and that they often sang songs on religious themes—in other words they belonged to the world of the sacred, not the ordinary. Of course, the difference between ordinary and sacred is both individually determined and historically conditioned; moreover, there is no indication in sources such as *Denryaku, Chōshūki,* or *Taiki,* for example, that the male patrons of *asobi* considered their experience to be a religious one.[68] I think that rather than demonstrating the religious nature of *asobi* or any connection with shamans, the evidence shows the interpenetration of sacred and secular realms—the permeability of the boundary between *hare* and *ke.* Instead of being stuffed in an airtight container, religious experience colored daily life and helped to produce its linguistic currency. If *asobi* had shunned the sacred, that would have been the surprise.

Why have theories associating shamans with *asobi* been so persistent despite the lack of historical evidence for a connection? Barbara Ruch has proposed several reasons why scholars have tended to confuse shamans, female entertainers, and prostitutes: all three were organized into small matrilineal (biological or adopted) groups; all three lacked husbands and tended to travel independently; and all three shared some of the same songs and dances.[69] Sekiguchi Hiroko, who does not accept the shaman-origin theory, maintains that both shamans and *asobi* belonged to "extraordinary" *(hinichijōteki)* realms not inhabited by ordinary women; when *asobi* traded their bodies for payment, their sexual activity was set apart from that of everyday wives. According to Sekiguchi, the making of music—one specific meaning of the word *asobi* in ancient times—served as a bridge between ordinary and extraordinary worlds and also as a common point shared by shamans and *asobi* as entertainers.[70] Sekiguchi does not define "extraordinary" as sacred, but her arguments do suggest some ways in which both shamans and *asobi* can be seen as different from other women.

Perhaps because the lives of shamans and *asobi* seem to have touched in many ways, it is tempting to posit an organic relationship between the two. *Asobi,* who set up shop near important shrines and visited them to pray for customers, were surely familiar with shamans. If shamans appear in the songs of *asobi* as sexual beings, it may have been because *asobi* recognized that frenzied kami possession often had an erotic component. Moreover, both *asobi* and shamans trod the margin between danger and subservience to male authority: *asobi* worked to please men but escaped the control of individual men, while the oracles of shamans could serve as political threats or tools. These are some ways one might connect shamans and *asobi,* without suggesting that one became or was equivalent to the other.

Ritual Pollution, the Female Body, and *Asobi*

The concept that women's bodies were ritually defiled suggests another possibility for positioning female sexual entertainers—whose profession depended on the intimate use of their bodies—along the axis of purity and pollution. Scholars rarely characterize sexual entertainers as ritually polluted, even while describing them as marginalized and transgressive.[71] Yet ironically, there is more historical evidence linking *asobi* and *kugutsu* with pollution and groups thought to be defiled than with sacrality and shamans. Although at first glance any notion that *asobi* were polluted seems to contradict the "shaman" theories discussed earlier, this interpretation too rests on locating certain sexual actors and some forms of sexual activity outside the everyday world. While in the end I think the interpretation must be rejected as a comprehensive explanation of the position of sexual entertainers in Heian and Kamakura Japan, it cannot be denied that *asobi* and *kugutsu* were sometimes blamed for causing pollution and sometimes categorized with low-status *hinin* who performed ritually polluting tasks.

As women, sexual entertainers were subjected to notions of female bodily pollution as well as female sinfulness in the Buddhist sense. As in many cultures, childbirth and menstruation were thought to defile the body. Since this pollution was considered contagious—along with defilement related to death—birthing or menstruating women were often quarantined for the perceived duration of their defilement. Although technically a woman's body was polluted only at certain times in her life, birth and menstruation pollution cast a shadow over the female body in general, reshaping the relationship between women and the sacred as well as increasing contempt for women within male society.

Birth, pregnancy, and menstruation taboos were codified in the *Engi shiki* (Procedures of the Engi era), a compilation of court rituals and procedures written in the early tenth century. The most serious concern was to prevent the defilement of the royal palace or important shrine festivals through the participation of those who were polluted, either directly or through contagion. The *Engi shiki* stipulated seven days of abstinence for anyone who had contracted pollution through witnessing a birth. While there were no such regulations for those who had come into contact with pregnant or menstruating women, pregnant shrine attendants were forbidden to participate in certain festivals and those who were menstruating were banned from the palace.[72] By the twelfth century, however, those who wished to participate in major festivals were advised to avoid both pregnant and menstruating women, indicating that these conditions were now seen as defiling to others. In time, these concepts of female bodily pollution intensified, increasing the ritual isolation of women at certain times of their lives.[73]

Although pregnancy and menstruation taboos contributed to the idea that the female body was defiled, birth pollution was probably the most threatening condition related to the female body. Iinuma Kenji argues that the concepts of menstrual and birth pollution were not originally associated: while menstrual pollution was a variety of blood pollution, birth taboos were associated with those of death, since both birth and death involved traffic between this world and the other.[74] Nishiguchi Junko, on the other hand, subscribes to the more standard view that birth pollution was related to the defilement of blood.[75] I suspect that people in fact associated birth with both death and blood, the gravest and most fundamental agents of defilement; already fraught with emotions of hope and anxiety, birth was thus doubly polluted.

Intriguing examples from picture scrolls indicate the conditions under which women gave birth and common perceptions of the dangers attending the process. A Kamakura-period scroll, *Kitano tenjin engi,* shows a battery of rituals for safe childbirth and the survival of a mother. A monk reads sutras, a female shaman prays to the kami, a man beneath the raised floor of the birthing room twangs a bowstring to ward off evil spirits, and a yin-yang master conducts purification rites.[76] *Gaki zōshi,* an illustrated scroll from the early Kamakura period, shows a woman who has just borne a child.[77] In the room with her are five other women, including one well along in years; perhaps she is the midwife and the others are her assistants or relatives of the mother. Outside the room there are a laywoman, a shaman wearing a red skirt but naked from the waist up, and a Buddhist monk. Both the latter, presumably, are present to offer prayers and spells for safe delivery. In the delivery room, however, crouches a being known as a hungry ghost *(gaki)*—in Buddhist lore, a creature condemned to a life of starvation in recompense for sins in former lives. The hungry ghost, invisible to all the human participants, crouches beside the birthing mat, ready to devour the child. The baby's dangerous transition from the world of the nonliving renders it vulnerable to such attacks, just as the mother's participation in crossing boundaries imperils and defiles her. The hungry ghost, who also haunts graveyards, seems an apt representative of the ritual pollution attending birth, as well as the very real dangers for both mother and newborn in premodern society. The abstract concept of pollution is personified by a creature from Buddhist mythology that represents human sinfulness: as punishment for killing his or her own children, the ghost is condemned in the next world to hunger after the children of others. The illustration suggests the overlap of notions of pollution and evil, marking both as dangers to the unwitting.

This woman seems to be giving birth in a room in someone's house, perhaps her own; but parturition huts separate from the household were also common. Another example cited by Iinuma is an illustration from the *Yūzū nenbutsu engi emaki,* begun in the late Kamakura period and revised and augmented in

Muromachi times. One scene shows such a hut facing a road in a commoner section of the capital. It is located next to a stable and looks out on a woman drawing water from a well and people passing by on foot and on horseback. The scene shows a difficult childbirth, as two women urge the mother to push the child out of her womb. A monk in the hut encourages the woman to say the *nenbutsu* and records her name in his register of the saved, since it is possible she will die.[78] By sending the woman away from home to give birth in a parturition hut, her family avoided both the pollution of birth and that of her possible death. The very real prospect that mother or child might die in the process of childbirth warranted such concentrated activity and supports Iinuma's contention that birth and death were intimately related, along with their attached pollution.

One locus for fused notions of pollution and moral transgression was the female body. Not only was it considered polluted at certain times, but the female person was thought to be inherently sinful. This concept was part of the Buddhist package imported into Japan from India via China and Korea, but Taira Masayuki argues that until the late Heian age it was accepted only in the abstract. Taira associates the acceptance of women's sinfulness as concrete reality with heightened fears of gender pollution. The exclusion of women from selected sacred places is often seen as an indicator of the extent to which society regarded the female body as ritually polluted. According to Taira, exclusion developed gradually over the Heian and Kamakura periods. At first women were excluded only when pregnant or menstruating. But when concepts of gender pollution fused with Buddhist ideas of female sinfulness, women were barred from many sacred places on a permanent basis. Taira maintains that it was considered possible to cleanse the temporary pollution that came from menstruation or childbirth, but the permanent uncleanness of women as women was impossible to remove.[79]

In contrast to childbirth, with at least indirect connections to death, sexual intercourse between women and men was not in itself regarded as defiling. It was, however, tabooed under certain circumstances: at times of abstinence and within sacred space. While this taboo was often ignored—as Fukutō Sanae points out, men and women commonly initiated sexual encounters at shrines[80]—violation was often thought to have serious consequences, an idea promoted in *setsuwa* literature. For example, a story that appears in both *Nihon ryōiki* and *Konjaku monogatarishū* tells of a professional sutra copier who was invited to a temple in Kawachi to produce a copy of the *Lotus Sutra.* Also participating in the ritual were some women whose job it was to add purified water to the ink. When a shower broke out, everyone crowded into the temple, men and women in the same small room.

> Then the scripture copier, burning with lust, crouched behind one of the women, lifted her skirt, and penetrated her. As his penis entered her vagina, they died together, the woman foaming at the mouth.

The *Nihon ryōiki* compiler comments: "Although your body and mind may burn with desire, do not let lust in your heart make you commit a defiling act."[81] The comment seems directed entirely at the man, and the woman's death is left unexplained. In *Konjaku,* the compiler notes that horrified observers dragged the two corpses out of the temple, and he goes on to provide his own explanation of the deaths:

> Even if the sutra copier burned with desire, even if his passions boiled within his breast, he ought to have suppressed them while copying and dedicating the sutra. However, he stupidly threw away his own life. Moreover, even though the sutra copier had such passions, the woman should not have yielded to him so quickly. Because they polluted the temple and did not revere the sutra, they were punished before everybody's eyes.[82]

As Hitomi Tonomura points out, in the later version of the tale the couple was punished for violating the purity of sacred space, even though the woman had been raped.[83] The compiler, in fact, seems to have strained to invent a moral reason for the woman's unjust punishment.

Several historical incidents illustrate the concept that sexual relations defiled sacred space. In 1003 at Mirokuji, a temple attached to Usa Hachiman shrine, shrine officials were informed that a couple was having intercourse in a chapel on the temple grounds. The officials surrounded the chapel and, before entering, conducted a purification rite to protect themselves against contamination through contact with a polluting act. When they burst inside, they found a Mirokuji monk in the embrace of a woman who had often worshipped at the temple. Officials demanded the resignation of the monk's teacher, a high-ranking cleric, on the grounds that such a serious offense was the result of the teacher's negligence.[84] Nishiguchi points out that not only did the monk violate the Buddhist precept against sexual relations with a woman, but the offense was thought to have polluted sacred ground; hence a purification ritual was conducted before officials confronted the offending couple. Among the reasons given for punishing the monk's teacher as well as the culprit himself was the exalted status of the chapel, which was sustained by public rice fields and had been constructed with donations from the court; in addition, rituals to defend the western region of Japan against foreign invasions were conducted there. In other words, the chapel was a holy site responsible to both the buddhas and the realm, requiring special purity.[85]

Kamakura-period sources also illustrate not only the taboo against sexual intercourse at sacred places but also the difficulties authorities had enforcing it. Two documents issued in 1261 by officials of Kasuga shrine complain that some priests and lay supporters had engaged in sexual relations with female pilgrims at the shrine. According to the documents, such activities produced deluding worldly attachments; they not only polluted the shrine but were "unprecedented acts of evil."[86] For monks and shrine officials, sexual activity on their sacred precincts was a serious offense indeed, and in 1285 Go-Uda Tennō issued an edict prohibiting men and women from mixing while worshipping at Iwashimizu shrine or staying overnight there.[87]

If female bodies were polluted, did exchanging sex indiscriminately or for payment make them even more so? In the Heian period, pilgrims sometimes avoided *asobi* on their way to sacred sites, but as noted earlier they did not do so consistently. For example, when Fujiwara Tadazane and his party were about to undergo penance during a visit of several days to Byōdōin, the *asobi* with whom they had been consorting on the trip were sent away.[88] Aristocratic pilgrims on their way to Mt. Kōya in 1048 turned back a band of *asobi* who approached their boat, telling them that consorting with them was forbidden and promising to patronize them on the way back from the sacred mountain.[89]

However, the men did not necessarily avoid contact with the *asobi* because the women were sexual professionals. Sexual relations of any type were usually prohibited for men en route to a temple or shrine or undergoing other forms of abstinence. It was because Fujiwara Yorinaga was at the gate of Shitennōji that he decided not to "penetrate" the male dancer he had invited to his quarters.[90] In the well-known Dōjōji story in *Konjaku monogatarishū,* a young monk refuses a lusty widow's advances, declaring: "In accord with a long-held vow, I have practiced abstinence these days to purify my mind and body and have set out on the long road to Kumano to pay reverence to the kami. If I suddenly break my vow here, something terrible will happen to both of us."[91] According to this tale, dire consequences would result from violating a vow of purity with any woman, not just a sexual professional.

Ritual taboos were not always observed, however, even when *asobi* were involved; the diary of Minamoto Morotoki suggests that some twelfth-century pilgrims casually violated abstinence to consort with *asobi.* In one late-twelfth-century episode recounted in *Azuma kagami,* moreover, blood and death pollution and Buddhist sanctions against killing were regarded far more seriously than any possible pollution through sexual contact with *asobi.* According to the account, in 1193 Minamoto Yoritomo and his retainers broke a hunting expedition for a day of abstinence and purification dictated by the Buddhist calendar. Instead of hunting—which would have required the men to take life in violation of the Buddhist precepts—Yoritomo and his retainers held an all-day banquet, summoning a group of *asobi* for entertainment and sexual pleasure.[92] Even though the men refrained from hunting on this day of abstinence, contact with *asobi* seems to have been permitted.

By the thirteenth century, some sources begin to associate *asobi* specifically with ritual pollution. One midcentury source notes that contributions from *asobi* and *kugutsu* defiled *(kegasu)* court poetry collections—in some sense sites of purity, since they had been commissioned by the monarch.[93] A second example appears in Kasuga shrine records dated 1246, which relate that *asobi* from Suita had polluted the sacred tree of Kasuga and were required to donate a horse to the shrine in compensation.[94] The records leave to the imagination the precise taboo violated by the *asobi,* but the fine of a horse, an expensive item, suggests that the violation was a serious one.

The issue of pollution appears in another complaint, submitted to the bakufu in 1268 by monks of Jissōji in Suruga province. A temple official was accused of patronizing *asobi* and *kugutsu* along with other gross misconduct. The culprit was the deputy of an abbot appointed from outside the monks' assembly. According to the monks, the deputy "welcomed *yūkun* to the abbot's residence, served meals of fish and fowl, and ordered the culture of silkworms." The monks complained that inviting "women who delight in making love *(irogonomi)*" to the residence—the site of monthly ceremonies to honor Jissōji's founder—was one factor causing the temple, in their words, to perish. Similarly, the deputy had dishonored the Fudō Chapel, built by the bakufu regent and temple patron Hōjō Yasutoki (1183–1242): by "summoning women just to carouse with wine, he has brought pollution upon this sacred place." The monks complained that the deputy had constantly taken pleasure in consorting with women and indulging in drunken revelry, fearing neither the authorities nor the Buddha.

After censuring the deputy for preparing fish for dinner by washing them in sacred water at one of the temple buildings, the monks returned to his excesses with women. They accused the culprit of disturbing monks at prayer or study to fetch female visitors. In addition, the deputy was blamed for making the temple a site of unseemly revelry:

> The resident monks lament the invitation of *keisei* [castle-topplers] and weep over *kugutsu* and *dengaku* performances that the deputy has arranged. But the spectators applaud and laugh, and this temple sanctified in ancient times is transformed into a den of pollution. Have demons brought this curse upon us? How could the Buddhist discourse fall into such disarray?[95]

The Jissōji monks' petition lists consorting with women, specifically sexual entertainers, in a series of complaints about waste and misspending by an official who was probably disliked primarily because he represented an outside authority. However, the document suggests that extravagant spending was not the only problem the women posed. The use of the terms *irogonomi* and *keisei* suggests that it was sexual activity, not just banquet entertainment, that offended the temple's celibate monks. Rather than describing the offense as only a violation of Buddhist precepts, the monks emphasized the defilement of sacred space, making their point even stronger by associating "consorting with women" with acts related to killing such as eating flesh and raising silkworms. Moral transgression and ritual pollution coalesced in the monks' forceful condemnation of the deputy and contemptuous denunciation of the women as one means for his villainy.

Given intensified concerns with the polluting nature of the female body, it is not surprising that sexual professionals could have been reproached occasionally for defiling a temple or shrine. The increasingly unfavorable evaluation of sexual entertainers, especially from the mid-Kamakura period, was based in part on negative judgments of all women, including those related to pollution. If *asobi* and *kugutsu* entered the realm of defilement sometime in the Kamakura period, they did not do so alone but in connection with the process by which all women's bodies were devalued. Any additional defilement depended, not on the women's status as sexual professionals, but on specific acts they performed in specific contexts. Although *asobi* could produce ritual pollution under some conditions, we cannot conclude that they were defiled because of their profession.

The *Asobi Chōja* Transformed and Other Edifying Tales

In the late Heian and Kamakura periods, miracle tales, saints' hagiographies, and Noh plays portrayed *asobi* in several ways. Some tales depicted them specifically as transgressors—presenting them either as obstructions to the religious practice of both monks and laymen or as paradoxical "expedient means" for men's salvation. Other tales avoided the label of transgressor but showed *asobi* attaining rebirth in paradise or as manifestations of bodhisattvas. Differences in these tales can be attributed partly to their time period—those generated later tended to emphasize the transgressiveness of *asobi*—and partly to the religious teaching that the tales were intended to promote.

Buddhist attitudes toward female sexuality were complex and contradictory,[96] but in medieval Japan the strongest characterization of sexual entertainers as transgressors comes from the Buddhist discourse. Nevertheless, Japanese Buddhist texts often refused to brand the women as deliberate wrongdoers; rather than focusing on the sex trade as a degraded occupation, many texts argued that the *asobi* themselves must be suffering and offered particular religious solutions for their pain. In some tales, *asobi* take vows as nuns and thereby achieve rebirth in paradise. Other tales, however, portray *asobi* as incarnations of bodhisattvas—not as an attempt to cast the sex trade as a wellspring of Buddhist virtue but as an illustration of the nondualism of absolute reality and the phenomena perceived by the senses. The purpose of these tales was evidently to promote concepts such as nondualism or practices such as the *nenbutsu* rather than point to the sale of sex as a moral problem or social evil. Yet as it evolved from the late Heian to the late Kamakura period, the overall effect of this Buddhist discourse was to devalorize female sexuality and present women in the sex trade as leading lives of transgression.

While stories about prostitutes who became nuns or revealed themselves as bodhisattvas appear in the Buddhist canon,[97] neither motif seems to have grasped the Japanese imagination until the end of the Heian period. I have found no comparable examples in earlier Heian miracle-tale collections such as *Hokke genki* or *Nihon ōjō gokuraku ki.* Such tales appear, however, in *Hōbutsushū,* compiled in the 1180s, as well as in the thirteenth-century collections *Kojidan, Hosshinshū,* and *Senjūshō,* and in early-fourteenth-century versions of hagiographies of Hōnen such as *Hōnen shōnin eden.* They are also dramatized in several Muromachi-period Noh plays.

The singing of *imayō* plays a central role in some of these tales. An episode in *Hōbutsushū* tells of one Toneguro, an *asobi* from Kamusaki who "enjoyed sexual pleasure for many years and was ignorant of the Buddhist law. She passed her life in a boat on the waves, consigning her body to travelers." Like *asobi* in Heian texts, Toneguro becomes a sad example of ephemerality and inconstancy, but *Hōbutsushū* also marks her as a religiously benighted being ignorant of Buddhism. The tale relates that on a sea voyage to western Japan, Toneguro's boat was attacked by pirates who fatally stabbed her. She recited the following *imayō:*

> When I wonder why we must grow old,
> it makes me sorrowful.
> Now I shall contemplate the vow of Amida
> in the Western Paradise.

Having entrusted herself to Amida, who had vowed to save all who called on him, Toneguro was welcomed in death by the purple clouds that signified rebirth in paradise.[98] This tale is one example of a genre in which the singing of a religious lyric expressing faith in Amida becomes a mechanism to assure the salvation of even an unworthy person.[99] The phenomenon that Imahori Taitsu terms *"imayō ōjō"* also appears in a tale in an early version of Hōnen's biography. Reciting the same *imayō* as Toneguro, an elderly *chōja,* inspired by the proximity of a holy man, is welcomed to paradise by sublime music and the emblematic purple clouds.[100]

In another story, an *asobi* reveals herself as an incarnation of a bodhisattva. The tale appears in several versions, the earliest in *Kojidan* (compiled 1212–1215):

> The holy man Shosha [Shōkū, 910–1007] prayed that he might be granted a vision of the living body of the bodhisattva Fugen. He obtained his answer in a dream:

> "If you wish to be granted a vision of Fugen, you must visit the *chōja* of the Kamusaki *asobi.*" Rejoicing, he headed for Kamusaki.
>
> When he inquired at the *chōja*'s dwelling, he found that some travelers from the capital had already gathered there, and they were all having a good time carousing and dancing riotously. The *chōja* occupied the seat of honor, beating on a drum and singing in rhythm: "As the wind blows over the sacred pool at Suō Murozumi, it raises little ripples on the surface."
>
> Struck with wonder, the holy man closed his eyes and clasped his hands in prayer. The *chōja* appeared as a manifestation of Fugen riding on a white elephant with six tusks. A light glowed between the bodhisattva's eyebrows, shining on monks and laity alike. In a soft and melodious voice, Fugen explained: "Although the wind of the five sensory illusions and six desires does not disturb the great undefiled sea of absolute reality, there is no occasion when the waves of the conditioned phenomenal world do not arise on its surface." Feeling the rise of religious devotion in his heart, the holy man venerated the bodhisattva as he wiped away tears of gratitude. When he opened his eyes, he saw what he had seen before, a woman beating out the Suō Murozumi song. But when he closed his eyes again the bodhisattva's form was revealed to him once more, reciting verses from the Buddhist scriptures.
>
> After he had venerated the bodhisattva many times, the holy man headed for home in tears. When he left, the *chōja* unexpectedly rose from her seat and followed him along the narrow path to his dwelling. "Don't reveal this to anyone," she said, and died. I've heard that a wonderful fragrance immediately filled the air, and at the banquet frivolity froze to a halt at the *chōja*'s sudden disappearance.[101]

This famous tale can be interpreted in several ways. Perhaps most obviously, it illustrates Tendai teachings on nondualism. The *chōja*'s song refers to Murozumi Bay in Suō province,[102] the location of a temple dedicated to Fugen. The water imagery suggests the *asobi* boat trade, and the syllables *"mu-ro-tsu (zu)"* buried in the song spell out the name of a port in Harima province famous for *asobi.* In Shōkū's meditative trance, the song is transformed into Buddhist scripture explaining that worldly phenomena arise like surface waves on the "great undefiled *(muro)* sea" of absolute reality—even though that sea itself remains untouched by desire or objects of desire.[103]

Yet another way to look at this tale—as does Michele Marra—is to cast the *asobi chōja* as a shaman-intermediary between the deity, Fugen, and the human holy man. Focusing on this and other tales that depict *asobi* as guides to salvation, Marra argues that Buddhist institutions cast themselves as conquerors of both pollution and shamanism, personified in the defiled bodies of *asobi*-shamans: "In order to insulate the community from the potential assault of religious competitors—either shamanistic, Shintoist, or Taoist—Buddhist mythographers first represented these 'pagan' priestesses as courtesans, eventually transforming them into manifestations of a bodhisattva."[104] If one follows this interpretation, the story—rather than relating the manifestation of a deity in human form—tells of deity possession, demonstrating that very powerful religious phenomenon in Buddhist harness. (An actual historical connection between *asobi* and shamans is not required.) Or, following Terry Kawashima, one can focus on the *imayō* sung by the *chōja* that effects both Shōkū's trance and the *chōja*'s transformation.[105] The song itself becomes a formula that transports both to another world.

Two subsequent versions of this tale differ in minor details and in one important way—the later the version, the more specifically it points to the *asobi* as a transgressor. As Kawashima points out, the *Kojidan* version of the Shōkū-*chōja* story does not cast the *asobi* as a transgressor: the holy man is neither reluctant to visit the pleasure quarters at Kamusaki nor startled when the *chōja* reveals herself as a manifestation of Fugen. In a similar tale in the somewhat later collection *Senjūshō,* however, Shōkū does seem somewhat surprised, and the compiler remarks that it is sad that one could gaze on the holy form of the bodhisattva and see an *asobi.*[106] In a third version, in *Jikkinshō* (1252), the compiler declares:

> Since this *chōja* was a woman and a professional sexual entertainer, who would have recognized her as the incarnation of the bodhisattva? When pursuing expedient means to lead deluded beings to salvation, their compassionate vows cause buddhas and bodhisattvas to manifest themselves in various forms—whether or not these are despised beings. This is something people should understand from this example.[107]

Although the story expresses increasing contempt for the *chōja*'s profession in the two later versions, in none of the three does the *chōja* express remorse for the way she makes a living. I argue, however, that the power of all versions comes from something unstated in any of them: the revelation that the manifestation of the bodhisattva in the phenomenal world is a potent symbol of sexual desire and therefore illusion and danger. The contrast between *asobi* and bodhisattva creates the unlikely equation essential to deliver the tale's message—that distinctions cannot be made between the phenomenal world (represented by the *asobi*) and absolute reality (represented by the bodhisattva). In addition, the story suggests the conquest of female sexuality by transforming the *asobi* from an avatar of desire to one of Buddhist salvation. It is difficult to imagine that the tale would be so powerful if the transformed being had manifested itself as an ordinary wife or daughter.

Several tales from the early thirteenth century or later point specifically to *asobi* as prostitutes, portraying them as obstructions to the religious practice of both monks and laymen. Using terms such as *zaigō omoki mi, tsumi fukaki mi,* and *zaigō fukaki mi*—a body burdened with or immersed in sin—the tales depict *asobi* as those whose lives are encumbered by their transgressions.[108] Since *mi* can mean body as well as life, the language points to the physical nature of the *asobi*'s misdeeds. While such a characterization is more likely to be found in Kamakura-period than in Heian-period tales, it does appear as early as the late twelfth century: in *Ryōjin hishō kudenshū,* the retired sovereign Go-Shirakawa claims that *asobi* are mired in sin *(tsumi ni shizumite)* but acknowledges that even they can attain salvation if faith is awakened in their hearts.[109] The proposition informs Buddhist tale literature such as *Hosshinshū* by Kamo no Chōmei (1153?–1216), which depicts an *asobi* at the port of Muro who approaches a holy man's boat and recites the famous poem by Izumi Shikibu:

> From darkness
> into the path of darkness
> I must enter—
> Far away the moon
> shines over the mountain crest.

She then laments the karmic fate that has given her a "body immersed in sin" and asks the holy man to help her attain salvation.[110]

The biography of the Pure Land Buddhist master Hōnen (1133–1212), presented in several versions in illustrated scrolls dating from the 1230s through the early fourteenth century, contains a depiction of an encounter between Hōnen and *asobi* from Muro.[111] Imahori Taitsu argues that the later the version, the stronger its negative portrayal of the *asobi.* He maintains that variations reflect not only factional differences among Hōnen's followers but also changes in attitude toward *asobi* in the society at large. While early versions do not depict the *asobi* as transgressors, later ones censure them explicitly, taking advantage of the women's perceived sinfulness to illustrate the efficacy of the *nenbutsu* for rescuing even the unworthy. Imahori pinpoints the change in the Hōnen tales as occurring at the turn of the fourteenth century.[112] However, examples from *Ryōjin hishō kudenshū* and *Hosshinshū* demonstrate that the concept that the bodies of *asobi* were "immersed in sin" had begun to invade the Buddhist discourse considerably earlier.

In a late version of the Hōnen tales, from the early-fourteenth-century illustrated scroll *Hōnen shōnin eden,* a visual depiction of merriment contrasts with the tale of penitence that appears in the accompanying text. When Hōnen visited the port of Muro, so the story goes, his boat was approached by three *asobi.* The illustration of the tale shows three alluring young women in a small skiff alongside a boatful of men. Although the *asobi* are elegantly and tastefully dressed, their uncovered faces make it clear that they are not court ladies on an outing. One woman poles the skiff, one holds a parasol, and the third has a small drum tucked beneath her sleeve. Two groups of men gaze at the *asobi* from Hōnen's boat: laymen cheer on the women with encouraging gestures and laughter; monks look upon them with solemn expressions. The brilliant colors of the illustration, the laymen's delighted faces, and the obvious youth and beauty of the women suggest a scene of gaiety and pleasure, but the text presents a far more sober picture. The women have not approached Hōnen's boat to offer him pleasure. Instead they lament that they are "burdened with transgressions" and implore his help for their salvation. "Truly the obstacles to salvation from living your lives in this way are not trivial ones," Hōnen replies. If they are not willing to risk starvation by abandoning their profession, their only hope, he advises, is to recite the *nenbutsu*—to call on the name of Amida Buddha and invoke his mercy. Thanking Hōnen tearfully, the *asobi* go on their way. Later they report to him that they have retired to a mountain village in order to devote themselves to the *nenbutsu* in hopes of rebirth in Amida's paradise.[113]

In one fourteenth-century version, *asobi* confess to the Pure Land master: "In the mornings we face the mirror and put on our makeup, and in the evenings we approach customers and capture their hearts," criticizing these acts as tempting and sinful.[114] In another version from the fourteenth century, Hōnen blames evil karma, not present moral failing, for the *asobi*'s fate,[115] an explanation that appears in other literary treatments of the women. For example, in *Senjūshō,* the poet Saigyō comes upon *asobi* dwellings at Eguchi and laments:

> They must have become sexual entertainers because of karma from their past lives. How sad it is that they try to maintain their brief lives for just a little while by committing deeds strictly forbidden by the Buddha! We cannot avoid blame for our own transgressions, but isn't it much worse to lead multitudes of others astray?

He then considers that some *asobi* may have achieved rebirth in paradise, and subsequently he encounters a former *asobi* who has taken religious orders.[116] Rather than condemning her, the tale demonstrates that she can abandon her sinful life, both for her own sake and for that of men she might entice.

Other stories use the sad lives of penitent *asobi* as evidence of the ephemerality of beauty and the hazards of desire. For example, in a second tale in *Senjūshō,* Saigyō meets an aging Eguchi *asobi* who laments her past, blaming it on the sinfulness of women and her own personal karma: "I understand that women are especially transgressive, and I realize that it is because of karma from my past lives that I have followed this occupation." The *asobi* then vows to retire from her profession and proceeds to instruct Saigyō on the Buddhist concept of impermanence.[117] Combining this story with the *Kojidan* episode, Kan'ami's Noh play *Eguchi* presents a reformed *asobi* who reveals herself as an incarnation of Fugen.[118]

In the view expressed in several of these texts, an *asobi*'s transgression was to violate men's control over their own sexuality, thereby obstructing their efforts to pursue enlightenment unhampered by sexual concerns. When *asobi* became Buddhist instructors, this transgression was turned on its head. Female sexuality was first used as a tool to win men's attention, then devalorized as the women themselves were transformed from agents of seduction into agents of salvation—a similar process, perhaps, to the one in Renaissance Italy described by Joan Kelly, in which "Love, Beauty, Woman, aestheticized as Botticelli's Venus and given cosmic import, were in effect denatured, robbed of body, sex, and passion by this elevation."[119] Paradoxically, the *asobi*'s profession may have enabled such a transformation: as Bernard Faure has pointed out, Buddhists conceived of the prostitute as a temptress but also saw her as one who had " 'left the world' and [could] see through its vanity."[120]

In her study of crimes committed by women in early modern Germany,

Ulinka Rublack has suggested that sexually free women were threatening in part because they "tempted men into sin, which questioned their self-control and thus the legitimacy of male dominance over women."[121] As discussed in the previous chapter, *setsuwa* tales—and to some extent bakufu law—extended this perceived danger to cover all women, whose very existence aroused natural passions seen as irresistible. To arouse these passions on purpose seemed even more threatening. The concern expressed in many *setsuwa* episodes, that sexual desire endangered monastic celibacy, appears transformed in the Kamakura-period tales discussed here, which blame sexual professionals for distracting laymen from seeking Buddhist enlightenment and suggest means to neutralize the threat—often involving the salvation or miraculous transformation of the "temptress" herself.

Although such stories are fictional, they reflect actual reform efforts made by monks such as Eizon, who claimed to have extracted a promise from seventeen hundred "lewd women" *(injo)* in Harima province to abstain from sexual intercourse once a month.[122] An aging female entertainer, moreover, may have had little option but to seek the protection of Buddhist institutions and live out her life as a nun—like the band of retired *asobi* on an island offshore Tomo port in Bingo province described by the thirteenth-century court lady Nijō. The women had fled their lives as *asobi* and were living in seclusion. One of them confesses to Nijō:

> I was the *chōja* of the *asobi* on this island. I gathered together many prostitutes *(keisei),* had them make up their faces, and waited for passing travelers. We rejoiced if they stopped and lamented if they rowed on by. We pledged ourselves to complete strangers for a thousand autumns or ten thousand years and encouraged them to drink and carouse in a moment of love amidst the flowers.[123]

Nijō blames fate and illusion for the women's misdeeds. Perhaps their situation struck a sympathetic chord with Nijō, no stranger herself to sexual transgression and exploitation.[124]

Tales of salvation and transformation provide the strongest evidence of an imagined connection between *asobi* and extraordinary worlds, one that was forged to demonstrate the potency of Buddhist teachings. Some tales may hint at an *asobi*'s shamanic powers, but I suspect this reflects the extent to which Buddhist and pre-Buddhist religious systems had merged by the twelfth and thirteenth centuries, rather than any conscious attempt to portray *asobi* as shamans or to cast Buddhism in a conquering role vis-à-vis other systems. Ritual pollution plays no obvious part in the stories—perhaps because it, as a variety of transgression, had merged with more strictly Buddhist concepts of sin as ignorance and illusion that leads one onto evil paths. The stories form part of a developing Buddhist discourse that viewed *asobi* more on an axis of illusion and enlightenment than on one of pollution and purity.

If the *asobi* in these tales does not appear polluted because of her profession—any more than she does in most other accounts of the sex trade in Heian and Kamakura Japan—there is no indication that her profession sacralizes her either. Repenting one's sins, recognizing the ephemeral nature of life in the present world, obtaining salvation by singing a religious *imayō,* or even revealing oneself as a bodhisattva or becoming a nun who expounds Buddhist teachings—all were used as evidence, not of the *asobi*'s sacred nature, but of the power of Buddhism to overcome the *asobi*'s transgression of willfully tempting men. Rather than considering *asobi* as *"hare no onnatachi"* ("sacred women," Saeki's designation) or *kegare no onnatachi,* I find it more useful to regard them as social actors who need to be analyzed in conjunction with such quotidian matters as marriage, law, and property—all part of the everyday world—as well as Buddhist concepts of illusion and desire. While the Buddhist discourse lamented the trade as an obstacle to enlightenment, such practical matters occupied the minds of many observers.

4 Constructing the Prostitute

> Since [the Kamusaki] *chōja* was a woman and a professional sexual entertainer, who would have recognized her as the incarnation of the bodhisattva? When pursuing expedient means to lead deluded beings to salvation, their compassionate vows cause buddhas and bodhisattvas to manifest themselves in various forms—whether or not these are despised beings.—*Jikkinshō*[1]

THE *SETSUWA* COLLECTION *Jikkinshō,* compiled in 1252, thus justifies the bodhisattva Fugen's assumption of an *asobi*'s body in the tale of the holy man Shōkū and the *asobi chōja.* While the earliest version of this story, in *Kojidan* (1212 – 1215), shows no need to explain the bodhisattva's incarnation as an *asobi, Jikkinshō* not only does so but also verifies the woman's lowly status.

The views expressed by the *Jikkinshō* compiler represent only one voice in the complex discourse about women in the sex trade in the middle and late Kamakura period, but it was a marginalizing voice that was growing stronger and would eventually join with others to affect public policy. This marginalizing process paralleled the efforts of authorities, particularly the bakufu, to regulate sexual behavior—efforts that had far more to do with issues of property and social order than with moral questions. In this climate, some female extramarital sexual activity was punished as a crime, and women who made a profession of sexual entertainment were subjected to increasing stigma and restrictions. However, the marginalization and stigmatization of sexual entertainers, as well as the loss of their romantic and idealized identity, proceeded slowly and irregularly and was often contested. In this chapter I explore several grounds—some rooted in the Heian period, some new to Kamakura—for stigmatizing sexual entertainers and constructing them as prostitutes.

In her study of *asobi,* Terry Kawashima suggests that the marginalization of these women was uncertain, inconsistent, and often driven by the idiosyncratic motivations of those who created the marginalizing discourses; by taking these discourses at face value, she contends, modern scholarship has made careless assumptions about the status of the women depicted.[2] While I agree with Kawashima that we need to consider the motivations and conditions under which texts were produced, we must also recognize that the texts did not simply describe marginalization but also contributed to its production. Moreover, an examination of evidence of various types shows that while at any single moment the evaluation of particular cohorts of women may be contested, we can also detect a long-term historical process by which women such as *asobi* were constructed as transgressors of social norms.

Japanese Scholars on Marginalization and Discrimination

In his discussion of marginal people in medieval Paris, Bronislaw Geremek defines them as those "who played no part in the processes of production" and "whose [lives] remained immune to the norms of behaviour in operation."[3] Japanese scholars have raised similar issues concerning female sexual entertainers, focusing on their social status and their treatment in legal decisions and property distribution.

Amino Yoshihiko and Wakita Haruko are among the prominent scholars who have debated the issue. Amino's argument—that *asobi, kugutsu,* and *shirabyōshi* were *shokunin* (people of skill such as performers or artisans)—emphasizes their role within a system of landholding and production that encompassed nonagricultural as well as agricultural occupations.[4] Amino maintains that some cohorts were originally under the control of a palace office and that many held rights to income from agricultural land and, like other *shokunin,* were licensed to travel by court or bakufu authorities.

Citing *Kairaishiki,* Wakita characterizes female entertainers as *rōnin* outside of standard hierarchies of authority and dependence. To support this contention, she points to the women's autonomous structures led by female *chōja.* In a recent work, she characterizes the *kugutsu,* who were explicitly described as itinerants and outlaws in Masafusa's essay, as hunting and fishing people who lived in the mountains and turned to performing arts as a way to make a living. Although she acknowledges that sexual entertainers were not necessarily held in contempt in the Heian and Kamakura periods, Wakita suggests that within their own organizations fictive kinship ties could disguise exploitation or even slavery.[5] The disagreement between Amino and Wakita is part of a larger debate within Japanese scholarship about the nature of the medieval status system and the position—within it or outside it—of nonagricultural people such as *shokunin* and the *hinin* who labored on construction projects or disposed of corpses. Wakita's arguments are compatible with those of Kuroda Toshio, who characterizes occupations unrelated to landholding and agricultural production as outside the medieval status system.[6] In her work, however, Wakita concentrates less on structural elements than on the degree to which individuals were "unfree" or otherwise subject to exploitation.

Amino and Wakita have sometimes based their arguments on contrasting interpretations of the same evidence. For example, a document dated 1256 provides Amino with evidence that female entertainers could be powerful and wealthy and supplies Wakita with evidence of exploitation and servitude within entertainer society.[7] The document is a deposition filed by the *shirabyōshi* Tamaō with authorities at the Hōjō family holding of Kida in Mino province. Tamaō had acted as guarantor for Tokuishime, a woman indentured as security for a loan to her foster parent Saishin (of unknown gender and occupation). The lender Jitsurenbō sold Tokuishime's contract to one Ishikuma Tarō, perhaps the same Ishikuma associated with two *shirabyōshi* in moneylending activities earlier that year. If so, Ishikuma may have been professionally involved with a *shirabyōshi* troupe.[8] Tokuishime apparently absconded, or perhaps Saishin reclaimed her, and Ishikuma brought the case before the Kida authorities, who ruled that he should have his money back. When Jitsurenbō refused to act on the matter, Tamaō herself redeemed the contract.

While Amino uses the document as evidence for the wealth and power of Tamaō, Wakita focuses on Tokuishime's situation. She argues that the adoptive relationship between Tokuishime and Saishin was a disguise for the sale of human beings that characterized the entertainment professions. Although Wakita's suggestion is provocative, it assumes that Saishin and Tokuishime were *shirabyōshi*. The document does not state this, nor does it indicate the services Tokuishime was expected to provide Jitsurenbō and Ishikuma. In a more recent discussion of this document, however, Wakita offers an argument for regarding Tokuishime, at least, as a *shirabyōshi:* the price of her services for five years. At fourteen *kan,* this was a considerably higher price than paid for an ordinary laborer—in another document, a payment of one and a half *kan* was made for the services of an eighteen-year-old male for fifteen years. Wakita also cites another source in which a fee of fourteen *kan* was paid for the services of a *shirabyōshi;* she suggests that this may have been the set price for such an entertainer's contract.[9] Wakita's argument assumes, of course, that the fourteen-*kan* loan to Saishin, for which Tokuishime served as guarantee, was actually a payment for her services and was not expected to be returned. Whatever her situation, Tokuishime was treated as property throughout. If she was in fact a *shirabyōshi,* Tamaō's deposition indicates that performers could be hierarchically organized under leaders with considerable power to dispose of the services of its members, some of whom were not free. Tokuishime's circumstances, in other words, may suggest a different picture of *shirabyōshi* than Tamaō's.

In some sense the differences between Wakita and Amino are more apparent than real: Wakita recognizes the relatively high status of some sexual entertainers prior to the fourteenth century, and more recent work by Amino locates the beginning of the women's decline in status between the mid-thirteenth and fourteenth centuries rather than in the fifteenth—without, however, rejecting the strong evidence for incorporation into the system of production that supported his earlier contentions.[10] The differences between the two scholars may lie, as Toyonaga Satomi has argued, in the complexity of an entertainer society that included women with wealth, power, and privilege as well as those without.[11]

In most of his work concerning sexual entertainers, Amino argues that they were incorporated into the production process at various levels: as recognized artisans or landholders or as persons of means allowed to file lawsuits and otherwise treated with respect by authorities. Heian and Kamakura sources present conflicting evidence on this issue and on others related to marginalization, such as the categorization of sexual entertainers as itinerants, criminals, or low-status persons. It should be noted, however, that the sources say far more about others' perceptions of female entertainers than about their actual lives.

Public Policies and Male Control

Scholars studying the sex trade in medieval Europe sometimes begin by examining government and ecclesiastical policies. In her study of prostitution in medieval Languedoc, Leah Otis categorizes public policies toward the profession as repression, tolerance, or institutionalization, policies that differed according to time and place.[12] At no time in the period covered by her study did authorities simply ignore prostitution. She is thus able to construct a picture of the sex trade largely through evidence from law codes and court cases, as is Ruth Karras in her study of prostitution in late medieval England.[13]

Works such as these indicate that prostitution was very rarely prohibited outright, despite Christian support for the sanctity of monogamous marriage. Public acceptance of prostitution—based on the concept that it responded to and helped contain natural male lust—was combined with efforts to confine the sex trade spatially and to confine prostitutes socially by stigmatizing them. Perhaps one reason prostitution was not forbidden in medieval Europe was because it earned profits for governments and powerful individuals. In England, for instance, prostitutes paid fines that were, in fact, disguised taxes; on the continent, cities earned income from municipal brothels.[14]

In contrast to medieval Christian Europe, it is difficult to discern a public policy toward the sex trade in the Heian age, and only a handful of relevant edicts or court cases can be found in the Kamakura period, clustered mostly in its middle and late years. This raises the possibility that the sex trade and its practitioners—whether entertainers or not—were simply of no interest to authorities before mid-Kamakura times. It seems doubtful, however, that the *asobi* or *kugutsu* who catered to elite men were under no official surveillance at all, especially when most artisans and tradesmen were dependents of noble families or religious institutions or else licensees of the court. Lacking concrete evidence, we can only speculate on the agents and methods of surveillance. Heian-period *asobi* may have been supervised by a palace office such as the Naikyōbō (Office of Entertainment) or the Gagaku Bureau, as Amino suggests,[15] or by the Kebiishi (court police) who oversaw the port towns and highways where *asobi* congregated.[16] Since Heian sources do not mention *asobi* or *kugutsu* based in the capital, they may have been officially discouraged from setting up shop there and steered, instead, to locations outside the city, just as European prostitutes were sometimes forced outside the city walls.

While elite males obviously enjoyed the sexual companionship of *asobi* and *kugutsu,* there is no evidence that the sex trade was exploited economically in the same way as its European counterparts—there were no publicly owned brothels, for instance, and no licensing system disguised as fines.[17] Of course, it is not hard to imagine the different people who must have profited from the sex trade: the boatmen who carried customers to Eguchi; the innkeepers who sold the customers rooms; the makers of clothing, musical instruments, and perhaps even aphrodisiacs; the carvers who made repeated images of Hyaku Dayū.

In the thirteenth century, there is evidence that authorities had begun to develop an interest in overseeing the sex trade. While neither court nor bakufu made serious efforts to regulate sexual entertainers such as the *asobi,* two orders—one from the throne and the other from a provincial military overseer *(shugo)*—focused on the activities of go-betweens called *nakadachi* who arranged illicit liaisons. These orders indicate not only official concern but also the existence of a flourishing sex trade that was not limited to traditional entertainers' groups. In 1212, Juntoku Tennō issued the following order:

> Item: We must curb those sorts called *nakadachi* in the capital.
>
> Recently in our realm, some lower-class women called "*nakadachi*" have appeared in the capital. Their reputation is to turn their backs completely on the law; their scheme is to join thoughtlessly with criminals. They lure women of refinement to cohabit with men of mean status. They either falsely claim noble lineage [for their retinue] or deceptively plot [to imitate] Xi Shi or Byanhou.[18] They make a living solely by captivating men's hearts. Such lewd misdeeds are already noted in penal law. Does not deception accompany their heavy crimes? We command the Kebiishi to make note of their lodgings and to arrest and interrogate them in person.[19]

While Ishii Ryōsuke identifies *nakadachi* as marriage go-betweens,[20] the women singled out in the edict arranged far less respectable liaisons. Clearly some were involved in sexual entertainment. A later document—house rules issued by the Kamakura *gokenin* Utsunomiya family in 1283—prohibited retainers from inviting *shirabyōshi, asobi,* or *nakadachi* to their lodgings while they were in Kamakura;[21] and in the sixteenth century, *nakadachi* paid indirect taxes to the Kebiishi for the right to operate brothels.[22] The women cited in Juntoku's order seem to have been procurers involved in a version of the sex trade that may have had very little to do with artistic performance.

While the sex trade was not illegal in the thirteenth century, the *nakadachi* are accused of breaking the law. The edict does not clearly state how they did so, but an item in the Yōrō code prohibits arranging illicit unions, and a late-eighth-century Council of State memorial to the throne notes a ban on the marriage of "good" and "base" persons.[23] *Nakadachi*—or, more likely, their retinue—are compared to two women of ancient China who had sexual relations with men of much higher class: Xi Shi (J.: Seishi), a beautiful firewood peddler of the Spring/Autumn period in China who was used by the king of one country to seduce a rival kingdom's ruler, thereby bringing about his downfall; and Byanhou, a courtesan of the kingdom of Wei who became one ruler's concubine and the mother of another. By invoking Xi Shi, the edict not only underlines its charge of deception but also implies that the women endanger the polity as well as individual men. The Kebiishi are made responsible for regulating the *nakadachi,* perhaps indicating police involvement in the sex trade well before the sixteenth century.[24]

Juntoku's edict also expresses dismay that the *nakadachi* have lured "women of refinement"—in other words, women of respectable families—into improper sexual unions. Rather than pointing simply to the arrangement of marriages with men of lower status, I think this statement implies that the women were recruited into prostitution. The order issued in 1242 by the *shugo* of Bungo province, discussed in Chapter 2, supports this interpretation. Here I quote the item in full:

> *Nakadachi*
>
> Except for designated women, to entice wives and unmarried women into secret liaisons is a basis for disorder and must cease. If violators remain, whatever their status or gender, their offense must be punished.[25]

The "designated women" were probably sexual professionals,[26] whose activities were tolerated by the Bungo authorities; the "disorder" was no doubt caused by slander when amateurs used the *nakadachi*'s services or joined their retinues.

Although neither the order of 1212 nor that of 1242 goes very far toward controlling the sex trade or even toward defining it as a potential object of control, both may be seen as attempts to set boundaries—the first between social classes and both between professionals and amateurs. Both orders suggest a sex trade beyond the coteries of sexual entertainers at inns and ports. *Nakadachi* link an old class of professionals with both amateur recruits and criminal activities. The public image of the sexual entertainment trade was changing from that of a service focused largely on the aristocratic traveler to one designed for a bigger, more heterogeneous audience. The documents suggest a thriving underground trade in the bodies of women, whether sexual professionals or amateurs.

The issue of male control divides the sex trade of the Heian period from that of Kamakura. In Heian times, it appears that the *asobi chōja* dealt directly with patrons and men were involved only as consumers. In the Kamakura period, men began to assume functions of intermediaries and managers. The appointment of Satomi Yoshinari as administrator in charge of *asobi (yūkun bettō),* recorded in an *Azuma kagami* entry of 1193,[27] is often cited as evidence that early in the Kamakura period *asobi (yūkun)* were brought under the control of the bakufu. According to this entry, on an occasion when *asobi* entertained the shogun Minamoto Yoritomo and his retainers, Yoritomo appointed Yoshinari to take charge of the women's legal disputes. At first glance this seems like a step toward regulation. But since the *yūkun bettō* post disappears from history after this reference, the appointment may have been nothing more than an ad hoc expedient to deal with a particular set of lawsuits.

Other evidence, however, suggests that some sexual entertainers were subjected to male supervision and even control—in one case from the court rather than the bakufu. According to an entry dated 1202/6/10 in Fujiwara Teika's diary *Meigetsuki,* one Tomoshige (no surname given) summoned some sixty *shirabyōshi* dancers and selected five of them to perform before the retired sovereign Go-Toba upon his pilgrimage to Iwashimizu Hachiman shrine. Tonomura Hisae believes that Tomoshige is Hida Tomoshige, an officer of the guards identified in the same source some two decades later as the *shirabyōshi bugyōnin* (supervisor).[28] According to Tonomura, Heian-period palace entertainers were supervised by the palace guards, so the involvement of an officer in selecting entertainers for Go-Toba is not at all surprising.[29] Nor is it surprising that *shirabyōshi* who entertained the retired sovereign were subjected to a rigorous audition. The 1202 entry depicts Tomoshige as a powerful individual with strong ties to *shirabyōshi* organizations, since he was able to summon so many potential candidates quickly.

Another indication of male control over female entertainers appears in the two documents of 1256 discussed earlier in this chapter. One document records payment of interest on loans of a hundred *mon* each to a man named Ishikuma and to two women whose names—Enmyō Gozen and Enjū Gozen—identify them as *shirabyōshi.* Interest payments were sent to addresses in the capital, indicating that the three lenders maintained residences there.[30] The second document is the deposition of the *shirabyōshi* Tamaō, which relates that Ishikuma Tarō, probably the same man as in the other document, purchased the indenture of Tokuishime. Wakita Haruko suggests that Ishikuma used the proceeds from moneylending to finance such purchases.[31] In any case, it is reasonable to speculate that Ishikuma had business dealings with *shirabyōshi* and may have managed a *shirabyōshi* troupe that performed in the capital, to which he hoped to add provincial entertainers—one of whom could have been Tokuishime. The earlier example of Hida Tomoshige suggests that Ishikuma's role may have been to recruit entertainers to perform for elite patrons. We cannot be certain about Ishikuma's status, but Hida Tomoshige was certainly a public figure acting in the service of the court. It is likely that the independence of female entertainers was eroding as men took on management and liaison roles, sometimes in an official capacity.

Official involvement, of course, was far from the sixteenth-century taxation of prostitution or the establishment of publicly controlled brothels in medieval Europe. Considering Leah Otis' three categories for government policy toward the sex trade—tolerance, institutionalization, or repression—Kamakura Japan was still an age of tolerance. At the same time, the sex trade had begun to inspire many unofficial complaints. Sometimes it was the women themselves who were censured; but sometimes it was their customers, and the women were viewed as a device for male wrongdoing or foolishness. As seen in the previous chapter, however, even the severest critics of sexual entertainment—the Buddhist clergy—mixed their censure with compassion, fascination, and the appropriation of the women's transgressions for religious aims.

Flaws in the Picture

Much of the Heian discussion of *asobi,* in particular, can be classified as "literature of appreciation" that described enjoyable experiences in the pleasure quarters and urged others to visit there.[32] Nonetheless, not all observers admired the *asobi,* and even those who did sometimes pointed out flaws in the women's character or deportment. Few early commentaries were as critical as that of Shitagō or even Yukitoki, who censured the *asobi*'s licentious behavior even while recognizing their appeal. Masafusa's *asobi* squabbled over the take, however, and the author of *Sarashina nikki,* despite enjoying the *asobi* perform at Mt. Ashigara, was surprised that their faces were not coarse or dirty. Such comments suggest that even while Heian observers promoted a romantic, idealized picture of *asobi,* they were nonetheless keenly aware of social and behavioral gaps between themselves and professional sexual entertainers.

The brevity and ephemerality of relations with *asobi* also troubled many observers, from Ōe Yukitoki to Murasaki Shikibu. In *The Tale of Genji,* Murasaki describes the fictional Prince Genji's visit to Sumiyoshi shrine:

> A group of *asobi* approached. Even among the highest-ranked courtiers there were young men who were fond of that sort of thing, and they all seemed to fix their eyes on the women. But Genji thought that whether a relationship was interesting or touching depended upon the woman, and that there was no advantage to getting oneself involved in even a casual affair with someone a bit inconstant. He found the coquetry of the *asobi* distasteful.[33]

Genji's negative judgment rests on the fickle nature of women who, because of their profession, had to share their bodies with many men—an ironic note for a prince not noted for his sexual fidelity. Issues of class difference and the impropriety of public seduction may have also been on Murasaki's mind.

Despite the atmosphere of cheerful slumming promoted by the Heian literature of appreciation, it is possible to sense an occasional hint of danger in consorting with *asobi.* Minamoto Michichika (1149–1202) describes an encounter between *asobi* and the party of the retired sovereign Go-Takakura on pilgrimage to Itsukushima shrine in 1180:

> We set up lodgings for the retired sovereign at the port of Muro. The sovereign disembarked and hot water was ordered for his bath. The *asobi* at the port gathered around us near the sovereign's lodgings, like foxes from some old grave mound that take the forms of women and seduce men as dusk is falling. Since no one was interested they went away.[34]

The description is quite damning: foxes who disguised themselves as women and seduced unsuspecting men were a standard emblem of deception and danger in late-Heian *setsuwa* literature. The passage prefigures the concern with deception expressed in Juntoku's edict against the *nakadachi.*

Nor was the art of sexual entertainers immune to criticism. The tale collection *Zoku kojidan,* compiled in 1219, quotes the following complaint about *shirabyōshi* dancing by Fujiwara Moronaga (1138–1192), a powerful courtier who at one point held the post of prime minister *(dajō daijin):*

> The minister, who had taken orders at Myōonin, declared: "It is a custom of China to watch dance and listen to music to learn whether the country is well administered or in disarray. There is a dance called *shirabyōshi* in our society. Its music is in the key of *shō* among the five keys; this key indicates the ruin of the country. As for the form of the dance, the performers scurry back and forth or stand staring at the sky. This style is thought to go too far, and the dance is disagreeable, along with the songs and the persons of the dancers."[35]

In a new take on old tropes, an anonymous traveler described his experiences at a rest station in Sagami province in the fourth month of 1223 in the travel diary *Kaidōki:*

> When we passed through the Sekimoto rest station, we found that the people who lived in the houses lined up along the road let out rooms to travelers, and *kunjo (asobi),* who sat at the windows singing, detained guests and made them their spouses. How pitiable to make a thousand-year pledge in one night of illusion at a traveler's inn! They indulge the urges of passersby in order to make a living. A proper marriage is not a night spent in their crimson bedchambers hung with emerald curtains, but rather a lifetime of happiness in a rude thatch hut with a brushwood door.[36]

While some two centuries earlier, the *asobi* boat trade had struck Yukitoki as both charming and morally suspect, this passage uses the metaphors of Yukitoki and others to construct a bleaker picture of regrettable license.

Other Kamakura sources indicate that the old Heian charm had not entirely faded away. Writing almost twenty years later than the author of *Kaidōki,* another anonymous traveler introduces an *asobi* he met at a Tōtōmi province rest station in 1242:

> At the Hashimoto station was an inn where we stayed for one night. It was a thatch hut with an old roof, and the moonlight leaked in through the holes. Among the

> crowd of *asobi (kimidomo)* was one who seemed a little older and more experienced than the others. She chanted quietly to herself, "All night in my bed I see the clear sky . . ." She seemed to be a person of genuine refinement.[37]

Individual entertainers are sometimes portrayed as women of good character; for example, the late-thirteenth-century *Shasekishū* tells of a married man who brings home an *asobi* and orders his wife to leave. The wife prepares so graciously for her replacement that the *asobi,* touched by her rival's consideration, insists that the man call her back and volunteers to live elsewhere instead.[38] Later, in Muromachi-period literature, famous *shirabyōshi* such as Shizuka Gozen, the mistress of the ill-fated Minamoto Yoshitsune, become exemplars of fidelity, an ironic twist in the construction of female entertainers as prostitutes.[39]

Sexual entertainers both delighted and troubled observers in the Heian and Kamakura periods. There was never a time when the sex trade was a completely acceptable profession, but there was never a time when it was totally stigmatized either. Observers regretted the inconstancy of sexual entertainers but took pleasure in their ready availability. Complaints about them were often linked to other problems. The women were associated with outlaws or low-status persons; or they were placed at the bottom of hierarchically ordered lists of positions and occupations; or they were linked to social problems such as itinerancy, the waste of valuable resources, or public disorder. Of course, as seen in the previous chapter, they were also censured for sexually enticing men and thereby distracting them from the pursuit of virtue and enlightenment. These complaints, laments, and censure must be considered within the context of the dominant Heian discourse on sexual entertainers, an idealized view that did not disappear completely in Kamakura times. On balance, appreciation outpaced complaints in Heian sources but the reverse became true from mid-Kamakura times on. Even though the negative judgments resulted only in a few official acts of discrimination against sexual entertainers rather than a consistent public policy to control them, the change in attitudes foreshadowed later attempts to regulate and limit the sex trade and contributed to a view of the women as prostitutes and their occupation as degraded.

Questions of Social Status

Several Heian and Kamakura sources directly address the social status of sexual entertainers. *Wamyōshō*'s categorization of *asobi* and *yahochi* as beggars and thieves means not only that their mode of living rendered them socially undesirable, but posits a place for them within tenth-century society. "Beggars and thieves" is the final listing under the main heading "people" *(jinrinbu)* following entries such as "hunters and fishers" and "people of despised status."[40] If these classifications are listed in descending status order—a standard method of organization found in other Heian texts—*asobi* and *yahochi* were placed even below such despised folk as boatmen or stablehands.

Yet this was an issue of status, not caste: the sex trade was never regarded as so degrading that women could not move between it and other occupations and positions. Heian sources made *asobi* famous for their ability to seduce men of high station; and as Masafusa indicates, long-term liaisons sometimes followed. There are numerous Heian-period examples of *asobi* and *kugutsu* who were mothers of children sired by courtiers or even monarchs and whose offspring were acknowledged by their fathers.[41] Women trained in rigorous performing traditions may have been reluctant to abandon them for other occupations; but it seems unlikely that stigma would have barred them from doing so, since it did not prevent such liaisons. On a lower social level, Masafusa suggests that serving women moved casually in and out of the boat trade with no apparent social approbation. In the Kamakura period, documents indicate that local estate officials and warriors sometimes took sexual entertainers as wives and concubines.[42]

Rajyashree Pandey maintains that *asobi (yūjo)* and court ladies had some features in common—both were accomplished musicians and poets, both had considerable sexual freedom, and both established sexual liaisons with male courtiers. She also argues that visual images of *asobi* depict the women wearing dress and hairstyles that were similar to those of court ladies. (Court ladies, however, were expected to cover their faces in public, if they let themselves be seen at all; the *asobi* pictured in *Hōnen shōnin eden* openly reveal their faces.) Nevertheless, Pandey sees *asobi* and court ladies as belonging to essentially different categories conflated only in later fictional treatments.[43]

In fact, the social origins of sexual entertainers were probably for the most part quite modest. The author of *Sarashina nikki* declares that the *asobi* of Mt.

Ashigara "were pleasing enough to be maidservants in a courtier's house"[44]—a status comparable to that of the part-time workers described by Masafusa. More precise information for later times comes from *Meigetsuki.* In reporting the death in childbirth of the retired sovereign's concubine, the *shirabyōshi* Tanba no Tsubone, Teika notes that she was the daughter of a maker of bamboo blinds—in other words, the daughter of a small artisan in the service of the aristocracy.[45] One Kamakura source, *Azuma kagami,* shows a palace serving woman substituting as an entertainer: she was summoned to perform *imayō* and other arts, ordinarily performed by sexual entertainers, to comfort Taira Shigehira on the eve of his execution.[46] We cannot know how typical these situations were, but the sources indicate a strong possibility that sexual entertainers and serving women occupied similar social strata. Both, moreover, specialized in offering personal services to elites, moving within circles of power without being powerful themselves.

Other sources, from somewhat later in the Kamakura period, place sexual entertainers lower on the social scale, suggesting base status and in one case comparing them to *hinin.* The bakufu's supplementary legislation dated 1267 characterized *kugutsu* and *shirabyōshi* as "base women," implying defiled status for the entertainers' groups.[47] *Jikkinshō* retells the *Yamato monogatari* story about the *asobi* Shirome, who entertained the retired sovereign Uda, remarking that:

> Even *asobi* and *kugutsu* of despised status excelled at popular singing, and those who favored *waka* were received by respectable people, and their poetry defiled imperial collections. . . .[48]
>
> The aged *yūkun* Higaki of Higo province was included in the *Gosenshū,* and the Kamusaki *asobi* Miyagi defiled the *Goshūishū.* The Aohaka *kugutsu* Nabiki was permitted to include her poem in *Shikashū,* and the Eguchi *asobi* Tae became a *Shinkokinshū* poet. Such a phenomenon was not limited to women—although Mibu Tadamine was a low-status retainer *(shajin* or *toneri),* he ranked among those who were included in the *Kokinshū,* and Yamada Hōshi was a *hinin* who defiled the same collection.[49]

While *Wamyōshō* associated the women with criminals, *Jikkinshō* links them with low-status groups that performed recognized functions in society—the *shajin* as servants or stablehands and the *hinin* as construction or graveyard workers. The passage also suggests that female sexual entertainers were regarded in some quarters as ritually polluted, a topic considered earlier. Taken as a whole, however, the passage also makes the point that low-status people such as *asobi* and *kugutsu* could invade surprising milieux, even court poetry collections. Thus the text both draws boundaries and blurs them, further suggesting the ambiguous social position of sexual entertainers.

A list of positions and occupations in two related fourteenth-century petitions indicates the low status assigned to at least some sexual professionals by the end of the Kamakura period. The petitions, filed by the lay functionaries *(jinin)* of Tōdaiji Hachimangū in 1332, complain of the improper diversion of tolls collected at Hyōgo port, a Tōdaiji holding in Settsu province, which had been earmarked for the shrine since 1308.[50] According to the petititions, the residents of the port "down to the *yūkun*" had joined in the complaint.[51] The documents suggest not only the position of the *yūkun* within the hierarchy of the holding but also their formal inclusion in its everyday business. Thus low status did not imply an outcast position. In my view, this example casts doubt on the validity of Amino's arguments, which are based largely on the premise that markers of community membership such as the rights to hold property and file lawsuits ruled out low status and occupation-based stigma.

By the mid-fourteenth century, entertainers such as *shirabyōshi* appear as social undesirables in close association with *hinin* and beggars. At a shrine festival depicted in *Suwa daimyōjin ekotoba,* an illustrated scroll dated 1356:

> Types such as *shirabyōshi, miko, dengaku* performers, reciters of spells, *sarugaku* performers, beggars, *hinin,* the blind, the deaf, and the infirm—bands of good-for-nothings—crowd together like so many stalks of bamboo and quarrel among themselves. Such people are amusing and contemptible.[52]

A final but very late example is the oft-cited reference in *Daijōin jisha zōjiki,* dated 1463, which lists *arukishirabyōshi* and *arukimiko* in a roster of wandering lower-class entertainers, the inclusion of each reinforcing the notion that all were some form of social undesirable.[53]

Many scholars agree that sexual entertainers lost status from the Heian to the Kamakura to the Muromachi period—leaving aside, of course, that inconvenient listing in *Wamyōshō.* In my view, the status of sexual entertainers was ambiguous at the outset; it did not simply decline but rather was clarified in a negative way. One engine for that process was a series of complaints on quite specific social issues—complaints that could be found in some cases in late-Heian sources but intensified and increased in number in the Kamakura years. Problems such as itinerancy, excess spending, and public disorder, as well as issues related to property distribution, contributed to the disapproval of sexual entertainers and helped eventually to construct them as transgressors of social norms.

Itinerancy and "Otherness"

Among the specific problems associated with sexual entertainers, itinerancy engendered some early concern—for example, in Masafusa's depiction of the *kugutsu* in *Kairaishiki. Kugutsu* who grew no rice and paid no taxes were uncomfortably like the absconded peasant who eroded the tax base by reducing the acreage under cultivation. Although much itinerancy in Heian and Kamakura times was controlled by a system of barrier tolls and licenses granting permission to travel, itinerants also included dangers to the social and political order such as bandits and heterodox holy men. By depicting *kugutsu* as vagabonds who neither farmed nor obeyed authorities, Masafusa points to some of these fears.

In *Kairaishiki,* Masafusa took great pains to depict the *kugutsu* as aliens as well as itinerants by comparing them to "northern barbarians"—the Xiong-nu, nomads who lived on the border of Han China and presented the archetypical threat to a settled agricultural society. The analogy alienates the *kugutsu* not only from Japanese society but also from the agrarian mainstream of all East Asia. References to animal-hair tents (a typical Xiong-nu dwelling) and to the Xiong-nu hunting style made certain that the reader would not miss the point. The *kugutsu* women, moreover, are doubly marginalized: first as members of an alien, itinerant tribe with curious antisocial customs and second as prostitutes whose very manner of seduction is transgressive. Masafusa's description of the women is lifted directly from Fan Ye's Chinese dynastic history *Hou han shu* (History of the Latter Han). The contrived eyebrows, false teardrops, seductive saunter, and pained smile that Masafusa attributes to *kugutsu* women appear first in a portrait of the coquettish wife of General Liang Ji and then in an account of women's fashions at the Chinese capital.[54] Far from recommending these fashions for emulation, however, Fan Ye characterizes them as bizarre; moreover, he portrays Liang Ji's wife as detestable and manipulative of her husband. The resulting image of *kugutsu* women in *Kairaishiki* reflects a negative aspect of Chinese female society.

How accurate was Masafusa's information? Since he lifted entire descriptive passages from Chinese sources, perhaps he was not very familiar with *kugutsu* and was writing about what he feared rather than what he knew. A sequence of Chinese poems (including one by Masafusa) in *Honchō mudaishi* depicts *kugutsu* in such terms as "ceaseless wanderers" and "vain mad troupes" who "wander far and wide," tying their physical itinerancy to ephemeral sexual relationships and the fate of aging without a settled home or marriage.[55] In other words, the lives of *kugutsu* are depicted as itinerant, outlaw, ephemeral, and ultimately sad.

According to Terry Kawashima, *kugutsu* were portrayed by "a dynamic yet limited set of literary devices" such as the ones cited here.[56] The poets of this *Honchō mudaishi* sequence were probably all associates of Masafusa, although several of them were quite a bit younger than he; their use of similar tropes may have been the result of communal poetic exercises rather than actual observation. No other source, in fact, depicts *kugutsu* as outlaws, although the issue of itinerancy is still open, as I will discuss shortly. Other sources, in fact, portray *kugutsu* as functioning members of society, even entertaining at the royal palace, according to Sei Shōnagon's *Pillow Book*.[57]

Focusing on the characterization of both male and female *kugutsu* as marginals, not on the women as sexual entertainers, Amino Yoshihiko argues that Masafusa's essay was not an accurate depiction. Rather than outlaw itinerants, Amino contends, *kugutsu* were, as *shokunin,* accepted members of Japanese society. As evidence he cites an episode of 1114 recounted in Fujiwara Munetada's diary *Chūyūki.* A low-ranked government official *(kodoneri)* seized horses and cotton textiles belonging to a *kugutsu* troupe. The official's followers also attacked and wounded several *kugutsu.* When the *kugutsu* complained to higher authorities, the official was forced to return the property and was dismissed from office.[58] Amino argues that the *kugutsu* were prosperous enough to have valuable textiles and horses. The episode also suggests to him that *kugutsu,* rather than being outside the law, could successfully bring legal complaints before government authorities—an argument he also used in the case of the *shirabyōshi* Tamaō. Another piece of evidence Amino uses to support his argument is a *Konjaku* episode about a scribe *(mokudai)* at a provincial governor's office. The man, distinguished by his diligence and reliability, turns out to be of *kugutsu* origin—when a *kugutsu* troupe visits the governor's mansion, the *mokudai* cannot help but join in their singing and dancing.[59] Not only were *kugutsu* welcome in the homes of the powerful, but men of *kugutsu* origin could hold respected official positions.

Amino also cites an incident, recorded in 1212 in *Meigetsuki,* that has some similarities to the episode of 1114 in *Chūyūki.* A group of *kugutsu* residing on one of Teika's estates charged that servants of an estate manager had intruded upon their fields and foraged their crops. After several days of listening to the *kugutsu*'s bitter complaints, Teika had the servants arrested.[60] The incident indicates, first, that the *kugutsu* had crops that could be foraged—therefore they were no longer gypsies who did not "cultivate a single field"—and, second, that they had rights vis-à-vis the higher-status estate manager which were upheld by Teika, the proprietor. Amino uses such evidence, along with other indications that *kugutsu* held land rights, to conclude that they had *shokunin* status and were not considered to be outlaws.[61]

While this may well have been the case, Amino's evidence does not necessarily show that *kugutsu* were settled in Masafusa's time; nor does it prove that they were not marginalized then or later. To begin, the humor in the *Konjaku* story comes from the incongruity between the *mokudai*'s position and sober character and his less than respectable family background. The episodes in both *Chūyūki* and *Meigetsuki* involved a three-way relationship among the *kugutsu,* high-status authorities or proprietors, and petty managers or officials. Proprietors like Teika often quarreled with local estate managers, and the interests of central government authorities and petty officials often conflicted; higher authorities might logically have sided with the *kugutsu,* marginalized or not. Moreover, the *Meigetsuki* text shows that the *kugutsu* lived, not among the general agricultural population of the estate, but in a special area, called a *shuku,* which may have been segregated from other areas. The term *shuku* also designates the dwelling place of low-status persons such as *hinin.* Since another meaning of *shuku* is a traveler's inn—often at a designated rest station along a highway—the word itself has overtones of itinerancy as well as marginalization. While the *Meigetsuki*'s *kugutsu* were no longer itinerants, they were not in the same category as ordinary estate residents.

The issue of itinerancy needs to be examined more closely. Wakita Haruko's view—that *kugutsu* were originally hunters who lived in the mountains and therefore were free of controls placed on agricultural people—is intriguing but difficult to prove.[62] It seems likely that troupes of *kugutsu,* rather than being "settled" or "vagrants" in any strict sense of either word, traveled over a limited area and perhaps seasonally, offering entertainment at the mansions of the wealthy, at temples and shrines, and perhaps at periodic markets. Since there were no permanent theaters, they could not have functioned in any other way. The *Konjaku* episode about the *mokudai,* in fact, indicates this very mode of operation; and in the *Chūyūki* account, the *kugutsu* were on the road, possibly on their way to their next performance. By the end of the Heian period, many *kugutsu* women were based at inns along the highway, but they may have traveled from time to time with troupes of both men and women. Perhaps they were similar to the other *shokunin* such as metal-casters who had the right to travel from place to place to peddle their wares.[63] In fact, in a badly damaged document thought to date from the late Kamakura age, licensed comb manufacturers complained that "Chinese and *kugutsu*" were poaching on their trade and territory in "all provinces and the seven circuits"—in other words, wandering from place to place selling combs rather than giving theatrical performances.[64] Licenses or no, authorities seem to have found it difficult to keep itinerancy entirely under control.

Even if Amino is correct in arguing that *kugutsu* were not outlaws and were not necessarily itinerants, Masafusa's essay still has considerable historical value and cannot be discarded out of hand. Jane Marie Law has made the provocative suggestion that *Kairaishiki* should be read neither as true history nor as bad history, but rather as a "piece of fanciful 'exotica' " intended as a didactic example of improper social behavior.[65] Thomas Keirstead, discussing both *Yūjoki* and *Kairaishiki,* makes a similar point: "Women and movement, the problems of the supernumerary sex and of being without house or field or other property that fixes one in place (fixes one's place), comprise the twin contradictions that inform Masafusa's ethnography, that motivate and necessitate his social commentary."[66] For Keirstead, images of itinerant women in Masafusa's writings are used to represent the alien other, thereby defining not only the other but also the settled male self.

Unlike Keirstead, I find substantial differences between the women who appear in *Yūjoki* and in *Kairaishiki.* Masafusa did not portray the *asobi* as alien; they are firmly grounded at home, along the familiar Yodo River route and at the familiar shrines of Sumiyoshi and Hirota; they consort with named members of the Heian elite, just like court women known to Masafusa and his friends. While Masafusa's *asobi* could be quarrelsome, his essay never depicts them in serious transgressions. In contrast, the *kugutsu* are rendered as members of a marginalized outlaw tribe, and the women are shown to be greedy prostitutes, not sirens who delighted high-status men.

What does it mean that some but not all women who performed popular songs and traded in sex were described as alien and transgressive? Was Masafusa, in his guise as public official, calling the court's attention to women whose unorthodox customs made both their activity in the sex trade and their congress with "ordinary" Japanese men seem dangerous? Masafusa's marginalization of the *kugutsu* women seems to depend, not on the transgressive nature of the sex trade itself, but on the social identity of those who practiced it. If Masafusa's essay is historically accurate, some of the threat that *kugutsu* posed may have come from the men who hunted on horseback, uncomfortably similar to Japan's own "northern barbarians," the Emishi. The near disappearance of *kugutsu* men from later sources suggests that the men eventually lost their connotations of danger; perhaps the women did so as well.

As for the *asobi,* a few sources describe them in terms that suggest itinerancy and therefore otherness. As Jacqueline Pigeot points out, themes of itinerancy and impermanence were standard features in poems depicting *asobi.* In a sequence on *asobi* in the late-twelfth-century *Shinsen rōeishū,* a poem by the Tang Chinese master Bo Ju-yi was even misquoted to produce the image of an itinerant courtesan.[67] In no case, however, is it clear that *asobi* were actual vagabonds. *Wamyōshō*'s claim that *asobi* "wander about in the daytime" could simply mean that they toured the local streets to hunt for customers. When some fifty years later Ōe Yukitoki found "vagabond" an apt name for *asobi,*[68] and in late Heian times the monk Kōen called Eguchi *asobi* "wandering women" *(yūkō no onna),*[69] they may not have been describing the entertainers' actual mode of life. Rather, they were probably using vagabondage as a metaphor for the women's ephemeral relationships or perhaps were engaging in wordplay on the character *yū* (*asobu* 遊), used in both observers' descriptive phrases as well as in the terms *asobi* and *ukareme.*

Whatever the situation may have been in Masafusa's time, by the end of the twelfth century both *asobi* and *kugutsu* seem to have settled down, lodging in port towns or at inns where they entertained travelers. Even if the women themselves were not on the move, however, their customers were—at least temporarily—and in a society based on stable corporate structures such as estate hierarchies and lineage, their professions maintained connections with itinerancy and impermanence.

The Spendthrift Patron

Another social problem associated with sexual entertainers was men's use of community resources to pay for their services. Like the tellers of medieval French fabliaux for whom prostitutes' threat lay in greed rather than sexuality,[70] Masafusa points out the unseemly desire of *kugutsu* women for brocade and gold. Most Heian and Kamakura sources, however, focused on the extravagance of men, especially those who embezzled common funds to support their habits.

Two *Konjaku* episodes with similar opening passages concern a temple administrator *(bettō)* who misappropriates temple property to consort with *asobi* and *kugutsu*. According to one:

> A long time ago, there was a temple south of Hōshōji called Jōhōji. Its *bettō* was a monk in appearance only; he did not revere the three treasures [the Buddha, the law, and the community of monks] and did not comprehend the laws of karmic retribution. He loved to play *go* and *sugoroku* and gathered professional gamblers together for his games. Moreover, he regularly invited female entertainers such as *asobi* and *kugutsu* to perform and frolic. He selfishly appropriated temple property for his own benefit, without performing a single good deed, and spent his days eating meat and drinking sake.[71]

The real culprit in this tale is the *bettō*. Many *bettō* were outsiders appointed by the government, rather than resident monks chosen by their colleagues, and thus were particularly vulnerable to resentment and criticism. While *Konjaku* censures the *bettō* for his moral failings, *asobi* and *kugutsu* are not criticized on similar grounds but are seen as an improper diversion—like drinking and gambling—that eats away temple resources.

Since *Konjaku* episodes were probably used as sermon material by Buddhist evangelists,[72] they expressed not only the concerns of their narrators but also those of a target audience that included cultivators, rural notables, and common city folk. In fact, accounts of similar real-life incidents in the Kamakura period suggest that the diversion of common funds for private pleasure, including parties with *asobi* and *kugutsu,* posed a very real problem in both secular and monastic society. For example, in 1227 residents of a Suō province estate charged the custodian, an appointee from the capital, with wasting their taxes on *kugutsu* entertainment.[73] In 1300, local holders and estate officials of Ōta estate in Bingo province complained that their custodian's numerous misdeeds included the summoning of "dozens of adult women" to his home "day and night"—perhaps a reference to sexual professionals.[74] The 1268 complaint of the Jissōji monks discussed in the previous chapter was directed at the deputy of an abbot appointed from outside the monks' assembly; he was charged with patronizing *asobi* and *kugutsu* along with other gross misconduct.[75] In this complaint, contempt for an outsider was complicated both by his extravagant spending and by his indulgence in sexual pleasures nominally forbidden to monks.

Even the highest aristocrats could not spend lavishly on *asobi* or *shirabyōshi* without incurring public criticism. In 1260, an anonymous libel sheet passed around the capital complained, "There are *shirabyōshi* at Ankamon'in's mansion," along with other disastrous circumstances such as natural calamities, corpses in the riverbed, and ghosts and goblins in the capital.[76] Probably written by an Onjōji monk, the complaint singled out Go-Horikawa Tennō's sister Ankamon'in, known for her extravagance. The late-fourteenth-century history *Masukagami* characterizes the princess' tastes as "extremely flamboyant" and notes that she hosted performances of *shirabyōshi* and *dengaku* dancing, "enjoying herself just as she pleased."[77] Ankamon'in's extravagance invoked censure although, strictly speaking, communal funds may not have been involved.

The complaint against Ankamon'in, moreover, hints that excessive revelry —not just sexual indulgence—was seen as a social problem. On the other hand, sexual entertainment was not necessarily blamed for public disorder, even when the two were associated. An *Azuma kagami* entry of 1241 reports that a quarrel broke out between two warrior parties, one of which had been drinking and carousing at a Kamakura brothel *(irogonomi no ie).* The entry mentions that the two parties involved usually got along, so this was not the eruption of a long-standing feud. The chronicler concludes: "I've heard that today's quarrel occurred because a demon entered the hearts of the combatants."[78] No connection was drawn between the quarrel and the revelry at the brothel.

Despite increasing censure of sexual entertainers in the later Kamakura period, little was done to punish them or mark them as "different" from the rest of the population. Unlike their European counterparts, they were not fined, shamed, forced to wear special clothing, or confined to brothel districts; in many cases they were treated with respect. As late as 1322, nuns at the Ritsu convent Hokkeji—many of whom were aristocrats of the highest station—read sutras for the death anniversaries of the *chōja* of Hashimoto inn and for the *chōja* of Kagami inn and both her parents. Although the relationship between Hokkeji and the *chōja* may have come from the temple's past connections with Eizon, who made it his business to minister to marginalized women and men, it is also clear that *asobi chōja* were not viewed as social outcasts.[79]

Complaints against sexual entertainers, though increasing in frequency after the middle of the Kamakura age, rarely resulted in policies of repression or control. In one arena, however, that of property inheritance, the women's occupation sometimes put them at a disadvantage. For inheritance to be a problem, of course, the women had to have the right and the opportunity to hold property in the first place. The next section of this chapter examines issues of landholding and inheritance rights, focusing on the middle and late Kamakura period.

Property and Inheritance

Nonagricultural people in Kamakura Japan frequently received compensation from rice or dry fields: in other words, from rights they held to land. These people included aristocrats and officials in the capital, as well as warriors, monks, and certain artisans. Temples and shrines, for example, distributed produce from their holdings to the people who crafted their ritual vessels, repaired their porches, or made umbrellas for their monks and priests. In some cases artisans were simply paid with a set amount of produce—a certain number of bushels of rice, for example—but in other cases they were assigned rights to a percentage of the produce from specific fields or fields within a specific estate.

Evidence that female entertainers possessed land rights lies at the heart of Amino's argument that they were not marginalized but were regarded as *shokunin* like carpenters or ironworkers. A record of tax-exempt fields connected to shrines and temples in the public holdings *(kokugaryō)* of Iyo province includes some that were assigned to *kugutsu* and to *kusemai* (another type of performer) as well as to other *shokunin.*[80] The document, dated 1255, shows that *kugutsu* received one *chō,*[81] the same allotment as that of coppersmiths, potters, and dyers. We do not know, however, how many persons each allotment was expected to support. Using such evidence, Amino argues that *kugutsu* of the Kamakura period received land allotments and were subject to taxation. Wakita Haruko suggests that the allotments were payments to those who performed at the provincial headquarters or at temples or shrines where provincial officials worshipped and thinks that the *kugutsu,* among others, were under the direct control of the provincial government.[82]

A bakufu legal judgment of 1249 concerning the land rights of *kugutsu* women in Suruga province provides Amino with further evidence for his claim that *kugutsu* were incorporated into the landholding system.[83] The *kugutsu* argued that, several generations in the past, they had been granted tax-exempt jurisdictions over two villages within a holding under the proprietary authority of the Buddhist temple Kuanjūryōin. More recently one of the *kugutsu,* a woman named Asoni, had been awarded a contract to cultivate rice fields within the holding. The representative of the temple argued that the proprietor had a right to collect taxes from both Asoni's fields and those originally allocated to the *kugutsu* group. He implied that the earlier tax exemptions were not of long standing but had been obtained by another *kugutsu,* Eiyōni, through her adopted son-in-law, an estate official. Despite this claim, the bakufu found for the *kugutsu* on all counts.[84]

Amino uses this document as evidence, not only that *kugutsu* possessed rights to agricultural land, but also that individual *kugutsu* women were powerful enough to win lawsuits and to take local notables such as the estate official into their families. Wakita Haruko, on the other hand, suggests that Eiyōni's daughter was the estate official's mistress rather than a legitimate wife; Wakita posits that the *kugutsu* women were operating a brothel in the area, staffed by some who were Eiyōni's relatives and others, sold into the profession, who were bound to her by fictive kinship ties.[85] In the absence of concrete evidence, this is speculation on Wakita's part. But it should be noted that the section of the estate on which the *kugutsu* lived was designated a *shuku,* suggesting that the women had *hinin*-like status.

Amino extends his argument that the *kugutsu* were *shokunin* with recognized rights and obligations to include the *asobi* and *shirabyōshi,* citing evidence that they too held land, filed lawsuits, and in general were treated as legitimate property holders by authorities. As examples he cites the cases of the *shirabyōshi* Tamaō, discussed earlier, and Gikō, a *yūkun (asobi)* from Yobikoura in Hizen province who purchased land from a *gokenin* in 1228.[86] Even when the property rights of female entertainers were challenged, this could be done on the same basis as any other lawsuit. For example, in a dispute between the Shima province *shirabyōshi* Kakuōshi and a monk, Kakuōshi's right to hold land was opposed on the grounds that her supporting documents had been forged, not because of her occupation.[87]

On occasion in the late Kamakura period, however, a sexual entertainer's occupation was sometimes used as a reason to deprive her of land rights. This was a time, of course, when bakufu decisions were restricting the inheritance rights of women in general as well as those of younger sons.[88] Nevertheless, the singling out of certain occupations for discriminatory treatment suggests a degree of marginalization based on negative judgments of certain types of female entertainers. One case in point is the bakufu edict of 1267 regulating the distribution of property owned by *gokenin,* discussed in detail in Chapter 2. To recapitulate: the edict restricted the rights of widows or divorced women to keep property given them by their husbands. Several categories of divorced women, including *kugutsu* and *shirabyōshi,* were not allowed to keep the property under any circumstance.[89] Even though this document is evidence that *kugutsu* and *shirabyōshi* could still marry high-status men in the mid-Kamakura period, it nevertheless stigmatizes the women by classifying them as "base women" and assuming that they "enticed" their husbands into giving them property, rather than acquiring it through legitimate means.

As the next example shows, moreover, a sexual entertainer could be denied an inheritance solely on the grounds of her occupation. In 1279 the former Dazaifu *yūkun* Akyō unsuccessfully sued to inherit her dead son Tome's holdings—Kanzaki village and Shiotsutome hamlet in Sashi village—two neighboring properties in Hizen province. Tome was the second son of the Hizen *gokenin* Sashi Shirōzaemon no jo Fusa, who had been killed in the first Mongol invasion of 1274 along with Tome and two other sons. The properties were also claimed by Fusa's widow, known by the Buddhist name Myōren; his minor grandson Yūtamaru, the offspring of his first son; and his granddaughter, the offspring of his third son (the child of Myōren). (See the accompany-

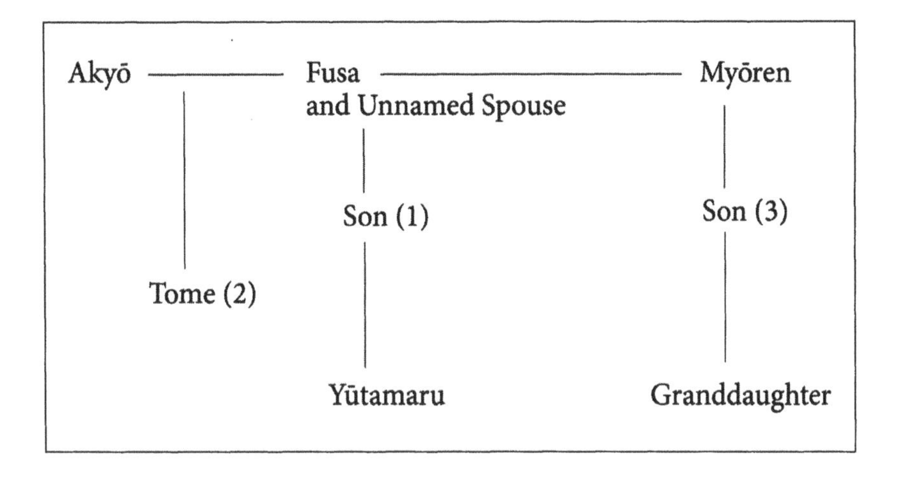

ing chart.) Akyō, who had borne Fusa's second son, was called a nun *(ama)* in the deposition, indicating that she had retired from her profession and had at least nominally taken Buddhist orders. Before his death Tome had been allotted the property rights in question, which had belonged to Fusa's father.

In her deposition, Akyō claimed Tome's inheritance as his only living relative, saying that she intended to use the income for memorial services for him. Myōren, however, argued that she should inherit the property, since she had adopted Tome and raised him as if he were her own son. Yūtamaru's deposition attacked Akyō's claim on the sole grounds that she was a *yūkun*. For the bakufu, this was a cogent argument: Akyō's claim was denied out of hand solely and explicitly for that reason. Since Myōren had died by the time the case was decided and the granddaughter was declared an inadequate overlord for unspecified reasons, but probably because of her gender, the bakufu decided in favor of Yūtamaru, even though the "maru" suffix in his name indicates that he was still a minor.[90] Not only did the bakufu ruling support the increasingly common practice of denying or restricting female inheritance rights, it also eliminated one claimant on the sole basis of her occupation as a sexual entertainer.

It would be dangerous to assume that this action meant that female entertainers were being deprived of property rights in general. The property in question was the object of a complex dispute that also involved the military land steward rights *(jitōshiki)* to Sashi, a village surrounded by land under the granddaughter's control. She and Yūtamaru had been at odds over the Sashi *jitōshiki* since 1277. While Akyō does not appear to have claimed the *jitōshiki*, the involvement of this very powerful right that carried obligations of military service to the bakufu may have tipped the judgment toward the single male claimant. Somewhat later, in fact, the bakufu prohibited female inheritance in Kyushu, where heavy fighting had taken place in the two Mongol invasions and the need for further defensive measures was anticipated.[91] Considered in this context, the decision in favor of Yūtamaru is not surprising; yet the out-of-hand denial of Akyō's claim and the bakufu edict discriminating against *kugutsu* and *shirabyōshi* suggest that in the arena of property rights, negative attitudes toward the sex trade had begun to make an impact.

As much evidence shows, work in the sex trade did not bar women from the landholding system, the fundamental socioeconomic structure of the day. Those who held land rights were undoubtedly included in the processes of "production," even if not directly engaged in agriculture. The term *shokunin* seems quite appropriate for them. Of course, since authorities were overwhelmingly concerned with landholding questions, landholders appear in documentary sources far out of proportion to their percentage in the population, and we do not know how common such *shokunin* actually were among women in the sex trade.

The meaning of inclusion needs to be reexamined, however. Even unchallenged land rights were not necessarily a mark of power or social acceptance. Not only did they fail to protect their holders from stigma and discrimination, they also curbed once-autonomous groups, settling them physically and obligating them to powerful male patrons and institutions. We do not know if authorities purposely sought such control, but they must have been aware of its value, just as was Masafusa at the turn of the late twelfth century when he contrasted the exotic but domesticated *asobi* with the outlaw, itinerant *kugutsu*.

Some changes in the position of sexual entertainers came from decisions by authorities, some from a general shift in moral perception and social context. To recapitulate: neither the Yōrō code nor subsequent legislation made prostitution illegal; in fact, "prostitution" was apparently not a concept defined in Nara, Heian, or Kamakura law. The contrast with China is instructive. Matthew Sommer has shown that in China prior to the early eighteenth century, prostitution was legally practiced by women of base status, in particular those who belonged to "music households" that performed despised occupations such as entertainment. When a woman of respectable commoner status engaged in prostitution, however, that act was punished as illicit sexual intercourse. Respectable women were expected to follow a moral code that demanded chastity; base people, on the other hand, were exempt from such requirements. In the eighteenth century, most of the distinctions between "good" and "base" people were eliminated and there no longer existed a caste of women who could legally sell their bodies. At that point prostitution per se became a crime.[92]

In Heian Japan, despite laws on the books prohibiting fornication and adultery, female chastity was given little importance. Moreover, occupations such as that of *asobi* could be practiced by women with respectable parentage, and sexual entertainers were not classified as base persons, either in law or in public perception. In the Kamakura period, however, elites began to draw connections between sexual entertainment and base status. Such connections may be found in literary sources such as *Jikkinshō* and in court and bakufu legislation. When *asobi* and *kugutsu* were associated with *hinin;* when the sovereign issued an edict forbidding *nakadachi* to bring together good and base persons; and when Kamakura legislation treated *kugutsu* and *shirabyōshi* as if they were base persons, sexual entertainers were pulled toward a stigmatized, despised status. At the same time, the bakufu was officially promoting concepts of marriage and family that closely resembled those set out in Chinese codes and government ideology. Yet prostitution was neither criminalized nor made the responsibility of a hereditary caste. Japanese concepts of appropriate sexual behavior were still an imperfect match with Chinese moral ideology and family structure.

New Conditions, New Terms, and Changing Definitions

By the middle of the Kamakura period, a flourishing sex trade could be found in various locations—in Kamakura and surrounding Sagami province; in Suruga, Tōtōmi, Owari, and Ōmi along the route from Kamakura to the capital; and in provinces far from either town, such as Shinano, Suō, Bungo, and Hizen.[93] While the *asobi* boat trade continued in operation until at least the 1280s,[94] Kamakura sources say little about Eguchi and Kamusaki after the first decades of the period; one possible reason is that frequent flooding along the Yodo River drove *asobi* elsewhere. In a *Meigetsuki* entry dated 1202/6/6, Teika remarks that *asobi* entertaining his party "wept bitterly" because of the heavy rain.[95] Other traditional locations seem to have declined as well. *Haru no shinsanji,* a travel diary written in 1280, describes the decline of the rest station at Mino Aohaka, famous for *kugutsu* and *asobi:* "In bygone days, the Aohaka rest station was a famous stopping-place, but now there are few houses there, and the *asobi* seem gone as well."[96]

The increasingly critical judgment of the sex trade in the Kamakura period may reflect its spread to new locations and its appeal to new classes of men as customers. The two phenomena were, of course, related: although a few Heian *asobi* could be found elsewhere, most gathered in locations such as those along the Yodo River patronized by retired sovereigns, regents, and provincial governors. Thirteenth- and fourteenth-century documents suggest, however, that the sex trade had begun to reorient itself toward travelers between Heian-kyō and Kamakura, warriors in distant locales such as Kyushu, and the hoi polloi in the capital. Sexual entertainment was evolving from play for a few aristocrats to a service for broad segments of society; as such it may have seemed a threat to authority and order. The numbers of women in the sex trade may have increased as well: even if Eizon's claim to have preached to some seventeen hundred *injo* (lewd women) is exaggerated, it suggests an obvious and disturbing presence.

The definition of sexual entertainers, moreover, broadened to include those who neither sang nor danced. A tale from the mid-thirteenth-century collection *Kokon chomonjū* introduces an *asobi* who is described purely as a prostitute:

> Not long ago, a low-status cleric traveling from Tennōji to the capital was joined on the road by a *yamabushi* [mountain ascetic] and an ironcaster. The three men walked along together, reaching the vicinity of Imazu just as the sun was starting to set. They sought lodgings at the same inn, whose keeper was an *asobi.* When the three guests retired, she retreated to her bedroom and went to sleep as well. After everyone was quiet, the *yamabushi* arose and arranged his hair in a layman's style. The ironcaster was fast asleep.
>
> The cleric had just pretended to go to sleep. As he watched, the *yamabushi* borrowed the slumbering ironcaster's cap and set it on top of his new coiffure. Then he approached the *asobi*'s bedroom and stealthily knocked on her door. She opened it immediately, saying: "Who is it?" The *yamabushi* replied, "I'm a guest at this inn.

I noticed that you had only one kettle instead of [the usual] two at your hearth. I thought you'd certainly like another. Since I'm an ironcaster, I'll make one for you—as payment, say . . ."

The *asobi* thought, "That seems like a good deal." The two of them immediately entered the sleeping room and went to bed together—the *yamabushi* being well versed in the ways of the boudoir. Afterward, leaving the ironcaster's cap on her pillow, he stepped out of the room as if he would return in a moment.

[Upon returning to his own sleeping quarters] the *yamabushi* rearranged his hair so that he looked once more like a mountain ascetic. "I ought to travel with you," he said to his two companions, "but I'm in a rush so I'll be on my way," ignoring their pleas to wait. After he was gone, the ironcaster looked for his cap and was puzzled because he could not find it.

The next morning the *asobi* got up and confronted the ironcaster, demanding: "Where's that kettle you promised me? Let me have it!" The ironcaster vehemently denied any knowledge of the matter. "Don't pretend you don't know what I'm talking about," said the *asobi*. "Here. I've got your cap. Don't think you can pull one over on me by blaming someone else for your doings. Now pay up on the spot!"

The ironcaster shouted furiously, "How can I possibly have promised to make you a kettle? How can you tell such a bald-faced lie?" But the *asobi* refused to listen, saying: "You old goat! Even though you're an old man you have a seven-inch cock and a thrust that would put a younger man to shame!"

Almost without thinking, the ironcaster replied, "Well thank the gods you brought that up! Here, take a look. Is this seven inches long?" When he showed her his tiny penis with its head completely hidden in the foreskin, the *asobi* ran out of the room without a word. Then, laughing in disgust, she bellowed for the entire neighborhood to hear, "It was that *yamabushi!*" The ironcaster, now out of danger, headed off to the capital.[97]

This humorous tale portrays a very different type of *asobi* than the seductive sirens of Masafusa's *Yūjoki* or the women who entertained Go-Toba. No mention is made of *imayō* or any other type of entertainment; the exchange is a simple quid pro quo: sex for a material reward. Instead of a sophisticated seductress of the likes of Michinaga, this *asobi* trades her favors for the promise to make a kettle. She is a sexual professional who caters to common men, providing sexual service as a side business to keeping an inn for ordinary travelers.

The tale is indicative of two developments: a loss of status for *asobi* and a general understanding that the term *"asobi"* includes a wider category of workers in the sex trade. Perhaps this "new" type of *asobi* reflects a change in circumstance, perhaps only in perception: if there were ordinary streetwalkers in Heian times, they were outside the purview of most elite observers and not enough of a threat to public order to arouse concern. A clear picture of the prostitute as one who simply traded in sex did not emerge until the Muromachi period, when brothel prostitutes *(zushikimi)* and streetwalkers *(tachigimi)* plied their trade in habitats called Hell's Corner (Jigoku-ga-Tsuji) and Pussy Alley (Kase-ga-Tsuji).[98] An image of the prostitute—one that cast her as a transgressor—was under construction long before that, however, and some of its raw materials may be found in Heian sources that list *asobi* as beggars or thieves or portray *kugutsu* who seduced men into giving up their wealth. In the Kamakura period, *injo, nakadachi,* and *keisei* cast shadows of transgression on female entertainers. When shorn of its association with the performing arts, the sex trade may have disturbed elites who had once accepted it as a partner of song and dance.

Keisei (castle-topplers) appear in several Kamakura sources, such as the tale in *Uji shūi monogatari* in which a man has sexual intercourse with a *keisei* at a festival-viewing stand along a main street in the capital.[99] Elsewhere the term appears as one name for the unwelcome guests who scandalized the Jissōji monks; in Lady Nijō's narrative, it refers to a pair of *shirabyōshi.*[100] In the Muromachi period, brothel prostitutes were organized under an office referred to as the Keisei no Tsubone,[101] making it clear that by that time at least, *keisei* were seen as prostitutes.

The characters read *keisei* in Japanese appear in Chinese sources as old as the *Book of Odes,* where they denote the seduction of a man in order to bring about his military defeat—in other words, the "toppling of his castle."[102] Unlike the occupational designations *asobi, shirabyōshi,* or *kugutsu,* the term *keisei* has an unmistakably pejorative cast, whether it refers to entertainers, to streetwalkers, or simply to women regarded as promiscuous seducers. The term suggests that men had begun to construct an image of a prostitute who threatened society because she diverted men from serious business such as warfare, land or temple management, and the pursuit of Buddhist enlightenment.

Nakadachi who appeared in thirteenth-century documents as shadowy figures, characters who arranged illicit sexual unions and recruited candidates for prostitution, were well-established brothel managers by the sixteenth century. At one time those in the capital paid a levy to the Seta family, representing the Kebiishi, but in 1528 a document regarding appointment to the Keisei no Tsubone entitled the Koga family to collect the taxes instead.[103] Sixteenth-century *nakadachi* were functionaries in an organized hierarchy, under official control and subject to taxation, and mark a policy to institutionalize and regulate prostitution.

By the late Kamakura period, the discourse on the sex trade had produced an image of the prostitute as a transgressor of social norms. Female entertainers were increasingly cast in that image. Through a variety of means, the women were marginalized, fixed at the bottom of society by the transgressive nature invented for their working lives. Yet authorities only rarely acted against them, attesting to the residual power of their appeal to elite men. Moreover, they could be included in fundamental institutions such as the landholding system and—at the price of their carnality—the Buddhist community of the saved. The contradictions in their lives and in men's views of them suggest the complex ways in which they served and troubled the social order as it moved toward patriarchy.

Conclusion

THE STREET AND BROTHEL prostitutes of Muromachi times are separated from earlier sexual entertainers both by time and by significant conceptual gaps, but the construction of identities as "prostitutes" was rooted in long-term social and economic developments. At the same time, the sex trade itself was changing—expanding geographically, appealing to broader social classes, and in some cases neglecting song and dance in favor of purely sexual functions. Or so it seems. The sources are fragmentary and do not tell us everything; the real "change" may be in what the documents note and not in what actually took place. The most we can say is that the sources reveal developments that were conspicuous and consistent enough to arouse the attention of literate observers and to impel authorities to act.

In her study of prostitution in medieval Languedoc, Leah Otis points out that changes in social structure and cultural values "determine and transform the shape of prostitution in a given society."[1] In the Japanese case, the construction of prostitution was part of conditions and changes in such areas as definitions of marriage, the preservation of order and status as new social classes lay claim to power, and assumptions regarding gender and class hierarchies and the dangers of female sexuality. Some developments in these areas can be traced to late Heian times, but the Kamakura period, with fundamental power alignments under way, was the real locus of change.

In medieval Europe, relations with a prostitute—assumed to be brief, for money, loveless, and unsanctioned by the church—were opposed to the only orthodox form of sexual relations: monogamous marriage. In Heian and to some extent Kamakura Japan, relations with sexual professionals may be considered the logical extension of the aristocracy's polygynous marriage system, in which a man's obligations to his female sexual partners declined in inverse proportion to their social status. Because marriage was a vaguely defined process rather than a fixed social institution, it was difficult to determine which sexual liaisons were acceptable and which were not. Change was under way, but not at all complete, by the end of the Kamakura age—in part a long-term promotion of male rights within the family,[2] in part the result of the bakufu's conscious efforts to manage and reshape family, descent, and inheritance patterns in order to control the way property was distributed and managed. Changing marriage patterns had implications for concepts of transgressive sexual activity on the part of women. While Heian wives were expected to be faithful to their husbands, penalties for adulterous wives were not always severe, and uxorilocal residence provided opportunities to conceal illicit affairs. In the Kamakura period, roots of the virilocal, patriarchal model can be found in bakufu legislation and court decisions, inheritance practices that favored men, and the common usage of categories of transgression such as *mittsū* and *bikkai.* Even with marriage patterns still in flux, bakufu legislation on adultery and widow remarriage drew firmer lines between orthodox and transgressive female sexual activity. As part of this process, distinctions were drawn between women who were sexual professionals and those who were not—for example, the "designated women" and "wives and unmarried women" of the Bungo *shugo*'s order of 1242 regarding *nakadachi.* In some cases, the occupation of sexual entertainer was enough to deny a woman inheritance rights.

The need to maintain order and hierarchy also played an important part in defining sexual transgression and cast an unfavorable light on aspects of the sex trade. The essence of the trade in Heian and early Kamakura times was the mixing of social classes: the women were mostly of low birth in comparison to their aristocratic patrons, who included even retired sovereigns. Go-Shirakawa welcomed *asobi* and *kugutsu* in part, perhaps, because they opened a window for him on a society to which he was otherwise denied access. Go-Toba indulged himself with *shirabyōshi* of "the lowest class," according to his somewhat prissy attendant Fujiwara Teika.[3] Only a few years later, however, an order from the throne complained of sexual liaisons that violated class boundaries, harking back to early-Heian legislation that prohibited marriage between "good" and "base" people. The concept of base status in relation to sexual entertainment appears as well in the bakufu edict of 1267 denying *kugutsu* and *shirabyōshi* inheritance rights granted more "respectable" women. This suggests the beginnings of an alignment between low social and low moral status.

In her analysis of prostitution in the modern United States, Laurie Shrage argues that the commercial sex industry is produced by, and reproduces, certain cultural myths: "the myth of a powerful human sex urge, the myth of male sexual and social dominance, the myth of female pollution through sexual contact, and the myth of the existence of a category of women we variously call 'harlots,' 'whores,' 'prostitutes,' and 'sluts.' " Shrage also suggests that in other cultures commercial sex may be based on other myths entirely—myths that cast sexuality as a civilizing force, or find commercial polyandry desirable, or posit "the sexual artistry, therapy, or wisdom of some women."[4] Although I prefer to use the term "assumption" rather than "myth," I find Shrage's proposition useful for an analysis of sexual entertainment in Heian and Kamakura Japan. What needs to be kept in mind, however, is the changing nature of the assumptions themselves and the simultaneous existence of contradictory ones.

At its high end, the Heian sex trade was fueled by the assumption of aristocratic superiority and allowed both noble men and women to demonstrate that superiority through distributing "gifts" to *asobi*. Shrage argues that in the modern United States, "[a] culturally produced belief in the natural, sexual, and fundamental dominance of men" is evident in the sex industry, which is oriented toward men as consumers.[5] However, the presence of female aristocrats in the "audience" of Heian *asobi* suggests that power relations were based as much on class as on gender.

A tangled set of inconsistent assumptions regarding male and female sexuality helped to shape sexual entertainment and attitudes toward it. Sexual activity was celebrated in folk and shrine religious practice, and sexual desire itself was seen as an irresistible force. In this context developed an open trade in which *asobi* publicly enticed unembarrassed male patrons who—if they needed to justify themselves—could simply point to the overwhelming power of their own desire. The assumption of irresistible male passions even helped to determine the location of the *asobi* boat trade: since male visitors to sacred sites were expected to indulge themselves after a few days' abstinence, *asobi* profitably located themselves along pilgrimage routes.

Somewhat later, assumptions of female bodily pollution and female sinfulness cast suspicion on women and their sexual functions. This gave Buddhist clerics a platform from which to attack sexual entertainers for compromising monastic purity and at the same time presented opportunities to promote the efficacy of their own teachings. Stories that showed "sinful" *asobi* attaining rebirth in paradise or revealing themselves as bodhisattvas depended on characterizing the women as transgressive, even when this assumption was unspoken. Or the assumption could be made explicit and the women openly portrayed as sinners in need of salvation. Specifically, Buddhist storytellers used the assumption of irresistible and pernicious male desire to censure *asobi,* who were accused of willingly tempting men and hindering their enlightenment. Portraying *asobi* as transgressors and then using them to prove religious points took place in the context of broad developments within Kamakura Buddhism—efforts to win adherents and raise funds by casting as wide a net as possible among the populace.[6]

These are some of the ways in which sexual entertainers came to be seen as a corrupting force, threatening male religious practice, the purity of sacred sites, the innocence of "respectable" women forced or lured into the trade, and public order overall. In comparison with developments in Otis' medieval Languedoc, however, changes in the way sexual entertainers were regarded and treated do not seem very substantial. Otis describes a historical process from the twelfth through sixteenth centuries in which prostitution was first largely tolerated, then institutionalized, and finally repressed. We can trace the same process in Japan, but over a longer period of time. Until the end of the medieval age, the sex trade was accepted by most authorities, although often with the caveats and misgivings that eventually contributed to the construction of the sexual entertainer as a prostitute who violated social norms. There was little effort to regulate the trade and none (that I know of) to forbid it in the Heian period; the legislation of Kamakura times was aimed at specific issues such as inheritance and inappropriate recruitment. Institutionalization of professional sexual entertainment began only in the sixteenth century—first with the taxation of some brothels and later with the establishment of licensed quarters by Toyotomi Hideyoshi. However, the sex trade was not actually prohibited throughout the entire country until 1956.[7] Wholesale repression, in other words, was a product of a modern capitalist state that had undergone recent occupation by the U.S. military.

In periods of tolerance or regulation, authorities and elites sometimes make arguments to justify prostitution. Both Saint Augustine and Saint Thomas Aquinas argued against abolishing prostitution on the grounds that it would give rise to uncontrolled sexual passions and abuses.[8] Similar arguments can be found much later in Japan—for example, in early modern and modern times, prostitution was justified by arguments that it channeled male lust and protected "honest" women from rape. The Meiji oligarch Itō Hirobumi even argued that prostitution enabled daughters of poor families to fulfill their filial duties to help their parents;[9] and the "comfort women" system in the countries Japan conquered during the Pacific War was infamously justified as a means of preventing rape. In the Heian and Kamakura periods, in contrast, few if any found it necessary to justify the sex trade—in other words, there was no effort to make excuses for the society that permitted the trade to exist. We cannot say the same, however, for sexual entertainers as individuals: once they were seen as prostitutes, justifying their actions seemed necessary; thus their choice of profession was often explained by the workings of karma.

Yet sexual entertainers were largely placed in an occupational rather than a moral or behavioral category. *Asobi* and other sexual entertainers were regarded not as promiscuous women but as professionals who made a living from a trade that included the sale of sex. Heian and Kamakura sources censured promiscuous women without equating them with sexual entertainers. The two are not confused, even though both are sometimes associated with licentiousness—sometimes signified by the term *irogonomi,* sometimes by combinations with the character *in.* Even Kamakura-period sources such as *Hōnen shōnin eden, Senjūshō,* and *Kaidōki,* which deplore sexual entertainment, refer to it as a trade, though one thought questionable and dangerous.

The defining feature of Heian- and Kamakura-period sexual entertainers (to paraphrase Ruth Mazo Karras) was their professional status: not just that they received payment for sexual play and intercourse, but that they made a living doing so. The features of their profession—how they behaved, how they dressed, what songs they sang and dances they performed—were as significant as their sexual services. The right of some *asobi* to approach high-status men freely—verified explicitly in *Tale of the Heike* as well as implicitly in courtiers' diaries—was one that would have been granted only to a specially defined group with specific skills and professional standards.[10] The erosion of these standards accompanies a shift from a set of entertainment trades that offered sexual services to a system of prostitution with brothels and procurers.

Notes

For a list of abbreviations used throughout the notes, see page 185 of the bibliography.

Introduction

1. In Western languages see Pigeot 2003; Kawashima 2001, pp. 27–119; Pandey 2004; and Marra 1993, pp. 87–95.

2. Otis 1985, p. 2.

3. *Nihon kokugo daijiten,* vol. 8, p. 828.

4. Bell 1994, pp. 1–2.

5. For example, see Hershatter 1997, pp. 34, 278, 507 (n. 41); Mahood 1990, p. 10; Karras 1996, pp. 10–11; Walkowitz 1980, pp. 14–15; and Corbin 1990, pp. 128–129.

6. Karras 1996, p. 10.

7. See the discussion in Tonomura 1997, pp. 159–161 and 418 (n. 92).

8. The term *teraiuru* (to display and sell) is used in *Asobi o miru* and *Fusō ryakki* (Jian 3 [1023]/10/29). In *Shinsarugakuki* (NST, vol. 8, pp. 146–147), Fujiwara Akihira describes an *asobi* as "selling her body" *(mi o urite).*

9. For representative samples of the two positions see Wakita 1982, pp. 93–99; Amino 1984, pp. 172–187; and Amino 1989, pp. 120–121.

10. As pointed out by Terry Kawashima (2001, chaps. 1–2).

11. For a discussion of Toda Yoshimi's views on the *ōchō* society, see the introduction to his article in Piggott 2006, pp. 245 – 247.

12. Jeffrey P. Mass (1992, pp. 158–162) challenges the common perception that in its time the Kamakura warrior administration was called the bakufu.

13. For male-male relations in the late Heian period, see Gomi 1995.

14. Tonomura 1994, pp. 135.

15. There is extensive English-language literature on marriage customs in the Heian period. See, for example, McCullough 1967; Wakita 1984; and Tonomura 1994.

16. See the discussion in Tonomura 1997, pp. 145–153.

17. See Ko, Haboush, and Piggott 2003, pp. 17–18. The article by Sekiguchi Hiroko in the same volume outlines the Chinese (Tang) family paradigm and discusses the degree to which it was accepted in eighth-century Japan.

Chapter 1: Delightful Sirens and Delighted Patrons

1. Imahori 1990, p. 255. The text does not say which circuit was fortunate enough to receive two princesses. The speculation is based at least partly on wordplay: the term

for princess *(himegimi)* and an alternative term for *asobi (yūkun)* both have the same second character. Correspondences of this type were given considerable credence in medieval Japan; see Klein 2002, pp. 26–29.

2. Takigawa 1965, pp. 14–18, 23–27.

3. Fukutō 1990, p. 217; Amino 1984, p. 181.

4. Matsumae 1992, pp. 23–25.

5. Yanagita 1962a, pp. 353–355, 1962b, pp. 293–296, 1963, pp. 486–492; Nakayama 1984b, pp. 469–488.

6. As noted specifically below, my argument draws on the research of Fukutō Sanae (1990) and Sekiguchi Hiroko (1993).

7. *Wamyōshō,* Jinrinbu (Benseisha ed., p. 16).

8. *Man'yōshū,* no. 966.

9. Fukutō 1990, p. 225.

10. Ibid., p. 230; Sekiguchi 1993, vol. 2, pp. 142–143.

11. For example, Takigawa 1965, p. 53.

12. Sekiguchi 1993, vol. 2, pp. 125–126. The term she uses for prostitution is *baibaishun.* Sekiguchi adopts the categories for family structure used by Lewis Morgan and Friedrich Engels; see Sekiguchi 1993, vol. 1, pp. 362–363.

13. Ibid., vol. 2, pp. 146–157. One exception is the *Kokinshū* poet Shirome, identified in several sources as the daughter of the *waka* poet and fourth-rank court official Ōe Tamabuchi.

14. Yamazaki port in Yamashiro, at the juncture of Yamashiro, Kawachi, and Settsu provinces. "Kaya" is also sometimes used to refer to the general area of the Yodo basin pleasure quarters.

15. *Asobi o miru. Yūkō,* the term I have translated as "vagabond," is made up of the first two characters of the four-character term for *ukareme.* See the Glossary.

16. From the notes to the SNKBT version of *Asobi o miru* (p. 61). For an alternative English translation see Dawson 1993, p. 33 (bk. 9, no. 18): "I have never come across anyone who admires virtue as much as he admires sexual attraction."

17. Sakamoto was at the foot of Mt. Hiei. I have not identified Kawakami, but since the term means "upriver" it may be the same as Yukitoki's Kaya, located upstream on the Yodo.

18. As noted in the thirteenth-century tale collection *Jikkinshō,* a poem by a Kamusaki *asobi* Miyagi appeared in the court poetry collection *Goshūishū,* the compilation of which was ordered in 1078. It is possible that the two were the same person. Kokarasu, Yakushi, and Naruto were apparently also famous *asobi,* but I cannot identify them further.

19. *Shinsarugakuki,* NST, vol. 8, pp. 146–147. For a *kanbun* version see GR, vol. 9, pp. 347–348. In preparing this translation, I benefited from the scholarship of Joan Piggott, who has completed an annotated translation of the entire *Shinsarugakuki* text.

20. *Ishinhō,* vol. 7, pp. 2576, 2602 (Levy and Ishihara 1989, pp. 36, 48–49, 56).

21. The correspondence appears in *Unshū shōsoku,* nos. 117–118 (Shigematsu, ed., 1982, pp. 173–174). The source is a collection of epistolary models; Jacqueline Pigeot (2003, pp. 19–20) thinks they were fictive letters, but I am not convinced. While the correspondents in this and other exchanges are not clearly identified, the author of the first letter signs himself "Chief of the Right Capital Fujiwara." This was a position held for some years by Akihira.

22. *Sarashina nikki* (Horiuchi, ed., 1977, pp. 87–88; see Morris 1971, p. 115). See also Morris for an English translation of the entire diary.

23. Besides his descriptions of *asobi* and *kugutsu,* discussed here, he also wrote essays on the popular dance called *dengaku* (see Raz 1985, pp. 297–298) and on fox spirits (see Smits 1996). For biographical information on Masafusa, see Ury 1993.

24. Ōsone Shōsuke, introduction to *Yūjoki,* NST, vol. 8, p. 153.

25. A *kakikudashi* version annotated by Ōsone Shōsuke appears in NST, vol. 8, pp. 154–156. For a *kanbun* version see GR, vol. 9, pp. 323–324. For an alternative English translation see Kawashima 2001, pp. 295–297.

26. The wording here is similar to that at the beginning of Yukitoki's essay.

27. Masafusa's geography is a little shaky. Since Eguchi is in Settsu, the traveler has already crossed the border into that province. Kamusaki and Kashima are located along the Yodo River tributary, the Kamusaki.

28. This sentence alludes to two poems in Chinese, one by Ōe Yukitoki in *Shinsen rōeishū* (GR, vol. 19, p. 332) and the other by Fujiwara Akihira in *Honchō mudaishi,* bk. 3, no. 173 (Honma, ed., 1992, vol. 1, p. 387). In Watanabe Shōgo's reading (1979, p. 34), the river is crowded with various types of boats, some fishing boats, others those of peddlers trying to hawk their wares to the customers of the *asobi.*

29. Ōsone Shōsuke (NST, vol. 8, p. 445, n.) suggests that Miyashiro may be the same person as Miyagi in *Shinsarugakuki*—in other words, a famous *asobi* of the past described in a text predating Masafusa's by several decades. This would mean that Masafusa was describing a situation from some time ago. However, names or portions of them may have been passed down from generation to generation, much the same as in the kabuki theater of later times.

30. Literally, "Hyaku Dayū . . . is one name for a roadside guardian deity."

31. An entry dated Enkyū 5 (1073)/2/28 in the history *Fusō ryakki* confirms Go-Sanjō's religious pilgrimage but does not mention the *asobi.*

32. *Shinsen,* literally deities (kami) and wizards.

33. A Han-dynasty figure who served as a cook at a banquet that was short of supplies.

34. This is a tentative interpretation of *tanzen* (hurried adjustment?).

35. This is a tentative interpretation of an obscure passage.

36. This passage follows Ōsone's tentative interpretation (NST, vol. 8, p. 156, n.), which substitutes the character *marui* (round) for *kyū* (nine) in the *kanbun* text. The

phrase *marui bun,* according to Ōsone, could refer to a circle divided in half, used as an emblem of some sort, perhaps the moons noted in *Eiga monogatari;* see below.

37. Ruch 1990, p. 527.

38. A Shirome appears in *Yūjoki.* We cannot assume the two were the same.

39. *Yamato monogatari,* no. 146 (Tahara 1980, pp. 92–93).

40. *Nihon kiryaku,* Eien 2 (988)/9/16. A *koku* is a measure of capacity that varied in size.

41. *Denryaku,* Chōji 2 (1105)/3/7.

42. *Nihon kiryaku,* Chōhō 2 (1000)/3/26.

43. For example, see *Nakatsukasa naishi no nikki,* 1285 (SNKBT, vol. 51, p. 232).

44. Foard 1982, p. 239.

45. Hur 2000.

46. For aspects of aristocratic pilgrimage in the Heian period, see Moerman 1997 and Ambros 1997.

47. Moerman 1997, p. 350.

48. *Nihon kiryaku,* Chōhō 2 (1000)/3/26.

49. *Sakeiki,* Chōgen 4 (1031)/9/24. See also Narahara 1998, pp. 15–16.

50. *Eiga monogatari,* bk. 31, no. 23. The source dates the visit Chōgen 4 (1031)/9/26.

51. See Pandey 2004, p. 63. In the Giō chapter of *Heike monogatari,* a *shirabyōshi* exercises this privilege at the home of Taira Kiyomori. In English see McCullough 1988, p. 31.

52. *Uji kanpaku Kōyasan gosankeiki,* Eishō 3 (1048)/10/11.

53. Text unclear.

54. The *asobi* were probably singing *imayō* on religious themes.

55. *Uji kanpaku Kōyasan gosankeiki,* Eishō 3 (1048)/10/20.

56. *Denryaku,* Chōji 1 (1104)/9/18–25; *Chōshūki,* Gan'ei 2 (1119)/9/3–6.

57. Identified in Toyonaga 1989, p. 408.

58. A playful interpretation of this phrase, based on puns, might read: "Amid melodies from the past . . ."

59. Names are rendered inconsistently because of Morotoki's carelessness or copyists' errors.

60. For Hirata see Takeuchi 1975–1976, vol. 1, p. 27, B3. I have not been able to identify the others.

61. The printed *Shiryō taisei* version initially uses the name Sonson but later calls her Sonboshi; a handwritten copy calls her Sonboshi throughout. Pigeot (2003, p. 54) suggests that this sentence reads: "The *chōja* (Kinju), Sonboshi, and Kumano were already on our boat." I think, however, that Sonboshi (or Sonson) was the Eguchi *chōja.*

62. The implications of the letter of transfer and the seal are not entirely clear and will be discussed later in the chapter.

63. Literally, Shibo 子母. I think that this is an error for [Son]boshi [孫]母子.

However, Jacqueline Pigeot's reading (2003, p. 51) is "Toto, daughter and mother *(fille et mere).*"

64. *Chōshūki,* Gen'ei 2 (1119)/9/3–6.

65. *Taiki,* Kyūan 4 (1148)/3/18–22.

66. A *kakikudashi* version annotated by Ōsone Shōsuke appears in NST, vol. 8, pp. 158–159. For a *kanbun* version see GR, vol. 9, pp. 324–325. For alternative English-language versions of this essay see Law 1997, p. 97, and Kawashima 2001, pp. 297–298.

67. Similar phrasing is used in the *Han shu* (vol. 94, pt. 1, *Xiong-nu chuan,* no. 64:1) to describe the Xiong-nu. See also *Nihon kokugo daijiten,* vol. 6, p. 309 *(suisō o ou).*

68. According to Law (1997, p. 98), these were spectacular performers who appeared first as lynxes, then transformed themselves into flounders and then into dragons.

69. This may mean "one hundred (myriad) kami," or it may refer to Hyaku Dayū, as Ōsone Shōsuke suggests (NST, vol. 8, p. 159, n.).

70. The story appears in writings attributed to Lie Zi, an ancient Chinese philosopher. See *Resshi,* p. 245. The *imayō* collection *Ryōjin hishō* takes the first two characters of its title, "dust on the rafters," from this story.

71. These are types of songs performed by *kugutsu.* I have not been able to identify all of these terms; *saibara* are Japanese lyrics sung to Chinese melodies, *tauta* are rice-planting songs, *kamiuta* are shrine songs, *saouta* are boatmen's songs, *fuzoku* are regional folk songs from the eastern provinces, and *zushi* are Buddhist incantations. See Kim Kwon 1986, p. 272, for some of these.

72. One example of a source that associates the two is *Konjaku,* bk. 13, no. 44.

73. Pigeot 2003, pp. 119, 162–163.

74. *Heike monogatari,* Giō chapter; McCullough 1988, pp. 30–37.

75. *Meigetsuki,* Shōji 2 (1200)/2/5; Kennin 1 (1201)/3/21; Kennin 2 (1202)/6/2 (1202)/7/17, 19.

76. Watanabe 1979, p. 44. The confiscated rights were *jitōshiki,* generally the prerogative of warriors.

77. *Meigetsuki,* Kennin 2 (1202)/6/2. See also Pigeot 2003, p. 190.

78. Watanabe 1979, p. 86.

79. *Eikyoku* is a category that includes *imayō* along with *rōei* (Chinese and Japanese poems set to music), *kagura* (shrine music), *saibara,* and *fuzoku.*

80. *Azuma kagami,* Bunji 3 (1187)/2/25; Kenkyū 1 (1190)/10/18; Kennin 1 (1201)/6/1; Kanki 1 (1229)/4/17.

81. *Sumiyoshi mōde,* GR, vol. 18, p. 554.

82. For Muro see *Hōnen shōnin eden,* vol. 34, 5th *dan* (ZNE, vol. 2, p. 211; NEZ, vol. 13, p. 127).

83. Otis 1985, p. 2.

84. Identification unclear. Both Horiuchi Hideaki (*Sarashina nikki,* 1985, p. 11, n.)

and Ivan Morris (1971, p. 47) think that Kohata was a famous *asobi* of the past; but no such name appears in accounts such as those of Masafusa or Akihira.

85. *Sarashina nikki,* Horiuchi, ed., 1985, pp. 11–12 (Morris 1971, pp. 47–48).

86. *Sarashina nikki,* Horiuchi, ed., 1985, p. 18 (Morris 1971, pp. 51–52).

87. For travel between capital and provinces, see Toda 2006, pp. 259–264.

88. *Chōshūki,* Gen'ei 2 (1119)/9/3.

89. *Azuma kagami,* Ninji 2 (1241)/11/29.

90. *Genji monogatari,* SNKBT, vol. 20, p. 116 (Seidensticker 1976, p. 284; Tyler 2001, vol. 1, p. 292).

91. For example, see *Taiki,* Kyūan 4 (1148)/3/22; *Chōshūki,* Gen'ei 2 (1119)/9/6; and *Unshū shōsoku,* no. 118.

92. *Gō shidai,* vol. 1, p. 341 (Hachijūshima *matsuri*). This is a photocopy of a handwritten manuscript; for a printed copy of the pertinent passage, see *Koji ruien,* 1968, vol. 46, p. 869.

93. Fukutō 1990, p. 232.

94. Toyonaga 1989, p. 408.

95. Ibid., p. 409.

96. *Azuma kagami,* Kenkyū 1 (1190)/10/29. Ōi also appears in *Heiji monogatari* (SNKBT, vol. 43, pp. 227–228) as Yoshitomo's mistress.

97. Narahara 1998, pp. 19–22.

98. Takigawa 1965, p. 306.

99. Toyonaga 1989, p. 409.

100. *Chōshūki,* Gen'ei 2 (1119)/9/6.

101. *Heiji monogatari,* SNKBT, vol. 43, pp. 227–228.

102. Iinuma Kenji (1990, pp. 46–47) discusses the instability of marriages at the time, and Wakita Haruko (1993, p. 86) points out women's insecure position within the Heian system.

103. *Sarashina nikki,* Horiuchi, ed., 1985, p. 11 (Morris 1971, p. 47).

104. *Saibara,* NKBZ, vol. 25, pp. 137–138 (no. 22, *kubo no na,* terms for female genitals).

105. *Azuma kagami,* Kenryaku 2 (1212)/11/14.

106. *Imayō* established a 7–5 metric text and quatrain form in the mid-twelfth century, according to Konishi Jin'ichi (1991, vol. 3, p. 350). Extant lyrics do not always follow this form, however.

107. Several editions of *Ryōjin hishō* are available. Many of its lyrics are translated in Kim 1994, which analyzes *Ryōjin hishō* and the *imayō* genre.

108. Kim 1994, pp. 14–15.

109. *Ryōjin hishō,* no. 375 (Kim 1994, p. 10). Shimae is probably Mishimae, located along the banks of the Yodo River, which furnished lodging for pilgrims on their way to Shitennōji and nearby sacred sites (*Nihon rekishi chimei taikei,* vol. 28:1, p. 161).

110. Kim (1994, p. 153) suggests that these two lyrics may depict exploitation of *asobi.*

111. *Ryōjin hishō,* no. 475 (Kim 1994, p. 118).
112. *Ryōjin hishō,* no. 408 (Kim 1994, p. 153).
113. See Kim 1994 and Kim Kwon 1990.
114. *Ryōjin hishō,* no. 380 (Kim 1994, p. 10).
115. Pigeot 2003, pp. 69–73.
116. Kawashima 2001, pp. 40–46.
117. Toyonaga 1989, p. 406.
118. Amino 1984, pp. 181–182.
119. See Wakita 2001, p. 73.
120. *Ryōjin hishō,* no. 473; Watanabe 1979, pp. 26–27. See also Kim 1994, p. 147.
121. *Ryōjin hishō,* no. 388; Watanabe 1979, p. 146. See also Kim 1994, p. 117.
122. *Uji shūi monogatari,* bk. 12, no. 24; Mills 1970, p. 377.

Chapter 2: Defining Transgression

1. For the changing rights of women to inherit, hold, and bequeath property, see Mass 1989 and Tonomura 1990.
2. Ruch 1990, pp. 501–502.
3. Perhaps the best-known proponent of this view in regard to sexual norms is Katsumata Shizuo; see Katsumata 1979. His arguments are examined later in this chapter.
4. Yoshie 2005, pp. 442–445; Yoshida 1988, p. 248.
5. For a discussion of this issue that focuses on the fourteenth century, see Tonomura 1999, pp. 145–153.
6. Yoshie 1986, pp. 4–5; Yoshida 1988, pp. 247–248; among others. For an English-language discussion of this topic, see Yoshie 2005, pp. 439–440. For Kamakura patterns in relationship to inheritance, see Tonomura 1990, pp. 607–608.
7. Yoshie 1986, pp. 3–4.
8. Sumi 1983, p. 84.
9. Yoshida 1976, pp. 156; 1988, pp. 240–242, 245–246; Yoshie 2005, p. 443.
10. *Genji monogatari,* esp. chaps. 9 ("Aoi") and 18 ("Matsu no kaze"); *Shinsarugakuki,* NST, vol. 8, pp. 135–137; *Konjaku,* bk. 30, no. 12.
11. Takamure 1963, pp. 67, 106–107. The wife's home is defined as one that she inherited from her parents or established on her own.
12. Tonomura 1990, pp. 605–606.
13. The following is based on Sekiguchi 1993, vol. 1, pp. 136–167.
14. *Nihon shoki,* Yūryaku 2/7 (Aston 1972, pt. 1, p. 338); Sekiguchi 1993, vol. 1, p. 141.
15. *Nihon shoki,* Yūryaku 3/4 (Aston 1972, pt. 1, p. 341); Sekiguchi 1993, vol. 1, p. 138.
16. Not all scholars agree that celibacy was required for female shamans. Countering arguments by Yoshie Akiko are presented in the next chapter.

17. Sekiguchi 1993, vol. 1, p. 167; 2003, pp. 39–40.
18. Sekiguchi 1993, vol. 1, p. 125.
19. *Hossō shiyōshō,* GR, vol. 6, p. 92.
20. *Ritsuryō, kōryō* (regulations on taxation and residence units), no. 25.
21. *Nihon kōki,* Enryaku 18 (799)/6/4.
22. *Ryō no gige,* section on *ko* (taxation units).
23. As Hitomi Tonomura (1994, p. 133) points out in regard to *Konjaku.*
24. For changes in the conjugal relationship see Yoshie 2005, pp. 442–445.
25. Tonomura 1994, pp. 151–154.
26. Faure 1998, pp. 144–206.
27. KI, vol. 4, pp. 54–56 (Doc. 1966).
28. *Uji shūi monogatari,* bk. 13, no. 14 (Mills 1970, pp. 396–397, no. 174).
29. *Uji shūi monogatari,* bk. 14, no. 1 (Mills 1970, pp. 397–398, no. 175).
30. A provincial governor was too low in status to expect his daughter to become a consort of the sovereign.
31. Apparently a euphemism for the woman's letter.
32. *Konjaku,* bk. 30, no. 3.
33. *Yamato monogatari,* no. 105 (Tahara 1980, pp. 63–64).
34. *Konjaku,* bk. 20, no. 7.
35. In one *Konjaku* tale the rapist is criticized, not because he raped his victim, but because he stole her clothing (Tonomura 1994, p. 150).
36. *Kokon chomonjū,* no. 329.
37. For a discussion of the relationship between *avadāna* and Japanese tales, see Dykstra 1983, pp. 9–20.
38. Rotman 2003.
39. *Konjaku,* bk. 26, no. 21; bk. 29, no. 22; bk. 30, no. 8.
40. *Nihon ryōiki,* bk. 3, no. 16 (Nakamura 1973, pp. 242–243).
41. *Nihon ryōiki,* bk. 2, no. 2 (Nakamura 1973, pp. 160–161).
42. Yoshie 2005, p. 443.
43. A linear measure; a very rough equivalent would be a foot.
44. *Kokon chomonjū,* no. 330.
45. *Konjaku,* bk. 13, no. 12.
46. Literally, "Mara's coming! Mara's coming!" Mara (Skt.: Māra) is the demon king who tried to tempt the Buddha, but the word is also a euphemism for the penis.
47. *Kokon chomonjū,* no. 552.
48. Wakita 1982, pp. 78–79.
49. *Konjaku,* bk. 17, no. 28; bk. 17, no. 29.
50. *Uji shūi monogatari,* bk. 3, no. 15 (Mills 1970, pp. 206–209).
51. Quoted in Wakita 1982, p. 78.
52. *Goshūi ōjōden,* bk. 3, no. 24; Pigeot 2003, pp. 129–130.
53. Tonomura 1994, p. 135, referring to *Konjaku,* bk. 26, no. 21.

54. *Kokon chomonjū,* no. 551.

55. *Konjaku,* bk. 24, no. 14. For a discussion of this and other *Konjaku* episodes on the same theme, see Hoshino 1998, pp. 261–268.

56. *Zenge iki,* quoted in the mid-Heian *Seiji yōryaku,* KST, vol. 28, pp. 711–712. *Zenge iki* was compiled by Miyoshi Kiyoyuki (847–918), probably in the later years of his life.

57. *Konjaku,* bk. 29, no. 13.

58. *Konjaku,* bk. 29, no. 14.

59. Katsumata 1979, p. 8; Hoshino 1998, p. 267.

60. *Konjaku,* bk. 26, no. 22.

61. *Hōshi* is a term that often refers to a man who has taken clerical vows but continues to live as a layman.

62. *Kokon chomonjū,* no. 339. Hachiman had been adopted as the tutelary deity by the Seiwa Genji, Yoshiie's family, and was considered a martial kami.

63. HI, vol. 2, pp. 672–674 (Doc. 495).

64. *Azuma kagami,* Shōji 2 (1200)/4/8.

65. *Taiki,* Kōji 1 (1142)/6/7.

66. Tonomura 1999, p. 139.

67. *Azuma kagami,* Shōji 2 (1200)/4/10.

68. *Azuma kagami,* Shōji 2 (1200)/4/8.

69. See Tonomura 1999, p. 140.

70. King Zhuang reigned 614–591 BCE. According to the ancient Chinese text *Shuo yuan,* the retainer, who had had too much to drink at a royal banquet, pulled off the robe of the king's favorite. She yanked off the cords of the culprit's cap and showed it to the king. But he, not wanting to humiliate the retainer, had all the others pull off their cords and did not punish the culprit. (*Kokon chomonjū,* ed. Nishi and Kobayashi, vol. 1, p. 406, n. 7.)

71. *Kokon chomonjū,* no. 331.

72. Wakita 1982, p. 78.

73. *Meigetsuki,* Kenryaku 2 (1212)/6/6. See Katsumata 1979, p. 31 (n. 11).

74. *Torikaebaya monogatari,* SNKBZ, vol. 39, pp. 331–333 (bk. 3, no. 9) (Willig 1983, pp. 120–121).

75. Takamure 1963, pp. 167–169.

76. *Hyakurenshō,* Angen 1 (1175)/int. 9/29; Angen 2 (1176)/2/20.

77. *Meigetsuki,* Karoku 2 (1226)/6/23.

78. *Meigetsuki,* Karoku 1 (1225)/2/13.

79. Takamure 1963, pp. 167–168.

80. *Azuma kagami,* Jōgen 3 (1209)/12/11.

81. The Utaishō was Minamoto Yoritomo.

82. *Goseibai shikimoku,* clause 34; in *Kamakura bakufu hō,* pp. 48–49. The more common modern reading for *bikkai* is *mikkai.*

83. Tsuikahō, clause 292; in *Kamakura bakufu hō,* pp. 174–175. The term *hyakushō* is hard to define; there is no general agreement on when the term took on its meaning as cultivator. In the ninth through thirteenth centuries, according to Thomas Conlan, "the term *hyakushō* came to designate provincials who possessed surnames and were entrusted with *shiki* office, or who were holders of local public office"; the first reference to the term designating cultivators is from the late thirteenth century (Conlan 2003, pp. 253–254). The electronic version of the dictionary *Kojien,* however, cites an example from the twelfth-century *Konjaku monogatarishū* in which *hyakushō* refers to cultivators *(nōmin).* The implication that the *hyakushō* could afford to pay fines indicates that they had some economic status in provincial society.

84. See the argument in Tonomura 1999, pp. 138–139.

85. Kasamatsu 1981, p. 408.

86. *Jingikan kudashibumi,* nos. 13–14.

87. Tonomura 1999, p. 142.

88. Kasamatsu 1981, p. 409.

89. Tonomura (1999, p. 142) points out that the primary concerns of the bakufu judicial process were property transmission and the social order.

90. Katsumata 1979, pp. 3–12.

91. *Shasekishū,* bk. 9, no. 12 (Morrell 1985, pp. 241–242).

92. *Shasekishū,* bk. 7, no. 1 (Morrell 1985, p. 198).

93. Tonomura 1994, p. 138.

94. *Nihon shoki,* Keikō 4/2/11 (Aston, pt. 1, p. 192).

95. *Azuma kagami,* Kennin 2 (1202)/8/15.

96. Tonomura 1994, p. 138.

97. Several of these examples were cited by Katsumata, suggesting that he regards them as exceptions.

98. *Azuma kagami,* Ninji 2 (1241)/6/16.

99. KI, vol. 9, pp. 55–57 (Doc. 6266).

100. *Azuma kagami,* Kangen 2 (1244)/7/20, 8/3.

101. Michitoki is identified as Kyōren's son in one place in the document and his grandson in the other. In context, however, it is more reasonable to suppose that he was Kyōren's son.

102. *Goseibai shikimoku,* clause 24; in *Kamakura bakufu hō,* p. 16.

103. KI, vol. 15, pp. 47–49 (Doc. 11167); Seno 1998, pp. 274–275.

104. See Mass 1989, pp. 90–93.

105. As mandated by law. See *Kamakura bakufu hō,* pp. 226–227 (Tsuikahō, no. 435).

106. KI, vol. 37, pp. 358–360 (Doc. 29167).

107. The discussion in this section is based on Seno 1998.

108. *Konjaku,* bk. 30, no. 13.

109. See Tonomura 1990, p. 618.

110. *Goseibai shikimoku,* clause 24; in *Kamakura bakufu hō,* p. 16. As Seno (1998, p. 269) points out, the children who benefited from property confiscation were usually not those of the widows in question.

111. For examples see Seno 1998, pp. 269–273.

112. Seno 1998, p. 276; *Kamakura bakufu hō,* p. 116 (Tsuikahō, no. 121).

113. Seno 1998, p. 277; Tonomura 1990, pp. 602–603, 614; in *Kamakura bakufu hō,* p. 275 (Tsuikahō, no. 597).

114. Seno 1998, p. 277.

115. See Mass 1989, chap. 4; and Tonomura 1990, pp. 614, 622.

116. *Goseibai shikimoku jū,* ZZGR, vol. 7, p. 224 (discussed in Faure 1998, pp. 177–178). Standard reference works do not attempt to date this commentary, which includes notes added by various parties postdating the main text. The latter cannot have been written prior to 1253, since it cites legislation promulgated in that year. The oldest known copy dates from the early Muromachi period.

117. KI, vol. 8, p. 328 (Doc. 5979); *Kamakura bakufu hō,* p. 136 (Tsuikahō, no. 185).

118. See Hotate 1990, p. 236.

119. *Kamakura bakufu hō,* pp. 225–227, 229 (Tsuikahō, nos. 433–435, 443–444).

120. *Kamakura bakufu hō,* pp. 226–227 (Tsuikahō, no. 435).

Chapter 3: Sacred Sex or Sexual Pollution?

1. For the poem see *Tōhokuin shokunin utaawase,* no. 5, GR, vol. 28, p. 443. The illustration can be found in Amino 1992, p. 93.

2. For example, see Namihira 1987, pp. S65–S72; Ohnuki-Tierney 1987, pp. 140–144.

3. Sakurai 1974, pp. 220–221.

4. Yamaguchi 1987, p. S7.

5. For example, Tonomura 1994, pp. 133–134.

6. Matsumae 1991, p. 343.

7. Ibid., pp. 338–339.

8. Yoshie 2004, pp. 160–161.

9. Ibid., p. 102.

10. Saeki 1987, pp. 27–28.

11. *Masurao,* a term that can also be represented by the characters for *dayū,* as in Hyaku Dayū. Generally the term can also mean a powerful man.

12. Similar, perhaps, to the cords of the caps mentioned in *Kairaishiki.*

13. These are rituals to worship kami and buddhas, respectively.

14. *Honchō seiki,* Tengyō 1 (938)/9/2; *Fusō ryakki,* Tengyō 2 (939)/9/2. Both sources are histories compiled at the end of the Heian period. One of the dates is obviously a mistake. The versions are identical except for two characters; I have followed the *Honchō seiki* version in both cases because it makes more sense.

15. *Unshū shōsoku,* no. 19.
16. Fukutō 1995, p. 29.
17. For example, see Hotate 1998, p. 263.
18. Yanagita 1962a, pp. 353–355; 1962b, pp. 293–296; 1963, pp. 486–492.
19. Orikuchi 1971a, p. 292.
20. Nakayama 1984a, pp. 76–81; 1984b, pp. 472–473.
21. Nakayama 1984b, p. 474. *Shōmonki* ("Shinnō senshō," in Kajihara, ed., 1976, vol. 2, p. 82) uses the following characters: 昌伎, probably read *shōgi,* a combination that does not appear in dictionaries; however, scholars have made the reasonable assumption that the term is equivalent to 娼妓 or 倡伎 (for example Kajihara Masaaki, who annotated the edition cited above [vol. 2, p. 86]). If that is the case, then the oracle was an entertainer and could have been an *asobi.*
22. Nakayama 1984b, pp. 482–483. See also Kim 1994, pp. 7, 123; Ōwa 1993, p. 176; and Yamakami 1980, p. 159.
23. Gorai 1982, pp. 103–118.
24. Saeki 1987, pp. 35–41.
25. Ibid., pp. 41–43.
26. Ibid., pp. 15–27.
27. Orikuchi 1971b, pp. 192–193.
28. Blacker 1986, pp. 104–108.
29. Yamakami 1980, p. 156.
30. Kuroda 1998, pp. 236–240; Nishiguchi 1987, p. 59.
31. *Gaki zōshi,* 2nd *dan,* in *Nihon no emaki,* vol. 7, pp. 4–5.
32. Yamakami 1980, pp. 8, 123–152.
33. Borgen 1986, pp. 319–320. Michizane, then minister of the right, was ousted as a chief adviser to Daigo Tennō (r. 897–930) by the northern (regents') branch of the Fujiwara family, in a coup that firmly established Fujiwara dominance of the court. Michizane was named governor-general of the court outpost at Dazaifu in far-off Kyushu, an appointment regarded at the time as tantamount to exile.
34. Yamakami 1980, p. 146. The Shidara no Kami incident was probably related to the movement for deification of Michizane; see Borgen 1986, pp. 319–320.
35. Nishiguchi 1987, pp. 226–227.
36. *Ruijū sandai kyaku,* KT, vol. 25, p. 590; Yamakami 1980, p. 136.
37. Yamakami 1980, p. 163.
38. *History of the Kingdom of Wei,* in Tsunoda and Goodrich 1951, p. 13.
39. *Nihon shoki,* Jingū (Chūai) 9 (Aston 1972, pt. 1, pp. 224–253).
40. Yoshie 2004, pp. 128, 161.
41. Yoshie 1996, pp. 8–20; the quotation appears on p. 20.
42. *Ruijū sandai kyaku,* KT, vol. 25, pp. 31–35; Sekiguchi 1993, vol. 1, pp. 140, 146; Nishiguchi 1987, p. 38.
43. Saeki 1987, p. 18; Yamakami 1980, pp. 158–159.

44. *Ruijū sandai kyaku,* KT, vol. 25, p. 21.
45. Yamakami 1980, pp. 158–159.
46. Nakayama 1984b, p. 473.
47. *Shinsarugakuki,* NST, vol. 8, p. 134.
48. Ibid., p. 139.
49. Yanagita 1963, p. 489.
50. Fukutō 1995, p. 72.
51. Kim 1994, p. 5.
52. Kim 1994, pp. 6–7.
53. Yamakami 1980, pp. 153–167; Ōwa 1993, pp. 170–186.
54. Kawashima 2001, pp. 98–112.
55. *Ryōjin hishō,* no. 265 (Kim 1994, p. 6); *Ryōjin hishō,* no. 324 (Kim 1994, p. 51).
56. *Ryōjin hishō,* no. 273 (Kim 1994, p. 123).
57. Nakayama 1984b, pp. 482–483; Ōwa 1993, pp. 176–177; Kim 1994, p. 123.
58. Yamakami 1980, p. 163. Several locations have the name Matsugasaki, and commentators have not been able positively to identify the place in the poem.
59. *Ryōjin hishō,* no. 541. For a discussion and alternative translation see Kim 1994, p. 123.
60. *Ryōjin hishō,* no. 559; Ōwa 1993, p. 180; Yamakami 1980, p. 159.
61. *Ryōjin hishō,* no. 360 (Kim 1994, pp. 123–124).
62. *Ryōjin hishō,* no. 362 (Kim 1994, pp. 122–123).
63. *Ryōjin hishō,* no. 364. For alternative translations see Kim 1994, p. 7, and Ruch 1990, p. 521.
64. Nakayama 1984b, p. 483; Ōwa 1993, pp. 183–184.
65. Ruch 1990, pp. 521–523.
66. For example, see KI, vol. 12, pp. 128–129 (Docs. 8732–8733, dated 1261).
67. Ōwa 1993, p. 182. Gorai (1982, p. 130) has the same view.
68. See Pigeot 2003, p. 234.
69. Ruch 1990, p. 526.
70. Sekiguchi 1993, vol. 2, pp. 165, 198 (n. 191).
71. One exception is Michele Marra (1993). I will take up his argument in the next section when I discuss the Buddhist textual sources on which it is based.
72. Nishiguchi 1987, pp. 23–24.
73. Iinuma 1990, p. 40.
74. Ibid., pp. 58–59.
75. Nishiguchi 1987, p. 36.
76. Ibid., p. 58; *Kitano tenjin engi,* vol. 8, in *ZNE,* vol. 15, p. 41.
77. *Gaki zōshi,* 2nd *dan,* in *Nihon no emaki,* vol. 7, pp. 4–5.
78. *Yūzū nenbutsu engi,* 9th *dan,* in ZNE, vol. 21, pp. 68–69.
79. Taira 1990, pp. 79–83.
80. Fukutō 1995, p. 29.

81. *Nihon ryōiki,* bk. 3, no. 18 (Nakamura 1973, pp. 245–246).
82. *Konjaku,* bk. 14, no. 26.
83. Tonomura 1994, p. 151.
84. HI, vol. 9, pp. 3501–3507 (Doc. 4599).
85. Nishiguchi 1987, pp. 37–39.
86. KI, vol. 12, pp. 128–129 (Docs. 8732–8733).
87. KI, vol. 21, pp. 4–5 (Doc. 15732).
88. *Denryaku,* Chōji 1 (1104)/9/25.
89. *Uji kanpaku Kōyasan gosankeiki,* Eishō 3 (1048)/10/11.
90. *Taiki,* Kyūan 4 (1148)/3/18 (see Chapter 1).
91. *Konjaku,* bk. 14, no. 3 (Ury 1979, pp. 93–96).
92. *Azuma kagami,* Kenkyū 4 (1193)/5/15.
93. *Jikkinshō,* bk. 10, no. 50.
94. *Kasugasha kiroku,* vol. 1, p. 369 (Kangen 4 [1246]/5/25).
95. KI, vol. 13, pp. 416–422 (Doc. 10298); the text for the direct quotation appears on p. 421. *Dengaku* was a form of popular entertainment derived from rice-planting songs and dances.
96. See Faure 1998 and Faure 2003.
97. Faure 1998, pp. 43, 121, 136, 158.
98. *Hōbutsushū,* SNKBT, vol. 40, pp. 345–346.
99. According to Terry Kawashima, this version of the tale illustrates in particular the teaching of the *Daihōshaku Sūtra* that even one who does not merit salvation can attain it through upholding the sutra. See Kawashima 2001, pp. 113–118, for a discussion and compete translation of the story.
100. Imahori 1990, pp. 207–208.
101. *Kojidan,* no. 291.
102. *Kojidan* (ed. Kobayashi Yasuharu) 1981, vol. 1, p. 304 (n. 9).
103. For a discussion of nondualism see LaFleur 1983, pp. 20–25.
104. Marra 1993, pp. 87–95; the quotation appears on p. 88.
105. Kawashima 2001, p. 52.
106. *Senjūshō,* bk. 6, no. 10 (no. 58). *Senjūshō* purports to be the work of the poet Saigyō (1118–1190), but it probably dates from the mid-Kamakura period. See the introduction to the translation by Jean Moore (1986, p. 127).
107. *Jikkinshō,* bk. 3, no. 15. For a discussion of various versions of the Shōkū-*asobi* story see Kawashima 2001, pp. 53–57. For a full translation of the *Jikkinshō* version see Kawashima 2001, pp. 301–302.
108. *Hōnen shōnin eden,* vol. 34, 5th *dan* (ZNE, vol. 2, p. 211; NEZ, vol. 13, p. 127); *Hosshinshū,* no. 41; and *Eguchi* (NKBZ, vol. 33, p. 268), respectively.
109. For a translation of *Kudenshū* see Kim Kwon 1986; the relevant passage appears on p. 297.
110. *Hosshinshū,* no. 41.

111. Imahori 1990, pp. 194–275.
112. Ibid., pp. 200–201 and passim.
113. *Hōnen shōnin eden,* vol. 34, 5th *dan* (ZNE, vol. 2, p. 211; NEZ, vol. 13, p. 127). See the frontispiece illustration.
114. Imahori 1990, p. 255.
115. Ibid., p. 256.
116. *Senjūshō,* bk. 5, no. 11 (no. 44) (Moore 1986, pp. 164–166).
117. *Senjūshō,* bk. 9, no. 8 (no. 118) (Moore 1986, pp. 168–171); LaFleur 1983, pp. 69–79.
118. *Eguchi,* NKBZ, vol. 33, pp. 260–270. For a discussion and partial translation of the play see LaFleur 1983, pp. 71–74.
119. Kelly 1984, pp. 40–41.
120. Faure 1998, p. 131.
121. Rublack 1999, p. 162.
122. *Kongō busshi Eizon kanshingaku shōki,* Kōan 8 (1285)/8/13; in the Nara Kokuritsu Bunkazai Kenkyūjo ed., p. 61. The source does not state that these women were sexual professionals, but given their location in Harima, where the *asobi* boat trade was still in operation, I suspect that they were.
123. *Towazugatari,* bk. 5 (SNKBT, vol. 50, pp. 213–214; Brazell 1973, p. 228). We cannot know, of course, whether or not Nijō embellished this episode to make a point, or even if it ever occurred at all.
124. Nijō was forced into a sexual relationship with the retired sovereign Go-Fukakusa, who initially raped her with the collusion of her father. She had several affairs with other men, including one that resulted in a pregnancy; Go-Fukakusa seems to have taken a prurient interest in her relationships with other men and in fact sometimes encouraged them. See Brazell 1973, pp. xvi–xvii.

Chapter 4: Constructing the Prostitute

1. *Jikkinshō,* bk. 3, no. 15. See also Kawashima 2001, pp. 53–57; for an English translation of this entire episode, see pp. 301–302.
2. Kawashima 2001, intro., chaps. 1–2.
3. Geremek 1987, p. 2.
4. Amino 1984, pp. 172–187.
5. Wakita 1982, pp. 93–99; 2001, p. 170.
6. Kuroda 1995, pp. 221–222.
7. Amino 1984, pp. 184–185; Wakita 1982, p. 96. The document appears in KI, vol. 11, pp. 156–157 (Doc. 7992).
8. KI, vol. 11, p. 140 (Doc. 7960). The reverse sides of this document and Tamaō's deposition were used as paper for the Shinfukuji copy of *Wamyō ruijushō* (Wakita 2001, p. 141), suggesting that the documents themselves had been transmitted and

stored together. This increases the likelihood that the two Ishikuma were in fact the same person. Documents accidentally preserved in this way are known as *uramonjo;* for the significance of this method of preservation for understanding the provenance and context of documents, see Toda 2006, p. 259.

9. Wakita 2001, p. 141.

10. Amino 1989, pp. 120–121.

11. Toyonaga 1989, p. 406.

12. Otis 1985, p. 9.

13. Karras 1996, pp. 13–31.

14. Karras 1996, p. 20; Otis 1985, p. 102. Otis (1985, p. 56) also notes that municipal brothels were sometimes unprofitable and were operated as a public service.

15. Amino 1989, p. 115.

16. Fukutō 1990, p. 238.

17. As we shall see, there may have been informal exploitation in the sense of demanding bribes.

18. Shortly I discuss these two women of ancient China. Hotate Michihisa (1990, p. 237) suggests that the characters 卞蔡 in the text should be 卞后, Byanhou.

19. KI, vol. 4, p. 27 (Doc. 1921).

20. Ishii 1977, p. 12.

21. *Utsunomiya ke shikijō,* no. 57; Pigeot 2003, p. 204.

22. Amino 1986, p. 20. The characters for *nakadachi* in the sixteenth-century source were different from those in the thirteenth-century source, but they probably designated members of the same profession, as Amino argues. (See the Glossary.)

23. Hotate 1990, p. 237; *Ritsuryō* (Yōrō code), miscellaneous law no. 27; Council of State memorial to the throne dated Enryaku 8 (789)/5/18, in *Ruijū sandai kyaku,* KT, vol. 25, p. 522.

24. Hotate 1990, p. 236.

25. KI, vol. 8, p. 328 (Doc. 5979); *Kamakura bakufu hō,* p. 136 (Tsuikahō, no. 185).

26. As suggested by Hotate (1990, p. 236).

27. *Azuma kagami,* Kenkyū 4 (1193)/5/15.

28. *Meigetsuki,* Kennin 2 (1202)/6/10, Karoku 2 (1226)/1/24.

29. Tonomura 1996, p. 161.

30. Wakita 2001, pp. 141–142; KI, vol. 11, p. 140 (Doc. 7960). The document is actually undated, but *Kamakura ibun* compiler Takeuchi Rizō has placed it between two other documents dated 1256/2.

31. Wakita 2001, p. 142.

32. This phrase was used by Gail Hershatter (1997, p. 8) to describe guidebooks, memoirs, and tabloid accounts of twentieth-century Chinese prostitutes. Some of the Heian accounts of the sex trade are remarkably similar to the far more recent material that Hershatter discusses.

33. *Genji monogatari,* SNKBT, vol. 20, p. 116. For other translations of this passage

see Kawashima 2001, p. 71; Seidensticker 1976, p. 284; and Tyler 2001, vol. 1, p. 292. According to Seidensticker, this is the only reference to *asobi* in the text.

34. *Takakura-in Itsukushima gokōki,* SNKBT, vol. 51, p. 14. See also Pigeot 2003, p. 241.

35. *Zoku kojidan,* bk. 2, GR, vol. 27, pp. 651–652. See also Pigeot 2001, p. 184. The source does not date the quotation, and there is no guarantee that it is accurate—in other words, it may express the views of the compiler in the early Kamakura period, not those of Moronaga himself.

36. *Kaidōki,* Jōō 2 (1223)/4/16.

37. *Tōkan kikō,* no. 16. According to n. 25 in the SNKBT version (vol. 51, p. 121), the *asobi*'s poem alludes to a poem in *Wakan rōeishū.* See also Pigeot 2003, pp. 47–48.

38. *Shasekishū,* bk. 7, no. 1 (Morrell 1985, pp. 196–197).

39. See the discussion in Pigeot 2003, pp. 220–226. Yoshitsune was the brother of the shogun Minamoto Yoritomo and a heroic general of the Genpei War that brought Yoritomo to power. The two brothers later clashed and Yoritomo pursued Yoshitsune, who was eventually forced to commit suicide.

40. *Wamyōshō,* Benseisha ed., pp. 15–16.

41. Amino 1984, p. 183.

42. KI, vol. 10, pp. 106–108 (Doc. 7093, Kenchō 1 (1249)/7/23); *Kamakura bakufu hō,* pp. 226–227 (Tsuikahō, no. 435).

43. Pandey 2004, pp. 62–64.

44. *Sarashina nikki,* ed. Horiuchi Hideaki, p. 12 (Morris 1971, p. 47).

45. *Meigetsuki,* Genkyū 2 (1205)/2/11.

46. *Azuma kagami,* Genryaku 1 (1184)/4/20; Pigeot 2003, p. 211.

47. *Kamakura bakufu hō,* pp. 226–227 (Tsuikahō, no. 435). See Chapter 2 for a detailed discussion of the law.

48. This is actually a conflation of two consecutive episodes in the earlier text: *Yamato monogatari,* nos. 145–146 (Tahara 1980, pp. 91–93).

49. *Jikkinshō,* bk. 10, no. 50. *Gosenshū* was ordered compiled in 951, *Goshūishū* in 1078, *Shikashū* in 1144, *Shinkokinshū* in 1205, and *Kokinshū* in 905, all under auspices of the throne. *Jikkinshō* also contains versions of the tales of Toneguro (bk. 10, no. 51) and of Shōkū and the Kamusaki *chōja* (bk. 3, no. 15).

50. The port had been under Tōdaiji control since the late twelfth century. See Hiraoka 1980, p. 399.

51. KI, vol. 41, pp. 110–111 (Doc. 31804), pp. 120–121 (Doc. 31836). The two petitions contain slightly different lists of participants, although both list the *yūkun* at the bottom. In one petition, they are "the military steward *(jitō)* of the east and the west, the custodian *(azukaridokoro),* and everyone from the residents *(domin)* down to the *yūkun*"; in the other, they are "the *jitō* of the east and west plus the proprietor *(ryōke)* and the residents from the *hyakushō* down to the *yūkun.*" The port community was obviously an extensive one that included cultivated fields and generated enough income to be divided between two *jitō.*

52. *Suwa daimyōjin ekotoba,* ZGR, vol. 3:2, p. 530.

53. *Daijōin jisha zōjiki,* Kanshō 4 (1463)/11/23.

54. *Hou han shu,* vol. 5, pp. 1180; vol. 11, pp. 3270–3271.

55. *Honchō mudaishi,* nos. 77–83. The term "ceaseless wanderers" is from Burton Watson's translation of poem 77 by Fujiwara Tadamichi (1097–1164) in Keene 1955, p. 166. The other two quotations are from poem 78 by Fujiwara Sanemitsu (active c. 1090–1130s). For the trope of the aging *kugutsu* see Kawashima 2001, pp. 41–42.

56. Kawashima 2001, pp. 40–41.

57. *Makura no sōshi* (Pillow book), no. 84.

58. *Chūyūki,* Eikyū 2 (1114)/4/6.

59. *Konjaku,* bk. 28, no. 27.

60. *Meigetsuki,* Kenryaku 2 (1212)/10/5–9.

61. Amino 1984, pp. 175–179.

62. Wakita 2001, pp. 87–88, 169–170.

63. For the seminal work on this topic see Amino 1975.

64. Amino 1980, pp. 147–150. Amino reproduces the extant portions of the document.

65. Law 1997, pp. 100–105.

66. Keirstead 1995, p. 85.

67. Pigeot 2003, pp. 80–82.

68. *Asobi o miru.*

69. *Fusō ryakki,* Jian 3 (1023)/10/29.

70. Karras 1996, pp. 89–90.

71. *Konjaku,* bk. 13, no. 44. The other tale is bk. 19, no. 22.

72. Ury 1979, p. 2.

73. KI, vol. 6, pp. 9–12 (Doc. 3580); Amino 1984, p. 176.

74. KI, vol. 27, pp. 140–143 (Doc. 20429). The women are literally described as "women who have put on the train"—in other words, those who have undergone their coming-of-age ceremony.

75. KI, vol. 13, pp. 416–422 (Doc. 10298).

76. *Shōgen ninen inrakusho;* Pigeot 2003, p. 197; Tonomura 1996, p. 163.

77. *Masukagami,* ed. Aoyama Naoharu, pp. 113–114.

78. *Azuma kagami,* Ninji 2 (1241)/11/29.

79. *Hokke metsusaiji nenjū gyōji,* in *Yamato koji taikan,* vol. 5, pp. 85–88 (Genkō 2 (1322)/2/25, 2/28, 3/3, 6/28, 11/2). I am grateful to Prof. Lori Meeks of the University of Southern California for introducing me to this source. Tanaka Minoru, in his comment on this document, suggests the connection between Eizon and Hokkeji activities on behalf of the *asobi.* Both inns mentioned here were at rest stations along the Tōkaidō route between Kyoto and Kamakura. Tanaka locates Kagami in Mino province, but maps show that it was actually in Ōmi. The text itself locates Hashimoto in Owari province but it was actually in Tōtōmi.

80. Amino 1984, p. 178; KI, vol. 11, p. 110 (Doc. 7912).

81. A *chō* is a unit of square measure equivalent to a little less than one acre.

82. Wakita 2001, pp. 93–94.

83. Amino 1984, pp. 176–177.

84. KI, vol. 10, pp. 106–108 (Doc. 7093).

85. Wakita 2001, pp. 92–93.

86. KI, vol. 11, pp. 156–157 (Doc. 7992) (Tamaō); *Hizen Matsuuratō Ariura monjo,* pp. 42–43 (1228 land sale).

87. *Kōmyōji monjo,* vol. 2, pp. 254–255 (Doc. 407, Engen 3 (1338)/int. 7/21), pp. 256–257 (Doc. 410, Kōkoku 3 (1342)/5); Amino 1984, pp. 182–185.

88. Mass 1989, pp. 101–106.

89. *Kamkura bakufu hō,* pp. 226–227 (Tsuikahō, no. 435).

90. KI, vol. 18, pp. 231–234 (Docs. 13730–13731).

91. Mass 1989, p. 101.

92. Sommer 2000, chap. 6.

93. See, for example, *Azuma kagami,* Ninji 2 (1241)/11/29 (Kamakura), Kennin 1 (1201)/6/1 (Sagami), Kenkyū 1 (1190)/10/18 (Tōtōmi), Bunji 3 (1187)/2/25 (Shinano); KI, vol. 13, pp. 416–422 (Doc. 10298, 1268, Suruga), vol. 6, pp. 9–12 (Doc. 3580, 1227, Suō), vol. 8, pp. 327–329 (Doc. 5979, 1243, Bungo), vol. 18, pp. 231–234 (Docs. 13730–13731, 1279, Hizen); *Hokke metsusaiji nenjū gyōji* (Ōmi, Tōtōmi).

94. *Nakatsukasa naishi nikki,* SNKBT, vol. 51, p. 232.

95. Watanabe 1979, p. 86; *Meigetsuki,* (1202)/6/6.

96. *Haru no shinsanji,* no. 43, NKBZ, vol. 48, p. 375.

97. *Kokon chomonjū,* no. 549.

98. Amino 1989, p. 121; Gotō 1984, pp. 170–171. Gotō (p. 173) argues that the term *kase* (clam shell) in Kase-ga-Tsuji is slang for the female genitals, but another possible interpretation for the term, based on the verb *kasegu,* is "working for a living."

99. *Uji shūi monogatari,* no. 160 (bk. 12, no. 24) (Mills 1970, p. 377).

100. *Towazugatari,* bk. 2, SNKBT, vol. 50, p. 112. The incident is dated in the eighth month of 1277. Karen Brazell (1973, p. 117) translates the term as "entertainers," but "prostitutes" is probably more to the point, as Hitomi Tonomura indicates (1997, p. 159).

101. Kitakōji 1964, pp. 38–39.

102. Morohashi 1955–1960, vol. 1, p. 914 (no. 1038:66).

103. Amino 1986, p. 20. The document is reproduced in Kitakōji 1964, pp. 38–39.

Conclusion

1. Otis 1985, p. 3.

2. Ko, Haboush, and Piggott 2003, p. 17.

3. *Meigetsuki,* Kennin 2 (1202)/7/19.

4. Shrage 1994, p. 141.

5. Ibid., p. 133.

6. For an examination of this process see Goodwin 1994.

7. It was prohibited at certain times in some of the domains in the Tokugawa period. On the Kaga domain see Leicester (forthcoming).

8. Otis 1985, pp. 12, 23.

9. Garon 1997, p. 102.

10. *Heike monogatari,* Giō chapter (McCullough 1988, p. 31). See also Pandey 2004, p. 63.

Glossary

This glossary includes specialized terms related to sexual entertainment; legal, religious, and common terms related to sexual norms; and selected personal and place names. It omits terms in common use in English-language textbooks on Japanese history, as well as those mentioned only once or twice in this book and unrelated to its main theme.

akugyō 悪行: wicked act, referring to brother-sister incest.

Aohaka 青墓: a rest station along the Tōsandō highway in Mino province, known for the *asobi* and *kugutsu* who performed at the inn there.

arukimiko 歩き巫: itinerant shamans, usually female.

asobi 遊女: Heian- and Kamakura-period sexual entertainers who specialized in singing popular songs and performing for the aristocracy. Many set up shop in port towns and used small skiffs to approach travelers' boats.

azukaridokoro 預所: a local landholder on a private estate (*shōen*), often the one who had commended the land to the proprietor in the first place; or the on-site custodian who represented the proprietor.

baibaishun 売買春: Sekiguchi Hiroko's term for prostitution.

baishō no onna 売笑の女: Orikuchi Shinobu's term for prostitute (a woman who sells smiles).

baishun 売春: a modern term for prostitution.

bettō 別当: an administrator; *bettō* of temples were often appointed by the government and were not necessarily resident monks of the temples in question.

bikkai 密懐: term used in the Kamakura bakufu's Jōei formulary of 1232 and in other documents to refer to illicit intercourse, usually adultery; also read *mikkai.*

chimata no kami 岐の神: a guardian figure set up along highways and at crossroads.

chōja 長者: the leader of an occupational group, such as *asobi. Chōja* appear frequently in references to sexual entertainment at inns along major highways; *asobi chōja* are mentioned in *Yūjoki* and *Chōshūki.*

danshu 団手: payment for the services of *asobi*, according to *Yūjoki.*

dengaku 田楽: dances originally performed at agricultural rituals; later performed by professionals at temples and elsewhere.

dōsojin 道祖神: a guardian figure set up along highways and at crossroads.

Eguchi 江口: Yodo River port in Settsu province where *asobi* gathered; perhaps the most famous of the pleasure districts in Heian and Kamakura times.

Gagakuryō 雅楽寮: under the *ritsuryō* codes, the bureau in charge of music and dancing in the palace.

gaki 餓鬼: a hungry ghost depicted in Buddhist lore and paintings. Hungry because they have tiny throats and huge bellies, *gaki* occupy the next-to-lowest position in the *rokudō* 六道, the six realms in which creatures can be born.

gōkan 強姦: the legal term for rape in both the eighth-century Yōrō code and the thirteenth-century Jōei formulary.

gokenin 御家人: vassals ("housemen") of the Kamakura bakufu.

goryō 御霊: spirits of the dead. In the Heian period, elaborate ceremonies (*goryōe* 御霊会) were held to propitiate angry *goryō*, who, it was feared, would attack their still-living enemies.

hajime 祖: a term used in *Yūjoki* for the leader of an *asobi* group.

hare 晴れ: ritual purity; sacrality. Anthropologists use this term, along with *ke* (ordinary) and *kegare* (polluted), to indicate the position of a particular person, object, event, or condition along the axis of purity and pollution.

himegimi 姫君: princess. The fact that the second character of this term is the same as the second character of *yūkun* (*asobi*) inspired an early theory (in *Hōnen shōnin eden*) that *asobi* originated as princesses.

hinin 非人: low-status persons who performed jobs such as construction labor and burying the dead.

Hirota Jinja 広田神社: a shrine in Settsu province that attracted many aristocratic pilgrims. *Asobi* stationed themselves along the route to Hirota and Sumiyoshi shrines.

hisoka ni aitotsugu 窃相嫁: to have secret sexual relations.

hoka no otto o totsugu 嫁他夫: to have intercourse with a man other than one's husband.

hōshi 法師: a Buddhist cleric; the term often refers to a low-status cleric or one who has a wife and family.

Hyaku Dayū 百大夫: kami revered by *asobi* and *kugutsu*; a type of *dōsojin* or *chimata no kami.*

Hyaku Kami 百神: a term that appears in *Kairaishiki* as the deity worshipped by *kugutsu*; probably another name for Hyaku Dayū.

hyakushō 百姓: provincial residents of some status; in the Kamakura period, the term may also refer to cultivators.

ie 家: the patrilineal stem family, which developed as the norm in Japan in the later medieval period.

imayō 今様: popular (literally, modern) songs performed for aristocratic patrons by *asobi* and *kugutsu. Imayō* lyrics ranged from sutra verses to witty descriptions of street life.

in 淫, 婬: licentiousness.

inbon 淫奔: term used in *Wamyō ruijushō* for the "licentious" sexual activities of *asobi* and *yahochi*.
injo 婬女: lewd women, probably sexual professionals; Eizon's term for some Harima province women to whom he ministered.
irogonomi 色好み: romance or sexual pleasure; or one skilled in romance or fond of sexual pleasure. The term was not necessarily used pejoratively.
irogonomi no ie 色好みの家: a brothel, according to an *Azuma kagami* reference.
Jigoku-ga-Tsuji 地獄辻: Hell's Corner; a brothel location in Muromachi-period Kyoto.
jitō 地頭: military stewards appointed to *shōen* by the Kamakura bakufu. Their job was to collect taxes, police the estate, and keep it under the purview of the bakufu. A *jitōshiki* 地頭職 refers to the right to this position, along with appropriate income from the estate.
kaihō 懐抱: embrace (implies sexual intercourse).
Kamegiku 亀菊: a *shirabyōshi* mistress of the retired sovereign Go-Toba.
kamunagi 巫: a shaman. (See *miko*.)
Kamusaki (Kanzaki) 神崎: a port famous for its *asobi*; in Settsu province on the Yodo River tributary the Kamusaki.
kan 奸, 姦: violation, generally a sexual one. (See *gōkan, wakan*.)
kannagi-asobi 巫遊 (reading uncertain): a figure in *Shinsarugakuki*. The term probably indicates one who sings and dances for the kami, but it can be interpreted as shrine-prostitute or shaman-entertainer.
Kase-ga-Tsuji 加世辻: Pussy Alley; a brothel location in Muromachi-period Kyoto.
Kashima 蟹島: a Settsu province port across the river from Kamusaki; also famous for *asobi*.
kataraitoru 語取: to seduce.
Kaya (or Kayō) 河陽: Yamazaki port in Yamashiro province, on the upper reaches of the Yodo River; famous for its *asobi*.
ke 褻: ordinary, everyday (as opposed to *hare* and *kegare*). (See *hare*.)
Kebiishi 検非違使: the royal police force, under the direction of the court. The main jurisdiction of the Kebiishi was the capital, but it also had authority elsewhere, for example in certain port towns.
kegare (*kegasu*) 汚れ, 穢れ (汚す, 穢す): ritual pollution (to pollute). (See *hare*.)
keisei 傾城: "castle-toppler"; pejorative term for sexual entertainers that casts them as prostitutes.
Keisei no Tsubone 傾城局: in a 1528 document, the agency in charge of taxing and regulating brothels.
kimidomo 君ども: a term for *asobi* that appears in the thirteenth-century *Tōkan kikō*.

kodoneri 小舎人: a low-ranked official in the service of the Kurōdodokoro (court secretariat).

kokugaryō 国衙領: agricultural lands under the direct control of the provincial governor (late Heian period and later). These lands were often managed as if they were *shōen*.

kugutsu 傀儡 (子): a puppeteer; a sexual entertainer originally belonging to a puppeteer troupe. In the late Heian period, *kugutsu* women entertained guests at inns, offering both song and sexual favors.

kuni no miyatsuko 国造: originally hereditary provincial officials. After the Taika reform of 645, the *kuni no miyatsuko* were made responsible for ritual matters only.

kunjo 君女: a term for *asobi* that appears in the thirteenth-century *Kaidōki*.

kusemai 曲舞: singers and dancers who performed to the beat of a drum; *kusemai* included men as well as women.

maotoko 間男: lover ("in-between man").

mi o urite 身をうりて: to sell one's body. A term used in a vignette about an *asobi* in the eleventh-century *Shinsarugakuki*.

miko 巫, 巫女, 御子: a shaman, often female. (See *kamunagi*.)

mippu 密夫: lover (secret spouse).

mitsu 密: secret, clandestine.

mitsugi 密儀: secret sexual affair.

mittsū 密通: illicit intercourse, especially adultery. The term appears in the eighth-century *Nihon shoki* and in a few Heian sources; by Kamakura times it is a common term for adultery.

mokudai 目代: the on-site representative of a provincial governor, who often served in absentia. In the *Konjaku* episode in which a *mokudai* appears, however, he seems to be functioning more as a scribe.

monoimi 物忌: a female ritualist at a shrine. The term can also refer to various types of ritual avoidance.

mune 宗: a term used in *Yūjoki* for the leader of an *asobi* group.

Muro 室: a port in Harima province famous for its *asobi*. The story of Hōnen preaching to the *asobi* (in *Hōnen shōnin eden*) takes place at Muro.

muro 無漏: a Buddhist term indicating a condition undefiled by worldly phenomena and passions. In a *Senjūshō* tale, the homonyms Muro and *muro* are used to indicate the Tendai teaching of nonduality.

myō 名: the unit of taxation on agricultural land.

myōshu 名主: a local land overseer who had the responsibility for paying the taxes on a particular plot of land on a *shōen*.

Naikyōbō 内教坊: office in charge of female entertainment (dancing and singing) in the palace in Nara and Heian times.

nakadachi, nakōdo 中媒: go-between, procurer (thirteenth-century sources).

nakadachi, nakōdo 仲人: go-between, procurer (sixteenth-century source).
nan'in 男淫: a woman's sexual intercourse with a man. The term appears in two paired tales in *Konjaku monogatarishū.*
nenbutsu 念仏: most commonly, the recitation of the name of Amida Buddha, thought to result in salvation for the reciter. The term can also mean contemplation of a buddha or recitation of another buddha's name.
ōchō kokka 王朝国家: the court-centered polity. In the mid-Heian period, the development of private landholding patterns and offices that were not specified in the law codes began to erode the *ritsuryō* polity. *Ōchō* politics were dominated by high-ranking courtiers with substantial landholdings and access to the throne.
Ōi 大炊: a *chōja* at the inn at Aohaka; the mistress of Minamoto Yoshitomo, she appears in *Azuma kagami* and *Heiji monogatari.*
ōjōden 往生伝: Buddhist tales of rebirth in paradise, especially by those who revered the *Lotus Sutra* or recited the name of Amida Buddha.
oni 鬼: a demon generally depicted with fangs and horns. *Oni* are known to eat people and commit other horrendous deeds.
reiroku 例禄: *roku* is the salary paid to a court official or functionary; in *Gō shidai* (eleventh century), *reiroku* is used for payment to *asobi.*
ritsuryō 律令: laws and regulations. The term generally refers to the eighth-century Taihō and Yōrō law codes, which were modeled on those of Tang China.
ritsuryō kokka 律令国家: Japanese governmental organization based on the eighth-century codes. The *ritsuryō kokka* took shape in the Nara period but began to disintegrate after early Heian times.
ryōke 領家: a *shōen* proprietor, usually an aristocratic individual or a temple or shrine.
saibara 催馬楽: Japanese lyrics set to Chinese (*gagaku*) melodies.
sekkai 窃会: clandestine meeting.
setsuwa 説話: an exemplary tale, often with religious flavoring. Many *setsuwa* collections were compiled in the Heian and Kamakura periods.
shajin, toneri 舎人: a low-level official or retainer of a noble.
shiki 職: an officially recognized right to position or income. On a *shōen*, those who possessed *shiki* had rights to income from the land.
shinsen 神仙: kami and wizards; a reference in *Yūjoki* to *asobi.*
shirabyōshi 白拍子: a sexual entertainer who specialized in dancing and singing. In the late Heian and Kamakura periods, *shirabyōshi* became the lovers of powerful men such as Taira Kiyomori and the retired sovereign Go-Toba.
shirabyōshi bugyōnin 白拍子奉行人: in the Kamakura period, the man in charge of recruiting *shirabyōshi* to entertain the retired monarch.
Shirome 白女: an *asobi* or *ukareme* who entertained the retired sovereign Uda, according to the tenth-century poem-tale *Yamato monogatari.*

Shitennōji 四天王寺: a temple in Settsu province said to have been founded in 623 by Prince Shōtoku. It was also known as Tennōji. In the Heian period, it was a popular pilgrimage destination.

Shō Kannon 小観音: an *asobi* who was patronized by Fujiwara Michinaga at the turn of the eleventh century.

shōen 荘園: privately held estates with multiple tenures. Superior rights to produce from *shōen* lands were held by members of the aristocracy and temples and shrines; rights were also held by their on-site representatives, by local managers, and, in the Kamakura period, by *jitō* as representatives of the bakufu.

shokunin 職人: a person of skill, especially an artisan or performer.

shugo 守護: a province-level officer responsible for liaison between the bakufu and its vassals in an entire province.

shuku 宿: an inn, often one located at a rest station along a major highway, where *asobi* or *kugutsu* performed; also an area where people of low or "special" status resided.

Sonboshi 孫母子: apparently the Eguchi *chōja* in *Chōshūki*.

suisan 推参: the privilege of approaching a high-status person without an invitation.

Sumiyoshi Jinja 住吉神社: a shrine in Settsu province that attracted many aristocratic pilgrims. *Asobi* stationed themselves along the route to Sumiyoshi and Hirota shrines.

tachigimi 立君: streetwalkers (Muromachi period).

Takahama 高浜: a port on the Yodo River where *asobi* gathered.

tanin no tsuma o bikkai 密懐他人妻: to secretly embrace another man's wife.

tanzen 湍繕: meaning unclear; possibly "hurried adjustment" (*Yūjoki*).

tentō 纏頭: rewards to singers and dancers.

teraiuru 衒ひ売る: to display and sell. The term is used in *Asobi o miru* (tenth century) and *Fusō ryakki* (twelfth century) to refer to the sale of sexual services by *asobi*.

totsugu 嫁ぐ: to marry virilocally; to have intercourse.

tsuma o okasu 妻を犯す: to violate someone else's wife.

tsumi fukaki mi 罪深き身: a body immersed in sin; a term used in the early Kamakura-period tale collection *Hosshinshū* by Kamo no Chōmei.

tsumi ni shizumite 罪に沈みて: to be mired in sin; a term used in the twelfth-century *Ryōjin hishō kudenshū* by the retired sovereign Go-Shirakawa.

tsūzu 通ず: to penetrate sexually.

Uji 宇治: a port on the Uji River south of Heian-kyō; the location of Byōdō-in, a temple that attracted pilgrims; and a place where *asobi* gathered.

uji 氏: a lineage or extended kinship group based on bilateral principles. The dominant form of kinship organization in early Japan, it was gradually replaced in medieval times by the *ie* or patrilineal stem family.

ukareme 遊行女児: itinerant female banquet entertainers. They often entertained at provincial headquarters during the Nara period. Many were literate, and some have poems in the *Man'yōshū*. They were probably predecessors of the *asobi*.

uneme 采女: women from the provinces chosen to serve in the palace. In one order from the throne reproduced in *Ruijū sandai kyaku*, the *uneme* were female attendants at Izumo shrine.

wakan 和姦: consensual sexual violation (e.g., fornication or adultery). A term used in both the Yōrō and the Jōei codes.

wayo 和与: a compromise settlement in a land dispute.

yahochi 夜発: a type of sexual entertainer or prostitute who appears in two mid-Heian sources, *Wamyō ruijushō* and *Shinsarugakuki*.

yūkō 遊行: vagabond; a reference to *asobi* in the tenth-century *Asobi o miru*.

yūkō no onna 遊行之女: itinerant women; a reference to *asobi* in the late-Heian-period *Fusō ryakki*.

yūkun 遊君: another term for *asobi*.

yuzuribumi 譲文: document transferring rights or property.

zaigō fukaki mi 罪業深き身: a body immersed in sin, according to the Noh play *Eguchi*.

zaigō omoki mi 罪業重き身: a body burdened with sin, according to the early-fourteenth-century *Hōnen shōnin eden*.

zushikimi 辻君: brothel prostitutes (Muromachi period); also pronounced *tsujigimi*.

Bibliography

Abbreviations

GR *Gunsho ruijū* 群書類従. 29 vols. Zoku Gunsho Ruijū Kanseikai, 1928–1934.

HI *Heian ibun* 平安遺文. Ed. Takeuchi Rizō 竹内理三. 13 vols. Tōkyōdō Shuppan, 1963–1968.

KI *Kamakura ibun, komonjo hen* 鎌倉遺文, 古文書遍. Ed. Takeuchi Rizō 竹内理三. 46 vols. Tōkyōdō Shuppan, 1971–1995.

KST *Shintei zōho kokushi taikei* 新訂増補国史大系. Ed. Kuroita Katsumi 黒板勝美. 66 vols. Yoshikawa Kōbunkan, 1929–1967.

NEZ *Nihon emakimono zenshū* 日本絵巻物全集. Ed. Tanaka Ichimatsu 田中一松. 24 vols. Kadokawa Shoten, 1958–1969.

NJR *Nihon joseishi ronshū* 日本女性史論集. Ed. Sōgō Joseishi Kenkyūkai 総合女性史研究会. 10 vols. Yoshikawa Kōbunkan, 1997–1998.

NKBT *Nihon koten bungaku taikei* 日本古典文学大系. 100 vols. + index. Iwanami Shoten, 1957–1967.

NKBZ *Nihon koten bungaku zenshū* 日本古典文学全集. 51 vols. Shōgakukan, 1970–1976.

NST *Nihon shisō taikei* 日本思想大系. 67 vols. Iwanami Shoten, 1970–1982.

SNKBT *Shin Nihon koten bungaku taikei* 新日本古典文学大系. 100 vols. to date. Iwanami Shoten, 1989–.

SNKBZ *Shinpen Nihon koten bungaku zenshū* 新編日本古典文学全集. 88 vols. to date. Shōgakukan, 1994–.

ST *Zōho Shiryō taisei* 増補史料大成. 48 vols. Rinsen Shoten, 1980.

ZGR *Zoku gunsho ruijū* 続群書類従. 71 vols. Zoku Gunsho Ruijū Kanseikai. 1872–1929.

ZNE *Zoku Nihon no emaki* 続日本の絵巻. Ed. Komatsu Shigemi 小松茂美. 21 vols. Chūō Kōronsha, 1990–1993.

ZST *Zōho zoku shiryō taisei* 増補続史料大成. Ed. Takeuchi Rizō 竹内理三. 51 vols. Rinsen Shoten, 1967–1982.

ZZGR *Zokuzoku gunsho ruijū* 続続群書類従. 16 vols. Kokusho Kankōkai, 1906–1909.

Reference Works

Koji ruien 古事類苑. 60 vols. Koji Ruien Kankōkai, 1931–1936.
Kōjien 広辞苑. Electronic version of the fifth edition. Iwanami Shoten, 1999.
Morohashi Tetsuji 諸橋轍次. *Dai kanwa jiten* 大漢和辞典. 13 vols. Taishūkan Shoten, 1955–1960.
Nihon kokugo daijiten 日本国語大辞典. 10 vols. Shōgakukan, 1972–1976.
Nihon rekishi chimei taikei 日本歴史地名大系. 50 vols. to date. Heibonsha, 1979–.

Primary Sources

Asobi o miru 見遊女 (Seeing *asobi*). An essay by Ōe Yukitoki 大江以言, probably dated toward the end of the tenth century. Included in vol. 9 (Shijo 詩序 pt. 2, no. 238) of *Honchō monzui* 本朝文粋 (Choice literary selections of our realm), a collection of Chinese-language essays compiled by Fujiwara Akihira 藤原明衡. Ed. Ōsone Shōsuke 大曽根章介, Kinpara Tadashi 金原理, and Gotō Akio 後藤昭雄. Vol. 27 of SNKBT, 1992.
Azuma kagami 吾妻鏡 (Mirror of the east). The official chronicle of the Kamakura bakufu, covering the years 1180–1266. Compiled between the second half of the thirteenth century and the beginning of the fourteenth century. *Zen'yaku azuma kagami* 全訳吾妻鏡, ed. Kishi Shōzō 貴志正造 and Nagahara Keiji 永原慶二. 6 vols. Shin Jinbutsu Ōraisha, 1976–1979.
Chōshūki 長秋記 (Record of a long autumn). The diary of the courtier Minamoto Morotoki 源師時. Covers the years 1087–1136, with many missing sections. Vols. 16–17 of ST, 1980.
Chūyūki 中右記. The diary of the courtier Fujiwara Munetada 藤原宗忠. Covers the years 1087–1138. Vols. 8–14 of *Shiryō tsūran* 史料通覧, ed. Sasagawa Tanerō 笹川種郎. Nihon Shiseki Hōzonkai, 1915.
Daijōin jisha zōjiki 大乗院寺社雑事記 (Miscellaneous records of temples and shrines at Daijōin). The diary of Jinson 尋尊, the aristocratic abbot (*monzeki*) of the temple Daijōin at Kōfukuji. Covers the years 1450–1508. Ed. Takeuchi Rizō 竹内理三. Vols. 26–37 of ZST, 1978.
Denryaku 殿暦. The diary of Fujiwara Tadazane 藤原忠実, regent to the throne, 1107–1113. Covers the years 1097–1118. 5 vols. In *Dai Nihon kokiroku* 大日本古記録, Series 13, comp. Tōkyō Daigaku Shiryō Hensanjo 東京大学史料編纂所. Iwanami Shoten, 1963.
Eguchi 江口. Noh play by Kan'ami 観阿弥 (1333–1384). In *Yōkyokushū* 謡曲集, vol. 1, ed. Koyama Hiroshi 小山弘志, Satō Kikuo 佐藤喜久雄, and Satō Ken'ichirō 佐藤健一郎. Vol. 33 of NKBZ, 1973.
Eiga monogatari 栄華物語 (Tale of flowering fortunes). Historical narrative written in the eleventh century, focusing on the career of Fujiwara Michinaga.

Eiga monogatari zen chūshaku sōsho 栄華物語全注釈叢書, ed. Matsumura Hiroji 松村博司. 8 vols. + supplement. Kadokawa Shoten, 1969–1982.

Fusō ryakki 扶桑略記 (Brief history of the eastern realm). History written in the late Heian period by the monk Kōen 皇円. Covers the reigns of Jinmu to Horikawa (to 1107). Vol. 12 of KST, 1932.

Gaki zōshi 餓鬼草紙 (Illustrated scroll of hungry ghosts). Early Kamakura-period picture scroll depicting the sufferings of those who have fallen into the realm of hungry ghosts. In vol. 7 of *Nihon no emaki* 日本の絵巻, ed. Komatsu Shigemi 小松茂美. Chūō Kōronsha, 1987.

Genji monogatari 源氏物語 (Tale of Genji). By Murasaki Shikibu 紫式部. The classic mid-Heian tale of court romance and intrigue, focusing on the career of the fictional Prince Genji. Ed. Yanai Shigeshi 柳井滋 et al. 5 vols.; vols. 19–23 of SNKBT, 1993–1997.

Gō (or *Gōke*) *shidai* 江(家)次第 (Records of the Ōe family). By Ōe Masafusa 大江匡房. Description of court affairs and ceremonies, compiled by order of the regent Fujiwara Moromichi. Ed. Maeda Ikutoku Kai Sonkeikaku Bunko 前田育徳会尊経閣文庫. 3 vols. Yagi Shoin, 1996–1997.

Goseibai shikimoku jū 御成敗式目注 (Notes on the administrative law of the Kamakura bakufu). Commentaries on the law codes of the Kamakura bakufu, compiled in the late Kamakura or early Muromachi period. In vol. 7 of ZZGR, 1907.

Goshūi ōjōden 後拾遺往生伝 (Collected tales of rebirth in paradise, continued). By Miyoshi Tameyasu 三善為康. Mid-twelfth-century collection. In *Ōjōden, Hokke genki* 往生伝, 法華験記, ed. Inoue Mitsusada 井上光貞 and Ōsone Shōsuke 大曽根章介. Vol. 7 of NST, 1974.

Han shu 漢書 (History of the Han dynasty). Chinese dynastic history of the Former Han (206 BCE–8 CE), by Ban Gu 班固. Vol. 11 of this version contains the *Xiong-nu chuan* 匈奴傳, records of the nomadic Xiong-nu people, who lived on China's northern border. Xianggang Zhong Hua Shu Ju, 1970.

Haru no shinsanji 春の深山路 (The mountain road in springtime). Written in 1280 by Asukai Masaari 飛鳥井雅有; includes an account of his journey from Kyoto to Kamakura. In *Chūsei nikki kikō shū* 中世日記紀行集, ed. Nagasaki Ken 長崎健 et al. Vol. 48 of SNKBZ, 1994.

Heiji monogatari 平治物語 (Tale of the Heiji era). Early Kamakura war tale that depicts the Heiji uprising of 1159. In *Hōgen monogatari, Heiji monogatari, Jōkyūki* 保元物語, 平治物語, 承久記. Ed. Tochigi Yoshitada 栃木孝惟 et al. Vol. 43 of SNKBT, 1992.

Heike monogatari 平家物語 (Tale of the Heike). Mid-Kamakura war tale focusing on the fate of the house of Taira Kiyomori, especially in the Genpei conflict of 1180–1185. Ed. Kajihara Masaaki 梶原政昭 and Yamashita Hiroaki 山下宏明. 2 vols. Vols. 44–45 of SNKBT, 1991–1993.

Hizen Matsuuratō Ariura monjo 肥前松浦党有浦文書 (Documents of the Ariura family of the Matsuura warrior league in Hizen province). Documents focusing on Kyushu, dated from 1235 to the early Edo period. Ed. Fukuda Ikuo 福田以久 and Murai Shōsuke 村井章介. Seibundō Shuppan, 1982.

Hōbutsushū 宝物集 (Collection of treasures). An early Kamakura-period *setsuwa* collection compiled by Taira Yasuyori 平康頼. In *Hōbutsushū, Kankyō no tomo, Hirasan kojin reitaku* 宝物集, 閑居友, 比良山古人霊託. Ed. Koizumi Hiroshi 小泉弘 et al. Vol. 40 of SNKBT, 1993.

Hokke metsusaiji nenjū gyōji 法華滅罪寺年中行事 (Ritual calendar of Hokke Metsusai temple). Liturgical calendar of the Nara nunnery Hokkeji for the year 1322. In vol. 5 of *Yamato koji taikan* 大和古寺大観. Ed. Ōta Hirotarō 太田博太郎 et al. Iwanami Shoten, 1978.

Honchō mudaishi 本朝無題詩 (Miscellaneous Chinese poetry of our realm). A collection of Japanese poetry in Chinese compiled in the mid-twelfth century. *Honchō mudaishi zen chūshaku* 本朝無題詩全注釈. Ed. Honma Yōichi 本間洋一. 4 vols. Shintensha, 1992.

Honchō seiki 本朝世紀 (The times of our realm). History compiled in the late Heian period by Fujiwara Michinori 藤原通憲. Covers the years 935–1153. In vol. 9 of KST, 1933.

Hōnen shōnin eden 法然上人絵伝 (Illustrated biography of St. Hōnen). 3 vols. Illustrated scroll depicting the life of Hōnen, founder of the Japanese Jōdo school. Several versions exist; the one cited here dates from the early fourteenth century. Vol. 13 of NEZ, 1961; also vols. 1–3 of ZNE, 1990.

Hosshinshū 発心集 (Tales of religious awakening). Early Kamakura Buddhist tale collection by Kamo no Chōmei 鴨長明. Ed. Yanase Kazuo 梁瀬一雄. Koten Bunko, 1962.

Hossō shiyōshō 法曹至要抄 (Essentials of legal scholarship). Legal commentary on the *ritsuryō* codes and supplementary legislation, dating from the late Heian or early Kamakura period. In vol. 6 of GR, 1932.

Hou han shu 後漢書 (History of the Latter Han). Chinese dynastic history of the Latter Han (25–220) by Fan Ye 范曄. 12 vols. Zhonghua Shu Ju, 1965.

Hyakurenshō 百錬抄. History compiled in the late Kamakura period, covering the years 968–1259. In vol. 11 of KST, 1929.

Ishinhō 医心方 (The essence of medical knowledge). Medical text compiled in 984 by Tanba Yasuyori 丹波康頼. Vols. 1–7 of *Nihon koten zenshū* 日本古典全集, Series 5. Nihon Koten Zenshū Kankōkai, 1935.

Jikkinshō 十訓抄 (Notes on ten precepts). *Setsuwa* collection compiled in 1252. Ed. Asami Kazuhiko 浅見和彦. Vol. 51 of SNKBZ, 1997.

Jingikan kudashibumi 神祇官下文 (Order of the Bureau of Shrines). An order from the Bureau of Shrines to Hirota shrine dated 1263. In *Chūsei seiji shakai shisō* 中世政治社会思想, vol. 2, ed. Kasamatsu Hiroshi 笠松宏至, Satō

Shin'ichi 佐藤進一, and Momose Kesao 百瀬今朝雄. Vol. 22 of NST, 1981.

Kaidōki 海道記 (Records of the road by the sea). Records of an unknown traveler's journey from Kyoto to Kamakura and back in 1223. In *Chūsei nikki kikō shū* 中世日記紀行集, ed. Nagasaki Ken 長崎健 et al. Vol. 48 of SNKBZ, Shōgakukan, 1994. Also in *Chūsei nikki kikō shū* 中世日記紀行集, ed. Fukuda Hideichi 福田秀一 et al. Vol. 51 of SNKBT, 1990.

Kairaishiki 傀儡子記 (An account of *kugutsu*). An essay on *kugutsu*, written by Ōe Masafusa 大江匡房, probably in the early twelfth century. Annot. Ōsone Shōsuke 大曽根章介. In *Kodai seiji shakai shisō* 古代政治社会思想, ed. Yamagishi Tokuhei 山岸徳平, Takeuchi Rizō 竹内理三, Ienaga Saburō 家永三郎, and Ōsone Shōsuke. Vol. 8 of NST, 1979. Also in vol. 9 of GR, 1928.

Kamakura bakufu hō 鎌倉幕府法 (Laws of the Kamakura bakufu). Includes the Jōei formulary of 1232 and subsequent supplementary legislation. Vol. 1 of *Chūsei hōsei shiryōshū* 中世法制史料集, ed. Satō Shin'ichi 佐藤進一 and Ikeuchi Yoshisuke 池内義資. Iwanami Shoten, 1955.

Kasugasha kiroku 春日社記録 (Records of Kasuga shrine). Records of an important shrine in Nara. Ed. Takeuchi Rizō 竹内理三. Vols. 47–50 of ZST, 1979.

Kitano tenjin engi 北野天神縁起 (History of the deity of Kitano shrine). Scroll painting relating the life of Sugawara Michizane and the history and traditions of Kitano shrine. The earliest version dates from the Kamakura period. Vol. 8 of NEZ, 1959.

Kojidan 故事談 (Tales of old times). *Setsuwa* collection compiled in 1212–1215 by Minamoto Akikane 源顕兼. Ed. Kobayashi Yasuharu 小林保治. 2 vols. Gendai Shichōsha, 1981.

Kokon chomonjū 古今著聞集 (Tales of ancient and modern times). A *setsuwa* collection compiled in 1254 by Tachibana Narisue 橘成季. Ed. Nishio Kōichi 西尾光一 and Kobayashi Yasuharu 小林保治. Shinchōsha, 1986.

Kōmyōji monjo 光明寺文書 (Documents of Kōmyō temple). Records of a temple in Shima province (present Mie prefecture). Includes documents from Heian, Kamakura, and Muromachi times. 2 vols. Zoku Gunshoruijū Kanseikai, 1985–1987.

Kongō busshi Eizon kanshingaku shōki 金剛仏子叡尊感身学正記. Autobiography of the thirteenth-century Ritsu monk Eizon 叡尊. In *Saidaiji Eizon denki shūsei* 西大寺叡尊伝記集成, ed. Nara Kokuritsu Bunkazai Kenkyūjo 奈良国立文化財研究所. Hōzōkan, 1977.

Konjaku monogatarishū 今昔物語集 (Tales of times now past). *Setsuwa* collection compiled in the early twelfth century, containing tales of India and China as well as Buddhist and secular tales of Japan. Ed. Mabuchi Kazuo 馬淵和夫, Kunisaki Fumimaro 国東文麿, and Konno Tōru 今野達. Vols. 21–24 of NKBZ, 1971–1976. Also: ed. Konno Tōru, Komine Kazuaki 小峯和明,

Ikegami Jun'ichi 池上旬一, and Mori Masato 森正人. Vols. 33–37 of SNKBT, 1993–1996.

Makura no sōshi 枕草子 (Pillow book). Recollections of court life by the mid-Heian court lady Sei Shōnagon 清少納言. Ed. Matsuo Satoshi 松尾聡 and Nagai Kazuko 永井和子. Vol. 11 of NKBZ, 1974.

Man'yōshū 万葉集 (Collection of ten thousand leaves). Collection of some 4,500 poems in Japanese compiled at the end of the eighth century. The oldest extant poetry collection in Japanese. Ed. Kojima Noriyuki 小島憲之, Kinoshita Masatoshi 木下正俊, and Tōno Haruyuki 東野治之. Vols. 6–9 of SNKBT, 1994–1996.

Masukagami 増鏡 (The clear mirror). Historical narrative, probably written in the late fourteenth century, covering the years 1180–1333. *Zen'yaku masukagami* 全訳増鏡, ed. Aoyama Naoharu 青山直治. Hatsune Shobō, 1970.

Meigetsuki 明月記 (Record of the full moon). The diary of poet and courtier Fujiwara Teika 藤原定家, covering the years 1180–1235. *Kundoku* version, ed. Imagawa Fumio 今川文雄. 6 vols. Kawade Shobō Shinsha, 1977.

Nakatsukasa naishi nikki 中務内侍日記 (Diary of a lady at court). The memoirs of the court lady Fujiwara Keishi 藤原経子, covering the years 1280–1292. In *Chūsei nikki kikō shū*. Vol. 51 of SNKBT, 1990. (See *Kaidōki* listing for publication details.)

Nihon kiryaku 日本紀略 (Abbreviated chronicles of Japan). Historical chronicle. Coverage begins with mythical times and ends with the reign of Ichijō Tennō (r. 986–1011). Vol. 11 of KST, 1929.

Nihon kōki 日本後記 (Later history of Japan). One of the Six Official Histories (*Rikkokushi*) of Japan, covering the years 792–833. In vol. 3 of KST, 1934.

Nihon ryōiki 日本霊異記 (Miraculous tales of Japan). Japan's oldest extant *setsuwa* collection, compiled in the early ninth century by the monk Kyōkai 景戒. *Nihon ryōiki zen yakuchū* 日本霊異記全訳注, ed. Nakada Norio 中田祝夫. 3 vols. Kodansha, 1978–1980.

Nihon shoki 日本書紀 (Chronicles of Japan). The first of Japan's Six Official Histories (*Rikkokushi*), compiled in 720 by order of the throne. Coverage begins in mythical times and ends with the reign of Jitō Tennō (r. 690–697). Ed. Kojima Noriyuki 小島憲之 et al. Vols. 2–4 of SNKBT, 1994–1998.

Resshi (*Lie Zi*) 列子. Purports to be the writings of Chinese philosopher Lie Zi, who lived in the Eastern Zhou period (771–256 BCE). Ed. Kobayashi Shinmei 小林信明. Vol. 22 of *Shinshaku kanbun taikei* 新釈漢文体系. Meiji Shoin, 1967.

Ritsuryō 律令. Laws and regulations issued in the early Nara period. Ed. Inoue Mitsusada 井上光貞 et al. Vol. 3 of NST, 1976.

Ruijū sandai kyaku 類聚三代格 (Edicts of three eras, organized topically). Collection of edicts and legal decisions from the Kōnin (810–823), Jōgan (859–

876), and Engi (901–922) eras. Probably compiled in the mid-Heian period. In vol. 25 of KST, 1936.

Ryō no gige 令義解 (Explanations of legal regulations). Commentary on the Yōrō codes, dated 834. Vol. 22 of KST, 1939.

Ryōjin hishō 梁塵秘抄 (Songs to make the dust dance). Collection of *imayō* lyrics thought to have been composed by the female entertainers who sang them. The collection was compiled in 1179 by the retired sovereign Go-Shirakawa 後白河 and includes his *Kudenshū* 口伝集, in which he discusses his patronage and practice of *imayō*. In *Kagurauta, Saibara, Ryōjin hishō, Kanginshū* 神楽歌, 催馬楽, 梁塵秘抄, 閑吟集, ed. Usuda Jingorō 臼田甚五郎 and Shinma Shin'ichi 新間進一. Vol. 25 of NKBZ, 1976.

Saibara 催馬楽. Japanese lyrics sung to Chinese melodies. In vol. 25 of NKBZ, 1976. (See the listing for *Ryōjin hishō*).

Sakeiki 左経記. The diary of Minamoto Tsuneyori 源経頼, covering the years 1016–1036, with many lacunae. Vol. 7 of ST, 1980.

Sarashina nikki 更級日記 (Diary of Sarashina). The diary of the daughter of Sugawara Takasue 菅原孝標の女. Written between 1058 and 1064, beginning with the diarist's recollections of returning home from Kazusa province with her father. Ed. Horiuchi Hideaki 堀内秀晃. Meiji Shoin, 1977.

Seiji yōryaku 政事要略 (Digest of government affairs). Mid-Heian legal text concerning court ceremonies, institutions, and official duties, compiled by Koremune Kotosuke 惟宗允亮. Includes quotations from lost sources such as *Zenge iki* 善家異記 by Miyoshi Kiyoyuki 三善清行 (847–918). Vol. 28 of KST, 1935.

Senjūshō 撰集抄 (Selected tales). Buddhist *setsuwa* collection compiled in the Kamakura period. Ed. Yasuda Takako 安田孝子 et al. 2 vols. Gendai Shichōsha, 1985–1987.

Shasekishū 沙石集 (Sand and pebbles). Buddhist *setsuwa* collection compiled by the monk Mujū Ichien 無住一円 between 1279 and 1283. Ed. Watanabe Tsunaya 渡辺綱也. Vol. 85 of NKBT, 1966.

Shinsarugakuki 新猿楽記 (Record of the new monkey music). Fujiwara Akihira's 藤原明衡 account of the large family of a fictional lieutenant of the guards. Annot. Ōsone Shōsuke 大曽根章介. In vol. 8 of NST. (See *Kairaishiki* for publication details.)

Shinsen rōeishū 新撰朗詠集 (Newly collected poems to sing). A collection of poetry in Japanese and Chinese compiled by Fujiwara Mototoshi 藤原基俊. In vol. 19 of GR, 1933.

Shōgen ninen inrakusho 正元二年院落書. An anonymous libel sheet passed around the capital in 1260. In *Chūsei seiji shakai shisō*, vol. 2. Vol. 22 of NST, 1981. (See *Jingikan kudashibumi* for publication details.)

Shōmonki 将門記 (Tale of Masakado). War tale about the rebellion of Taira

Masakado in the mid-tenth century. Ed. Kajihara Masaaki 梶原正昭. 2 vols. Heibonsha, 1976.

Sumiyoshi mōde 住吉詣 (Pilgrimage to Sumiyoshi shrine). Shogun Ashikaga Yoshiakira's 足利義詮 account of his pilgrimage to Sumiyoshi shrine in 1364. In vol. 18 of GR, 1928.

Suwa daimyōjin ekotoba 諏訪大明神絵詞 (Illustrated history of the deity of Suwa shrine). Illustrated scroll, dated 1356, relating the traditions of Suwa shrine in Shinano province (present Nagano prefecture). In vol. 3:2 of ZGR, 1903.

Taiki 台記. The diary of Fujiwara Yorinaga 藤原頼長, a high-ranking noble who attained the position of minister of the left. Covers the years 1136–1155. Vol. 1:1 of *Shiryō taikan* 史料大観, ed. Kurita Hiroshi 栗田寛 et al. Tetsugaku Shoin, 1898. For coverage through 1143, see also vol. 52 of *Shiryō sanshū kokirokuhen* 史料纂集古記録編, ed. Hashimoto Yoshihiko 橋本義彦 and Imae Hiromichi 今江広道. Zoku Gunshoruijū Kanseikai, 1976.

Takakura-in Itsukushima gokōki 高倉院厳島御幸記 (Retired sovereign Takakura's progress to Itsukushima shrine). Minamoto Michichika's 源通親 account of the retired sovereign Takakura's 1180 pilgrimage to Itsukushima shrine in Aki province (present Hiroshima prefecture). In *Chūsei nikki kikō shū.* Vol. 51 of SNKBT, 1990. (See *Kaidōki* for publication details.)

Tōhokuin shokunin utaawase 東北院職人歌合 (Poetry contest on the theme of artisans at Tōhokuin). Scroll painting depicting a poetry contest held in 1214. Contestants' poems about various artisans are illustrated by pictures of the artisans. Text only in vol. 28 of GR, 1933.

Tōkan kikō 東関紀行 (An account of travel to the east). Anonymous travel journal relating a voyage from the capital to Kamakura in 1242. In *Chūsei nikki kikō shū*, vol. 48 of SNKBZ, 1994. Also in *Chūsei nikki kikō shū*, vol. 51 of SNKBT, 1990. (See *Kaidōki* for publication details.)

Torikaebaya monogatari とりかへばや物語 (The changelings). Tale of cross-dressing and gender-switching in Heian Japan, probably written at the end of the Heian period. In *Sumiyoshi monogatari, Torikaebaya monogatari* 住吉物語, とりかへばや物語. Ed. Misumi Yōichi 三角洋一 and Ishino Keiko 石埜敬子. Vol. 39 of SNKBZ, 2002.

Towazugatari とわずがたり (Unrequested tales). Memoirs of a court lady known as Nijō 二条, concubine of the retired sovereign Go-Fukakusa. Covers the years 1271–1306. In *Towazugatari, Tamakiwaru* とはずがたり, たまきはる. Ed. Misumi Yōichi 三角洋一. Vol. 50 of SNKBT, 1994.

Uji kanpaku Kōyasan gosankeiki 宇治関白高野山御参詣記 (The Uji regent's pilgrimage to Mt. Kōya). An account of the regent Fujiwara Yorimichi's pilgrimage to the Shingon complex at Mt. Kōya in 1048. Written by Taira Norikuni 平範国. In vol. 5 of ZZGR, 1909.

Uji shūi monogatari 宇治拾遺物語 (Collection of tales from Uji). Ed. Kobayashi Chishō 小林智昭, Kobayashi Yasuharu 小林保治, and Masuko Kazuko 増古和子. 2 vols. Shōgakukan, 1986.

Unshū shōsoku 雲州消息 (Letters from Izumo). A collection of exemplary letters compiled by the eleventh-century courtier-literatus Fujiwara Akihira 藤原明衡. In *Shinsarugakuki • Unshū shōsoku* 新猿楽記・雲州消息, ed. Shigematsu Akihisa 重松明久. Gendai Shichōsha, 1982.

Utsunomiya ke shikijō 宇都宮家式条. Regulations of the Utsunomiya house, issued in 1283. In *Buke kahō* 武家家法, vol. 3 of *Chūsei hōsei shiryōshū* 中世法制史料衆, ed. Satō Shin'ichi 佐藤進一 and Ikeuchi Yoshisuke 池内義資. Iwanami Shoten, 1955.

Wamyō ruijushō (*Wamyōshō*) 倭名類聚鈔 (Topical collection of Japanese terms). A Chinese-to-Japanese dictionary compiled by Minamoto Shitagō 源順 in the Shōhei era (931–938). Benseisha, 1985. (Photographic reproduction of 1617 edition.)

Yamato monogatari 大和物語 (Tales of Yamato). A collection of poem-tales compiled by an unknown author in the tenth century. In *Taketori monogatari, Ise monogatari, Yamato monogatari, Heichū monogatari* 竹取物語, 伊勢物語, 大和物語, 平中物語, ed. Katagiri Yōichi 片桐洋一 et al. Vol. 8 of NKBZ, 1972.

Yūjoki 遊女記 (Account of *asobi*). An essay on *asobi* written in the twelfth century by Ōe Masafusa 大江匡房. Annot. Ōsone Shōsuke 大曽根章介. In vol. 8 of NST. (See *Kairaishiki* for publication details.) Also in vol. 9 of GR.

Yūzū nenbutsu engi 融通念仏縁起 (History of the Yūzū Nenbutsu school). Picture scroll illustrating the early history of the Yūzū Nenbutsu school of Buddhism. The earliest version dates from 1314. Vol. 21 of ZNE. Chūō Kōronsha, 1992.

Zoku kojidan 続古事談 (Tales of old times, continued). *Setsuwa* collection dated 1219. The compiler is unknown. In vol. 27 of GR, 1931.

Secondary Sources

Ambros, Barbara. 1997. "Liminal Journeys: Pilgrimages of Noblewomen in Mid-Heian Japan." *Japanese Journal of Religious Studies* (24) 3–4.

Amino Yoshihiko 網野義彦. 1975. "Chūsei shōki ni okeru imonoshi no sonzai keitai—Heian matsu • Kamakura shōki no tōro kugonin o chūshin ni—中世初期における鋳物師の存在形態—平安末・鎌倉初期の燈炉供御人を中心に—." In *Nagoya daigaku Nihonshi ronshū* 名古屋大学日本史論集, ed. Nagoya Daigaku Bungakubu Kokushigaku Kenkyūshitsu 名古屋大学文学部国史学研究室. Yoshikawa Kōbunkan.

———. 1980. *Nihon chūsei no minshū zō—heimin to shokunin*—日本中世の民衆像—平民と職人—. Iwanami Shoten.

———. 1984. *Hyōhaku to teichaku: Teijū shakai e no michi* 漂白と定着：定住社会への道. Shōgakukan.
———. 1986. "Kebiishi no shoryō 検非違使の所領." *Rekishigaku kenkyū* 歴史学研究 557.
———. 1989. "Asobi to hinin • kawaramono 遊女と非人・河原者." In *Sei to mibun* 性と身分, ed. Miyata Noboru 宮田登. Shunjūsha.
———. 1992. *Shokunin utaawase* 職人歌合. Iwanami Shoten.
Aston, W. G. 1972. *Nihongi: Chronicles of Japan from the Earliest Times to A.D. 697.* Charles E. Tuttle Company.
Bell, Shannon. 1994. *Reading, Writing, and Rewriting the Prostitute Body.* Indiana University Press.
Blacker, Carmen. 1986. *The Catalpa Bow: A Study of Shamanistic Practices in Japan.* George Allen & Unwin.
Borgen, Robert. 1986. *Sugawara no Michizane and the Early Heian Court.* Council on East Asian Studies, Harvard University.
Brazell, Karen, trans. 1973. *The Confessions of Lady Nijō.* (*Towazugatari.*) Anchor Press/Doubleday.
Conlan, Thomas Donald. 2003. *State of War: The Violent Order of Fourteenth-Century Japan.* Center for Japanese Studies, University of Michigan.
Corbin, Alain. 1990. *Women for Hire: Prostitution and Sexuality in France After 1850.* Trans. Alan Sheridan. Harvard University Press.
Dawson, Raymond, trans. 1993. Confucius, *The Analects.* Oxford University Press.
Dykstra, Yoshiko K. 1983. *Miraculous Tales of the Lotus Sutra from Ancient Japan: The Dainihonkoku Hokekyōkenki of Priest Chingen.* Kansai University of Foreign Studies.
Faure, Bernard. 1998. *The Red Thread: Buddhist Approaches to Sexuality.* Princeton University Press.
———. 2003. *The Power of Denial: Buddhism, Purity, and Gender.* Princeton University Press.
Foard, James H. 1982. "The Boundaries of Compassion: Buddhism and National Tradition in Japanese Pilgrimage." *Journal of Asian Studies* 41:2.
Fukutō Sanae 服藤早苗. 1990. "Ukareme kara asobi e 遊行女婦から遊女へ." In *Nihon josei seikatsushi* 日本女性生活史, vol. 1, *Genshi • kodai* 原始・古代. Ed. Joseishi Sōgō Kenkyūkai 女性史総合研究会. Tōkyō Daigaku Shuppankai.
———. 1995. *Heianchō no onna to otoko: Kizoku to shomin no sei to ai* 平安朝の女と男：貴族と庶民の性と愛. Chūō Kōron Shinsha.
Garon, Sheldon. 1997. *Molding Japanese Minds: The State in Everyday Life.* Princeton University Press.
Geremek, Bronislaw. 1987. *The Margins of Society in Late Medieval Paris.* Trans. Jean Birrell. Cambridge University Press.

Gomi Fumihiko 五味文彦. 1995. "Inseiki no sei to seiji • buryoku 院政期の性と政治・武力." *Bungaku* 文学 6:1.

Goodwin, Janet R. 1994. *Alms and Vagabonds: Buddhist Temples and Popular Patronage in Medieval Japan*. University of Hawai'i Press.

———. 2000. "Shadows of Transgression: Heian and Kamakura Constructions of Prostitution." *Monumenta Nipponica* 55:3.

Gorai Shigeru 五来重. 1982. "Chūsei josei no shūkyōsei to seikatsu 中世女性の宗教性と生活." In *Nihon joseishi* 日本女性史, vol. 2, *Chūsei* 中世. Ed. Joseishi Sōgō Kenkyūkai 女性史総合研究会. Tōkyō Daigaku Shuppankai.

Gotō Toshihiko 後藤紀彦. 1984. "Tsujikimi to zushikimi 辻君と辻子君." *Bungaku* 文学 52:3.

Hershatter, Gail. 1997. *Dangerous Pleasures: Prostitution and Modernity in Twentieth-Century Shanghai*. University of California Press.

Hiraoka Jōkai 平岡定海. 1980. *Tōdaiji jiten* 東大寺辞典. Tōkyōdō Shuppankai.

Hoshino Shizuko 星野志津子. 1998. "Chūsei zenki ni okeru bikkai no saikentō—*Konjaku monogatari* o chūshin toshite 中世前期における密懐の再検討—「今昔物語」を中心として—." In *Sei to shintai* 性と身体, vol. 9 of NJR. Yoshikawa Kōbunkan.

Hotate Michihisa 保立道久. 1990. "Nakadachi • nakōdo—toshi baishun no hassei 中媒・仲人—都市売春の発生." In *Nihon toshishi nyūmon* II: *Machi* 日本都市史入門 II: 町, ed. Takahashi Yasuo 高橋康夫 and Yoshida Nobuyuki 吉田伸之. Tōkyō Daigaku Shuppankai.

———. 1998. "Himen no onna to romen no onna—chūsei josei no 'soto aruki' 秘面の女と露面の女—中世女性の「外歩き」." In *Bunka to josei* 文化と女性, vol. 7 of NJR. Yoshikawa Kōbunkan.

Hur, Nam-lin. 2000. *Prayer and Play in Late Tokugawa Japan: Asakusa Sensōji and Edo Society*. Harvard University Asia Center.

Iinuma Kenji 飯沼賢司. 1990. "Chūsei zenki no josei no shōgai 中世前期の女性の生涯." In *Nihon josei seikatsushi* 日本女性生活史, vol. 2, *Chūsei* 中世. Ed. Joseishi Sōgō Kenkyūkai 女性史総合研究会. Tōkyō Daigaku Shuppankai.

Imahori Taitsu 今堀太逸. 1990. "Hōnen no emaki to asobi 法然の絵巻と遊女." In Imahori, *Jingi shinkō no tenkai to bukkyō* 神祇信仰の展開と仏教. Yoshikawa Kōbunkan.

Ishii Ryōsuke 石井良助. 1977. *Nihon kon'inhō shi* 日本婚姻法史. Sōbunsha.

Karras, Ruth Mazo. 1996. *Common Women: Prostitution and Sexuality in Medieval England*. Oxford University Press.

Kasamatsu Hiroshi 笠松宏至. 1981. "Kamakura kōki no kuge hō ni tsuite 鎌倉後期の公家法について." In *Chūsei seiji shakai shisō*, vol. 2. Vol. 22 of NST. (See *Jingikan kudashibumi* for publication details.)

Katsumata Shizuo 勝俣鎮夫. 1979. "Chūsei buke bikkai hō no tenkai 中世武家密懐法の展開." Chap. 1 of Katsumata, *Sengoku hō seiritsushi ron* 戦国法成立史論. Tōkyō Daigaku Shuppankai.

Kawashima, Terry. 2001. *Writing Margins: The Textual Construction of Gender in Heian and Kamakura Japan.* Harvard University Asia Center.

Keene, Donald, ed. 1955. *Anthology of Japanese Literature from the Earliest Era to the Mid-Nineteenth Century.* Grove Press.

Keirstead, Thomas. 1995. "The Gendering and Regendering of Medieval Japan." *U.S.-Japan Women's Journal, English Supplement* 9.

Kelly, Joan. 1984. "Did Women Have a Renaissance?" In *Women, History, and Theory: The Essays of Joan Kelly.* University of Chicago Press.

Kim, Yung-Hee. 1994. *Songs to Make the Dust Dance: The Ryōjin hishō of Twelfth-Century Japan.* University of California Press.

Kim Kwon, Yung-Hee. 1986. "The Emperor's Songs: Go-Shirakawa and *Ryōjin hishō Kudenshū* Book 10." *Monumenta Nipponica* 41:3.

———. 1990. "The Female Entertainment Tradition in Medieval Japan: The Case of *Asobi.*" In *Performing Feminisms: Feminist Critical Theory and Theatre*, ed. Sue-Ellen Case. Johns Hopkins University Press.

Kitakōji Ken 北小路健. 1964. *Yūjo: Sono rekishi to aikan* 遊女：その歴史と哀歓. Jinbutsu Ōraisha.

Klein, Susan Blakely. 2002. *Allegories of Desire: Esoteric Literary Commentaries of Medieval Japan.* Harvard University Asia Center.

Ko, Dorothy, JaHyun Kim Haboush, and Joan R. Piggott, eds. 2003. *Women and Confucian Cultures in Premodern China, Korea, and Japan.* University of California Press.

Konishi Jin'ichi. 1991. *A History of Japanese Literature*, vol. 3: *The High Middle Ages.* Trans. Aileen Gatten and Mark Harbison. Princeton University Press.

Kuroda Hideo 黒田日出男. 1998. "Miko no ime—ji 巫女のイメージ." In *Bunka to josei* 文化と女性, vol. 7 of NJR. Yoshikawa Kōbunkan.

Kuroda Toshio 黒田俊雄. 1995. "Chūsei mibunsei o meguru sho mondai 中世身分制をめぐる諸問題." In *Kuroda Toshio chosakushū* 黒田俊雄著作集, vol. 6, *Chūsei kyōdōtai ron • mibunsei ron* 中世共同体論・身分制論. Hōzōkan.

LaFleur, William R. 1983. *The Karma of Words: Buddhism and the Literary Arts in Medieval Japan.* University of California Press.

Law, Jane Marie. 1997. *Puppets of Nostalgia: The Life, Death, and Rebirth of the Japanese Awaji Ningyō Tradition.* Princeton University Press.

Leicester, Elizabeth. Forthcoming. "The Politics of Prostitution in Early Nineteenth Century Kanazawa." Ph.D. dissertation, UCLA, in progress.

Levy, Howard S., and Ishihara Akira, trans. 1989. Tanba Yasuyori, *The Tao of Sex: The Essence of Medical Prescriptions (Ishimpō).* 3rd rev. ed. Integral Publishing.

Mahood, Linda. 1990. *The Magdalenes*. Routledge.
Marra, Michele. 1993. *Representations of Power: The Literary Politics of Medieval Japan*. University of Hawai'i Press.
Mass, Jeffrey P. 1989. *Lordship and Inheritance in Early Medieval Japan: A Study of the Kamakura Sōryō System*. Stanford University Press.
———. 1992. *Antiquity and Anachronism in Japanese History*. Stanford University Press.
Matsumae Takeshi. 1991. "Early Kami Worship." Trans. Janet R. Goodwin. In *The Cambridge History of Japan*, vol. 1: *Ancient Japan*, ed. Delmer M. Brown. Cambridge University Press.
——— 松前健. 1992. "Tsukushi mai to kugutsu no dentō gei 筑紫舞とクグツの伝統芸." *Tsukushi mai kenmon* 筑紫舞見聞 3.
McCullough, Helen Craig, trans. 1988. *The Tale of the Heike*. Stanford University Press.
McCullough, William H. 1967. "Japanese Marriage Customs in the Heian Period." *Harvard Journal of Asiatic Studies* 27.
Mills, D. E., trans. 1970. *A Collection of Tales from Uji: A Study and Translation of Uji Shūi Monogatari*. Cambridge University Press.
Moerman, David. 1997. "The Ideology of Landscape and the Theater of State: Insei Pilgrimage to Kumano (1090–1220)." *Japanese Journal of Religious Studies* (24) 3–4.
Moore, Jean, trans. 1986. "*Senjūshō*: Buddhist Tales of Renunciation." *Monumenta Nipponica* 41:2.
Morrell, Robert E., trans. 1985. *Sand and Pebbles (Shasekishū): The Tales of Mujū Ichien, a Voice for Pluralism in Kamakura Buddhism*. State University of New York Press.
Morris, Ivan, trans. 1971. *As I Crossed the Bridge of Dreams: Recollections of a Woman in Eleventh-Century Japan*. (*Sarashina nikki*.) Dial Press.
Nakamura, Kyoko Motomachi, trans. 1973. *Miraculous Stories from the Japanese Buddhist Tradition: The Nihon ryōiki of the Monk Kyōkai*. Harvard University Press.
Nakayama Tarō 中山太郎. 1984a. *Baishun sanzennen shi* 売春三千年史. Parutosusha, 1984.
———. 1984b. *Nihon miko shi* 日本巫女史. Parutosusha.
Namihira, Emiko. 1987. "Pollution in the Folk Belief System." In *An Anthropological Profile of Japan, Current Anthropology* 28:4 supplement.
Narahara Junko 楢原潤子. 1998. "Chūsei zenki ni okeru asobi • kugutsu no 'ie' to chōja 中世前期における遊女・傀儡子の「家」と長者." In *Sei to shintai* 性と身体, vol. 9 of NJR. Yoshikawa Kōbunkan.
Nishiguchi Junko 西口順子. 1987. *Onna no chikara: Kodai no josei to bukkyō* 女の力：古代の女性と仏教. Heibonsha.

Ohnuki-Tierney, Emiko. 1987. *The Monkey as Mirror: Symbolic Transformations in Japanese History and Ritual.* Princeton University Press.

Orikuchi Shinobu 折口信夫. 1971a. "Shūki denshō 周期伝承." In vol. 7 of *Orikuchi Shinobu zenshū nōto hen*, 折口信夫全集ノート編. Chūō Kōronsha.

———. 1971b. "*Man'yōshū* kan jūroku kōgi 万葉集巻十六講義." In vol. 11 of *Orikuchi Shinobu zenshū nōto hen.* Chūō Kōronsha.

Otis, Leah L. 1985. *Prostitution in Medieval Society: The History of an Urban Institution in Languedoc.* University of Chicago Press.

Ōwa Iwao 大和岩雄. 1993. *Yūjo to tennō* 遊女と天皇. Hakusuisha.

Pandey, Rajyashree. 2004. "Poetry, Sex, and Salvation: The 'Courtesan' and the Noblewoman in Medieval Japanese Narratives." *Japanese Studies* 24:1.

Pigeot, Jacqueline. 2003. *Femmes galantes, femmes artistes dans le Japon ancien, XIe–XIIIe siècle.* Editions Gallimard.

Piggott, Joan R., ed. 2006. *Capital and Countryside in Japan, 300–1180: Japanese Historians Interpreted in English.* Cornell University Press.

Raz, Jacob. 1985. "Popular Entertainment and Politics: The Great *Dengaku* of 1096." *Monumenta Nipponica* 40:3.

Rotman, Andy. 2003. "The Erotics of Practice: Objects and Agency in Buddhist *Avadāna* Literature." *Journal of the American Academy of Religion* 71:3.

Rublack, Ulinka. 1999. *The Crimes of Women in Early Modern Germany.* Clarendon Press, Oxford.

Ruch, Barbara. 1990. "The Other Side of Culture in Medieval Japan." In *The Cambridge History of Japan*, vol. 3: *Medieval Japan*, ed. Kozo Yamamura. Cambridge University Press.

Saeki Junko 佐伯順子. 1987. *Yūjo no bunkashi: Hare no onnatachi* 遊女の文化史：ハレの女たち. Chūō Kōronsha.

Sakurai Tokutarō 桜井徳太郎. 1974. "Kesshū no genten 結衆の原点." In *Shisō no bōken—shakai no henka no atarashii paradaimu* 思想の冒険—社会の変化の新しいパラダイム, ed. Tsurumi Kazuko 鶴見和子 and Ichii Saburō 市井三郎. Chikuma Shobō.

Seidensticker, Edward G., trans. 1976. Murasaki Shikibu, *The Tale of Genji.* Alfred A. Knopf.

Sekiguchi Hiroko 関口裕子. 1993. *Nihon kodai kon'inshi no kenkyū* 日本古代婚姻史の研究. 2 vols. Hanawa Shobō.

———. 2003. "The Patriarchal Family Paradigm in Eighth-Century Japan." In *Women and Confucian Cultures in Premodern China, Korea, and Japan*, ed. Dorothy Ko, JaHyun Kim Haboush, and Joan R. Piggott. University of California Press.

Seno Seiichirō 瀬野精一郎. 1998. "Kamakura jidai ni okeru kaika to saikon 鎌倉時代における改嫁と再婚." In *Kon'in to josei* 婚姻と女性, vol. 4 of NJR. Yoshikawa Kōbunkan.

Shrage, Laurie. 1994. *Moral Dilemmas of Feminism: Prostitution, Adultery, and Abortion.* Routledge.

Smits, Ivo. 1996. "An Early Anthropologist? Ōe no Masafusa's *A Record of Fox Spirits.*" In *Religion in Japan: Arrows to Heaven and Earth*, ed. P. F. Kornicki and I. J. McMullen. Cambridge University Press.

Sommer, Matthew H. 2000. *Sex, Law, and Society in Late Imperial China.* Stanford University Press.

Sumi Tōyō 鷲見等曜. 1983. *Zenkindai Nihon kazoku no kōzō* 前近代日本家族の構造. Kōbundō.

Tahara, Mildred, trans. 1980. *Tales of Yamato: A Tenth Century Poem-tale.* (*Yamato monogatari.*) University Press of Hawai'i.

Taira Masayuki 平雅行. 1990. "Chūsei bukkyō to josei 中世仏教と女性." In *Nihon josei seikatsushi* 日本女性生活史, vol. 2, *Chūsei* 中世. Ed. Joseishi Sōgō Kenkyūkai 女性史総合研究会. Tōkyō Daigaku Shuppankai.

Takamure Itsue 高群逸枝. 1963. *Nihon kon'inshi* 日本婚姻史. Shibundō.

Takeuchi Rizō 竹内理三, ed. 1975–1976. *Shōen bunpu zu* 荘園分布図. 2 vols. Yoshikawa Kōbunkan.

Takigawa Masajirō 滝川政次郎. 1965. *Yūjo no rekishi* 遊女の歴史. Shibundō.

Toda Yoshimi. 2006. "Kyoto and the Estate System in the Heian Period." Trans. Janet R. Goodwin. In *Capital and Countryside in Japan, 300–1180*, ed. Joan R. Piggott. Cornell University Press.

Tonomura Hisae 外村久江. 1996. *Kamakura bunka no kenkyū—sōka sōzō o megutte* 鎌倉文化の研究—早歌創造をめぐって—. Miyai Shoten.

Tonomura, Hitomi. 1990. "Women and Inheritance in Japan's Early Warrior Society." *Comparative Studies in Society and History* 32:3.

———. 1994. "Black Hair and Red Trousers: Gendering the Flesh in Medieval Japan." *American Historical Review* 99:1.

———. 1997. "Re-envisioning Women in the Post-Kamakura Age." In *The Origins of Japan's Medieval World: Courtiers, Clerics, Warriors, and Peasants in the Fourteenth Century*, ed. Jeffrey P. Mass. Stanford University Press.

———. 1999. "Sexual Violence Against Women: Legal and Extralegal Treatment in Premodern Warrior Societies." In *Women and Class in Japanese History*, ed. Hitomi Tonomura, Anne Walthall, and Wakita Haruko. Center for Japanese Studies, University of Michigan.

Toyonaga Satomi 豊永聡美. 1989. "Chūsei ni okeru asobi no chōja ni tsuite 中世における遊女の長者について." In *Chūsei Nihon no shosō* 中世日本の諸相, vol. 2, ed. Yasuda Motohisa-sensei Tainin Kinen Ronshū Kankō Iinkai 安田元久先生退任記念論集刊行委員会. Yoshikawa Kōbunkan.

Tsunoda, Ryusaku, and L. Carrington Goodrich. 1951. *Japan in the Chinese Dynastic Histories.* P. D. and Ione Perkins.

Tyler, Royall, trans. 2001. Murasaki Shikibu, *The Tale of Genji*. 2 vols. Viking Penguin.

Ury, Marian, trans. 1979. *Tales of Times Now Past: Sixty-Two Stories from a Medieval Japanese Collection.* (*Konjaku monogatarishū.*) University of California Press.

———. 1993. "The Ōe Conversations." *Monumenta Nipponica* 48:3.

Wakita Haruko 脇田晴子. 1982. "Chūsei ni okeru seibetsu yakuwari buntan to joseikan 中世における性別役割分担と女性観." In *Nihon joseishi* 日本女性史, vol. 2, *Chūsei* 中世, ed. Joseishi Sōgō Kenkyūkai 女性史総合研究会. Tōkyō Daigaku Shuppankai.

———. 1984. "Marriage and Property in Premodern Japan from the Perspective of Women's History." *Journal of Japanese Studies* 10:1.

———. 1993. "Women and the Creation of the *Ie* in Japan: An Overview from the Medieval Period to the Present." *U.S.-Japan Women's Journal, English Supplement* 4.

———. 2001. *Josei geinō no genryū: Kugutsu • kusemai • shirabyōshi* 女性芸能の源流：傀儡子・曲舞・白拍子. Kadokawa Shoten.

Walkowitz, Judith R. 1980. *Prostitution and Victorian Society: Women, Class, and the State.* Cambridge University Press.

Watanabe Shōgo. 渡邊昭五. 1979. *Ryōjin hishō no fūzoku to bungei* 梁塵秘抄の風俗と文芸. Miyai Shoten.

Willig, Rosette F., trans. 1983. *The Changelings: A Classical Japanese Court Tale.* (*Torikaebaya monogatari.*) Stanford University Press.

Yamaguchi Masao. 1987. "The Dual Structure of Japanese Emperorship." In *An Anthropological Profile of Japan, Current Anthropology* 28:4 supplement.

Yamakami Izumo 山上伊豆母. 1980. *Miko no rekishi—Nihon shūkyō no botai* 巫女の歴史—日本宗教の母胎. Yūzankaku.

Yanagita Kunio 柳田国男. 1962a. "Ukareme 遊行女婦." In vol. 8 of *Teihon Yanagita Kunio zenshū* 定本柳田国男全集. Chikuma Shobō.

———. 1962b. "Mikokō 巫女考." In vol. 9 of *Teihon Yanagita Kunio zenshū*. Chikuma Shobō.

———. 1963. "'Itaka' oyobi 'sanka' 「イタカ」及び「サンカ」." In vol. 4 of *Teihon Yanagita Kunio zenshū*. Chikuma Shobō.

Yoshida Takashi 吉田孝. 1976. "Ritsuryōsei to sonraku 律令制と村落." In vol. 3 of *Iwanami kōza Nihon rekishi* 岩波講座日本歴史, *Kodai* 古代 3.

———. 1988. *Kodai kokka no ayumi* 古代国家の歩み. Vol. 3 of (*Taikei*) *Nihon no rekishi* (体系)日本の歴史. Iwanami Shoten.

Yoshie Akiko 義江明子. 1986. *Nihon kodai no uji to kōzō* 日本古代の氏の構造. Yoshikawa Kōbunkan.

———. 1996. *Nihon kodai no saishi to josei* 日本古代の祭祀と女性. Yoshikawa Kōbunkan.

———. 2004. *Kodai joseishi e no shōtai* 古代女性史への招待. Yoshikawa Kōbunkan.
———. 2005. "Gender in Early Classical Japan: Marriage, Leadership, and Political Status in Village and Palace." Trans. Janet R. Goodwin. *Monumenta Nipponica* 60:4.

Index

About the Author

A scholar of early medieval Japanese history, Janet R. Goodwin received her doctorate in Japanese history from the University of California, Berkeley. She was a member of the founding faculty of the University of Aizu in Aizu-Wakamatsu, Japan, and has taught at the University of California, Los Angeles, and the University of Southern California. She is the author of *Alms and Vagabonds: Buddhist Temples and Popular Patronage in Medieval Japan* (University of Hawai'i Press, 1994) as well as a number of articles and translations of work in Japanese. Her work on computer visualization of historical sites in Japan has been presented at conferences on archaeology and cultural heritage preservation. She is currently an editor of the H-Japan on-line discussion list.

HAWAI'I Production Notes for GOODWIN | SELLING SONGS AND SMILES

Cover and interior designed by April Leidig-Higgins in Garamond Premier Pro, with Zapfino ornaments

Composition by Copperline Book Services, Inc.

Printing and binding by The Maple-Vail Book Manufacturing Group

Printed on 60# Glatfelter Offset B18, 420 ppi

Lightning Source UK Ltd.
Milton Keynes UK
UKHW011531140722
405856UK00001B/126